Coastal Landforms
and Surface Features

Coastal Landforms and Surface Features

A Photographic Atlas and Glossary

Rodman E. Snead
University of New Mexico

Hutchinson Ross Publishing Company

Stroudsburg, Pennsylvania

This volume is dedicated to Richard J. Russell who spent his life studying coasts and alluvial valleys.

Copyright © 1982 by **Hutchinson Ross Publishing Company**
Library of Congress Catalog Card Number: 81-2949
ISBN: 0-87933-052-X

84 83 82   1   2   3   4   5
Manufactured in the United States of America.

Library of Congress Cataloging in Publication Data
Snead, Rodman E.
    Coastal landforms and surface features.
    Bibliography: p.
    Includes index.
    1. Coasts—Pictorial works.   2. Coasts—Dictionaries.
I. Title.
GB452.S64   551.4′57   81-2949
ISBN 0-87933-052-X   AACR2

Distributed world wide by Academic Press,
a subsidiary of Harcourt Brace Jovanovich,
Publishers.

Contents

Preface

This is a photographic compendium of the great variety of coastal landforms created by waves and currents as well as by structural movements along coastal regions. Although it does not cover every coastal landform feature, it does present most of the types of coasts found around the world. The atlas is topical rather than regional and uses the excellent coastal classification devised by Francis P. Shepard.

This atlas is needed because of the recently expanding interest in coastal regions stimulated by storm damage and pollution along the coasts of the United States and Europe. Barrier islands and bars as well as boat channels and harbors are constantly changing under the forces of waves, currents, and tides. A single storm in 1964, a "three-day northeaster," caused millions of dollars damage to the central portion of the east coast of the United States. The section on storm damage illustrates with photographs the power of wind and water to destroy or to move large structures.

The primary objective of this atlas is to present in a single source a photographic record of nearly all coastal features described during the development of the field of coastal geomorphology so that future workers on coastline problems can refer to these photographs for comparative and illustrative purposes. Also, it is hoped that this atlas will serve as an aid to those engaged in learning or teaching the fundamentals of geomorphology and its related fields such as geology and physiography. To this end I have attempted to create a book general enough to be useful even at the secondary school level but with sufficient detail to make it acceptable at the university level. By keeping this atlas as nontechnical as possible, it is hoped that it will appeal to the many nonprofessionals who are interested in the magnificent aspects of coastal phenomena. The description of coastal landforms reviews the general principles of coastal geomorphology from the point of view of their influence on the earth's scenery. I have cross-referenced the description with the photographic legends, making it possible to see the actual feature being described. The book also contains a detailed bibliography dealing with coastal geomorphology and a comprehensive glossary that describes the terms used throughout the book.

The geographic location of the photographs is presented (pp. ix-x) as a helpful guide. The breakdown is by continent, plus Oceania, followed by country, and then by province or territory. Because of the large number of photographs of U.S. coasts, I felt that the best method would be to follow south along the east coast of the United States from Maine to Florida, west along the Gulf Coast and then north from California to Alaska and across to Hawaii.

The atlas is designed to appeal to a wide audience. A space photograph of the southern coast of Florida will interest an elementary school student who can visualize the shape of Florida. A high school student can discern the symmetry of that same coast with its varied patterns of mangroves and barrier islands. And for the college student, that same space photograph illustrates a sequence of coastal changes that have taken place over a short period of time—the growth of spits and hooks, the filling in of bays, and the rapid growth of human-built structures. For the graduate student specializing in coastal landforms the photograph presents a story of sea-level change and coastal erosion and progradation.

I want to express sincere gratitude to the many people who contributed photographs to this volume and who gave advice and assistance in the preparation of the text. Whatever excellence this book has can be attributed to those contributors listed on pp. xvii-xx. In particular, I am indebted to Dr. Kenneth Boston, Dr. R. V. Fisher, Dr. Miles O. Hayes, Dr. Robin T. Holcomb, Dr. David Hopley, Dr. Robert Kirk, Dr. Stanley Morain, Dr. James P. Morgan, Dr. Antony R. Orme, Dr. William Ritchie, and Dr. Francis P. Shepard who permitted me to use their photographs. In compiling this book I have had the pleasure of contacting many other active workers in the field of geomorphology.

I wish to sincerely thank Dr. Rhodes W. Fairbridge for reviewing sections of the manuscript and to the graduate and undergraduate students at the University of New Mexico who helped in the compilation of this volume.

RODMAN E. SNEAD

Geographic Location
of the Photographs

List of Plates

List of Contributors

Aerial Photography Division ASCS
Western Laboratory
U.S. Department of Agriculture
2505 Parley's Way
Salt Lake City, Utah 84115

Air Photographs, Inc.
Library Sales Office
2421 Linden Lane
Silver Spring, Maryland 20907

Mr. Dennis Berg
Coastal Engineering Research Center
U.S. Department of the Army
Kingman Building
Fort Belvoir, Virginia 22060

Mr. Einar Bergh
Norwegian Information Service
825 Third Avenue
New York, New York 10022

Dr. Kenneth Boston
Department of Geography
Melbourne State College
757 Swanston Street
Carlton, Victoria, 3053
Australia

Dr. Leonard Bowden, deceased

British Tourist Authority
680 Fifth Avenue
New York, New York 10019

Mr. William G. Brooner
Earth Satellite Corporation
1747 Pennsylvania Avenue, N.W.
Washington, D.C. 20013

Mr. H. G. Chickering, Jr.
Consulting Photogrammetrist, Inc.
1190 Seventh Avenue West
P.O. Box 2767
Eugene, Oregon 97402

Dr. Donald R. Coates
Department of Geological Sciences
  and Environmental Studies
State University of New York
  at Binghamton
Binghamton, New York 13901

Department of Geography
Clark University
Worcester, Massachusetts 01610

Department of Geography
University of Aberdeen
Aberdeen, Scotland

Department of Geography
University of California, Los Angeles
Los Angeles, California 92521

Department of Lands and Surveys
Government of Australia
Canberra, Australia

Department of Mines and Technical Surveys
Geological Survey of Canada
Ottawa, Canada

Dr. Robert Dolan
Department of Environmental Sciences
University of Virginia
Charlottesville, Virginia 22901

Mr. Philip Durgin
U.S. Forest Service
Range and Experiment Station
Redwood Laboratory
Arcata, California 95521

Dr. D. J. Easterbrook
Department of Geography
Western Washington University
Bellingham, Washington 98225

Dr. John Estes
Department of Geography
University of California, Santa Barbara
Santa Barbara, California 93106

Dr. Rhodes W. Fairbridge
Department of Geology
Columbia University
New York, New York 10027

Fairchild Aeromaps, Inc.
14437 North 73rd Street
Scottsdale, Arizona 85251

Dr. R. V. Fisher
Department of Geology
University of California, Santa Barbara
Santa Barbara, California 93106

Mr. Steven Frishman
Institute of Marine Sciences
Port Aransas, Texas 78373

Dr. Roland Fuchs
Department of Geography
University of Hawaii
Honolulu, Hawaii 96822

General Electric Company
Space Division
P.O. Box 1726
Church Street Station
New York, New York 10022

Mr. Ralph Germann
623 Kumukalu Place
Honolulu, Hawaii 96825

Mr. Jack Green
McDonnell Douglas Corporation
Douglas Advanced Research Laboratories
Huntington Beach, California 92647

Mr. Warren Hamilton
U.S. Geological Survey
Denver Federal Center
Denver, Colorado 80225

Dr. John C. Hathaway
Office of Marine Geology
U.S. Geological Survey
Woods Hole, Massachusetts 02540

Dr. Miles O. Hayes
Department of Geology
University of South Carolina
Columbia, South Carolina 29208

Mr. Don Hewitt
Mountaintek, Inc.
7833 Lomas, N.E.
Albuquerque, New Mexico 87106

Dr. J. Edward Hoffmeister
Institute of Marine Science
University of Miami
Miami, Florida 33134

Dr. Robin T. Holcomb
Hawaiian Volcano Observatory
Geological Survey
Hawaii National Park, Hawaii 96718

Dr. David Hopley
Department of Geography
James Cook University of
    North Queensland
Queensland, Australia

Dr. Douglas L. Inman
Ocean Research Division
Scripps Institution of Oceanography
University of California, San Diego
La Jolla, California 92093

Irish Tourist Board
Baggot Street Bridge
Dublin 2, Ireland

Dr. Robert Kirk
Department of Geography
University of Canterbury
Christchurch, New Zealand

Dr. Tormod Klemsdal
Department of Geography
University of Oslo
Blindern, Oslo 3
Norway

Dr. F. A. Kohout
Ground Water Branch
U.S. Geological Survey
Reston, Virginia 22092

Mr. Larry Lee
General Electric Photo Engineering Lab
5030 Herzel Place
Beltsville, Maryland 20705

Mr. Baker Lemseffer
Moroccan National Tourist Office
550 South Grand Avenue
Los Angeles, California 90017

Dr. David S. McArthur
Department of Geography
San Diego State University
San Diego, California 92182

Map Information Office
U.S. Geological Survey
Reston, Virginia 22092

Dr. Stanley Morain
Technology Application Center
University of New Mexico
Albuquerque, New Mexico 87131

Dr. James P. Morgan
Department of Geology
Louisiana State University
Baton Rouge, Louisiana 70803

Dr. H. Gray Multer
Department of Geology
Fairleigh Dickinson University
Madison, New Jersey 07940

National Air Photographic Library
Department of Energy, Mines, and Resources
615 Booth Street
Ottawa, Canada

New Brunswick Department of Tourism
Fredericton, New Brunswick
Canada

Mr. F. T. Oliver, Jr.
Ammann International Corporation
223 Tenth Street
San Antonio, Texas 78215

Dr. Antony R. Orme
Department of Geography
University of California, Los Angeles
Los Angeles, California 90024

Dr. Clyde R. Patton
Department of Geography
University of Oregon
Eugene, Oregon 97403

Dr. Donald W. Peterson
Scientist in charge
Hawaiian Volcano Observatory
Hawaii National Park, Hawaii 96718

Dr. Norbert P. Psuty
Center for Coastal and Environmental Studies
Rutgers University
New Brunswick, New Jersey 08903

Dr. William Ritchie
Department of Geography
University of Aberdeen
St. Mary's High Street
Old Aberdeen, AB9 ZUF
Scotland

Royal Norwegian Embassy
Information Service
825 Third Avenue
New York, New York 10022

Dr. Maurice L. Schwartz
Department of Geology
Western Washington University
Bellingham, Washington 98225

Science Information Office
Office of Naval Research
Ballst Tower #1
860 N. Quincy Street
Arlington, Virginia 22210

Mr. John S. Shelton
P.O. Box 48
La Jolla, California 92093

Dr. Francis P. Shepard
Scripps Institution of Oceanography
University of California, San Diego
La Jolla, California 92093

Dr. Nicholas M. Short
Code 650.3 NASA
Goddard Space Flight Center
Greenbelt, Maryland 20770

Mr. Mark Shuster
Department of Geology
University of Wyoming
Laramie, Wyoming 82071

Soil Conservation Service
U.S. Department of Agriculture
Hyattsville, Maryland 20782

Dr. Arthur Strahler
1039 Cema Linda Lane
Santa Barbara, California 93102

Teledyne Geotronics
725 East Third Street
Long Beach, California 90802

Mr. Charles Theurer
Coastal Mapping Division
U.S. Department of Commerce
National Oceanic and Atmospheric Administration
National Ocean Survey
Rockville, Maryland 20850

Mr. J. V. A. Trumbull
c/o National Resources Laboratory
Box 9218
San Juan, Puerto Rico

Ventura Port District
Ventura, California 93001

Dr. Harley J. Walker
Department of Geography and Anthropology
Louisiana State University
Baton Rouge, Louisiana 70803

Mr. J. Richard Weggel
Coastal Engineering Research Center
U.S. Department of the Army
Kingman Building
Fort Belvoir, Virginia 22060

Mr. Robin Welch
2150 Shattuck Avenue
Berkeley, California 94704

Dr. Robert C. West
Department of Geography and Anthropology
Louisiana State University
Baton Rouge, Louisiana 70803

Dr. Everett A. Wingert
Department of Geography
University of Hawaii
Honolulu, Hawaii 96822

Mr. Inge Winkelmann
Danish Information Office
Consulate General of Denmark
280 Park Avenue
New York, New York 10017

Mr. John T. Wood
Chief, User Services Section
National Cartographic Information Center
507 National Center
Reston, Virginia 22092

Dr. Bobby Wright
Department of Geography
University of Aberdeen
Aberdeen, Scotland

Yugoslavian National Tourist Office
509 Madison Avenue
New York, New York 10022

Dr. John Zeigler
The Virginia Institute of Marine Sciences
Gloucester Point, Virginia 23607

Mr. Edward Zeitler
Earth Resources Division
NASA Manned Spacecraft Center
Greenbelt, Maryland 20770

Dr. Vsevold Pavlovich Zenkovich
Head of the Shore-Zone Lab
Institute of Geography
Staromonetry per 29
Academy of Sciences
Moscow, USSR

Coastal Landforms
and Surface Features

Description and Origin
of Coastal Landforms

INTRODUCTION

Coastal geomorphology is the study of a wide range of landforms that develop where the land meets the sea. The interaction of subaerial and marine processes on materials of widely differing structure, lithology, and resistance to erosion are so variable that the detailed evolution of a coastline is extremely complex. Wave action affects only a narrow littoral zone at any one moment of geological time, but factors such as fluctuations in sea level, extending throughout the Pleistocene and Holocene (Recent) periods, have left evidence of marine processes over wide regions of the overall coastal zone. Raised beaches occur well inland and former land surfaces, with their remains of terrestrial vegetation, can be found below present sea level. Therefore coastal geomorphology concerns itself with not only a narrow belt developing under present conditions but the much wider, larger zone over which the sea has migrated in the recent geological past. This volume is primarily concerned with present-day coastal landforms that are observable around the world. Photographs and captions give age and setting of significant landform features formed during the Pleistocene and Holocene (Recent) periods, but a detailed discussion of the evolutionary factors that contribute to the formation of coasts is beyond the scope and purpose of this volume.

One of the significant aspects of coastal geomorphology is the rapidity at which certain coastal features can change. In comparison with the development of inland scenery, coastal change is relatively rapid. A beach may disappear or a port may silt up within a human life span. Throughout history there have been reports of sudden and gradual coastal changes. Even in tideless seas such as the Mediterranean, ancient Egyptian, Greek, and Ro-

man writings mention that the coast was reforming. Leonardo da Vinci's interests included coastal studies. However, true scientific interest in coastlines began with the post-Renaissance development of navigation beyond the confines of the Mediterranean. The growth of interest in marine navigation provided a wealth of information on which investigation could be based, though much of this information was kept secret. For example, not until 1823 did British Admiralty charts become generally available. The United States Coast and Geodetic Survey was founded in 1807, but the United States Navy Hydrographic Office was not established until 1830.

At the time when marine influence passed from the Italian city states, first to Portugal and Spain, and then to France, Holland, and England, the freeing of the earth sciences from the strictly biblical concept of evolution began to take place. At this same time early geologists, including Hutton and Playfair did their work. Much of the early work done on waves, tides, and coasts originated in northwestern Europe. The first true tide gauge was set up in Amsterdam. The need to protect low-lying coastal land around the shores of the North Sea gave special emphasis to these studies. Some of the classic early nineteenth-century papers on wave motion and tidal fluctuations are still relevant. Coastal studies grew rapidly in the latter half of the nineteenth century and were carried out on both sides of the Atlantic Ocean. Much of this work was originated by coastal engineers and officers of various geological surveys. Johnson (1919) gathered together the results of these early works in his book *Shore Processes and Shoreline Development* where he summarized the subject as it stood in the first decades of the twentieth century. More recently Shepard (1948, 1963), Steers (1964), Guilcher (1954, 1958), King (1959), Russell (1967), and Fairbridge (1968) have contributed important reviews.

1

EVOLUTIONARY FACTORS IN COASTAL DEVELOPMENT

Although this work is primarily concerned with the origin and formation of present-day coastal types, a brief survey of evolutionary factors is needed to set the stage. We can say that present coastlines and shorelines are the sum of all the influences that have operated on them since they were originally established. Most of the world's coasts give clear evidence that the last major relative movements of land and sea have resulted in the drowning of a former land surface, corresponding in time to the melting of the last great ice sheet. The east coast of North America, with its branching, relatively shallow inlets such as Chesapeake Bay and Pamlico Sound, and the drowned mouth of the Hudson River reflect the eustatically rising sea level, which is believed to have reached its maximum about 6,000 years ago. About 9,000 years ago Britain was separated from the continent of Europe by the cutting of the straits of Dover as sea level rose. The chronology for sea-level changes is not entirely clear, especially during the last 7,000 years, despite (or maybe because of) the considerable amount of data that exists for this period. Although the various studies differ in detail, they show that sea level stood some 130 meters (426 feet) lower about 15,000 to 20,000 years ago than at present; that there was a rapid rise in sea level of 8 millimeters (0.31 feet) per year until about 7,000 years B.P. (before present); and then a slowing down to 1.4 millimeters (0.06 feet) per year in the rise until the sea reached approximately its present level some 2,000 to 4,000 years B.P. There has been considerable controversy over proposed higher sea levels during the past 7,000 years. Taking into account all the different investigations, higher sea levels amount to only some 2 to 3 meters (6.56 to 9.84 feet) above the present water line (Curray, 1960, 1961; Jelgersma, 1961; Fairbridge, 1961; Shepard 1963; Van Andel and Laborel, 1964; Bloch, 1965; Fujii and Fuji, 1967; Redfield, 1967; Shepard and Curray, 1967; Scholl and Stuvier, 1967; Milliman and Emery, 1968; Curray et al., 1970) Whether higher sea levels did not occur is still debatable. Either way, sea level has remained roughly at its present position for the last 4,000 years (Komai, 1976). Therefore, we can say that all the world's coasts are relatively new and that small amplitude eustatic oscillations have continued over the last few thousand years.

Glacial advance and retreat was accompanied by eustatic shifts of sea level as well as by movement of climatic belts with all that this implies in terms of variation in the exposure of coasts to waves, winds, and other influences quite different from those that are molding them today. For example, the western coasts of Hawaii and St. Helena were clifted during the low sea-level stages when they lay more in the belt of westerly winds. Today they lie in the trade-wind belts with winds more from the northeast and southeast, respectively.

Sea-level changes are but one of many factors that affect a coastal region. Many other factors also come into play. In a broad sense, many of the earth's coastlines originally date from great tectonic revolutions—such as the Alpine orogeny—that reached its peak in mid-Tertiary time. Some coasts even antedate this major revolution. Since the Miocene period there appears to have been many oscillations of sea level and the recent findings on continental drift point to the emergence and submergence of many coastal zones. The Fall Zone of the eastern United States, while meeting the sea in a recently drowned coast, is essentially an emergent coast. There is evidence that, even in recent historic times, changes have continued along the east coast of the United States. In England there is ample evidence of marine transgression in Roman British times and again in the late thirteenth century, but this pattern is complicated by the sinking of eastern England at the present time and is partially masked by upward isostatic readjustment and by sedimentation (Fairbridge, 1968).

COASTAL CLASSIFICATIONS

There is considerable difference of opinion, as well as some confusion, as to what characterizes existing classifications of coasts and shorelines. It may be questionable as to whether an entirely satisfactory classification is possible. The major problem is that relatively few present-day coasts are simple in nature. Because of the numerous oscillations of sea level that marked Pleistocene and Recent time, compound and multicyclic coasts predominate. Thus, present coastal configuration, except in areas of active diastrophism, is determined largely by postglacial rise of sea level.

Most proposed coastal classifications have fallen largely into two main types—those that are purely descriptive (morphological) and those that attempt to be genetic in nature. For most purposes, a genetic classification is the most useful provided the criteria used can be readily applied on a worldwide scale. Three factors must be taken into account in forming a coastal classification: the configuration of the land against which the sea abuts; the dominant recent relative movement of land and sea; and the modification of the coastline by marine geomorphic process (Thornbury, 1969).

In the past geographers and geologists have attempted to classify coasts according to whether they are submerging, emerging, or stable. Perhaps the best known of these early classifications was by Suess (1906) in which coasts were divided into two broad groups, the

Atlantic and Pacific types, with the general trend of the geological structures at right angles and parallel to the coast (see also Fairbridge, 1968, p. 34). Davis (1896) and Gulliver (1899) based their classification on a separation of coasts into those that had been drowned and those that were emergent. Dana (1849), Richthofen (1886) and Suess (1885-1909) had all recognized emergent and submergent coasts. However, these classifications were descriptive rather than genetic in concept. Martonne's (1909) classification combined the genetic and the morphological approach (Fairbridge, 1968).

Probably the best known shoreline classification is that by Johnson (1919, 1925) which was entirely genetic and retained, as major types, coasts of emergence and submergence but added neutral and compound coastlines as two additional categories. Neutral coastlines and shorelines were defined as those whose characteristics are dependent upon neither emergence nor submergence, and included deltaic, alluvial plain, volcanic, and coral reef coasts. Compound coasts are those whose features reflect the effects of both emergence and submergence.

A number of geomorphologists objected to Johnson's classification, particularly Shepard (1937, 1938, 1963) and Shepard and Wanless (1971). Shepard objected because he thought that Johnson's classification implied that barrier beaches and barrier islands, also known as offshore bars, are diagnostic of emerging coasts. Johnson maintained that this implication was not really intended but certainly many persons using his classification have inferred this. Shepard maintained that most coasts exhibit features associated with both emergence and submergence and, hence, would be compound coasts under Johnson's definition. It is also evident that Johnson failed to recognize the full significance of the eustatic changes in sea level that accompanied glaciation and deglaciation. Although this accusation was also denied by Johnson, the objection appears to be valid; there is no discussion of the effects of glacio-eustatic changes of sea level in his book *Shore Processes and Shoreline Development* (1919). In a later book, *The New England-Acadian Shoreline* (1925), only four pages are devoted to this most important influence on coastlines. Evidence shows that during the past million years sea level has been repeatedly both lower and possibly higher than at present. Thus, in addition to emergence and submergence of land areas, evidence of both emergence and submergence of seas is found along most of the coasts of the world. This certainly complicates any proposed classification (Fairbridge, 1968; Thornbury, 1969).

Valentin (1952) proposed a classification that has received considerable attention. He grouped the coasts of the world into what may be called configuration types. recognizing two main groups—those that have advanced and those that have retreated. Coastal advance may result from either emergence or constructional progradation and coastal retreat may result from either submergence or erosional retrogradation. Although Valentin's classification represents a genetic approach, it places emphasis on the changes coasts have undergone recently rather than on initial form. Such a classification tends to stress the idea that coastal characteristics are dynamic rather than static.

Cotton (1952) modified his original 1918 classification during the same year that Valentin made his proposal. Basically, Cotton regards all coasts as compound in origin but with one or another evolutionary factor having a dominant influence. He separates coasts into those in stable regions and those in so-called mobile regions. In the latter, coasts are affected by diastrophism as well as by the eustatic changes of base level that are important in stable regions.

Each of the above classifications has something to offer and appears to be partly correct. It may be too much to expect that a satisfactory simple classification of coasts taking all the numerous factors into account can ever be devised. As Thornbury says in his *Principles of Geomorphology* (1969), "Coastal evolution over the world has been so complex as to make it extremely difficult to devise a classification that is both simple and readily applicable."

Problems with a Coastal Explanatory Description

One of the problems encountered in developing a coastal classification system is how to treat time as a direct variable. Should it be measured in years or in stages of sequential changes? What is the rate, or tempo, of coastal landscape evolution? Some coasts have evolved rapidly in postglacial time; others have been only slightly modified by marine processes (Bloom, 1978, p. 479). Coasts with a rapid tempo of evolution are in many ways similar to Shepard's secondary coasts (Part III), and the slowly changing coasts can be compared with Shepard's primary class (Part II). There are significant differences, however, that must be pointed out. If steep cliffs were cut by the sea at a lower level, they might at the present time "plunge" and reflect rather than refract incoming waves. Thus plunging cliffs might presently change at a very slow tempo, even though they could have been shaped by marine erosion at a lower sea level. On the other hand, where the bedding plane refracts incoming waves, erosion can be much more rapid (Plate 87).

The concept of tempo or rate of coastal change is usually applied to erosional coasts but it could be extended to prograded coasts as well. Deltas, coral reefs, and lava flows have extended some coasts seaward despite postglacial submergence. A rapid tempo of accumulation can quickly offset the effects of submergence just as a rapid tempo of coastal erosion can offset the effects of tectonic emergence. The growth of the Mississippi Delta helps to offset the effects of geosynclinal sinking (Plate 34) while retreat by marine erosion of the California coast from Ensenada, Mexico to Los Angeles offsets the effects of tectonic emergence (Plate 59). Tempo is not, therefore, a very promising base for a geomorphic classification of coasts, because rapid tempo might be the result of high wave energy, or weak structures, or changing sea levels. We find, as more and more studies are carried out, that too many variables could have combined to produce the same observed results. The concept of tempo in coastal evolution is very important in the field of applied research on coasts. Coasts undergoing rapid change, either by erosion or progradation, present many problems for human use and development. Many of the examples used here may be undergoing more than one process—marine erosion may appear to be the dominant sequential change, but submergence may be contributing more significantly to the overall changes.

Another problem that must be considered is relict landscapes. Most modern coral reefs appear to be veneers of Holocene limestone about 10 meters (33 feet) thick, deposited during the last 8,000 years or less on foundations that date from the last interglacial. But we do not know what portion of other modern coastal landscapes is relict, because we have no dating techniques suitable for nonreef coasts. Thus, many broad shore platforms, barriers, and reefs that appear to be in equilibrium with modern sea level and wave energy may be only slightly modified inherited forms. This brings us back to the original problem of separating active from relict forms (Bloom, 1978, pp. 479-480).

Shepard's Classification

I have saved for the last a coastal classification proposed by Francis P. Shepard, because this is the one to be used throughout this book. Far from being a perfect classification, it does come the closest to combining the numerous factors that must be taken into account when organizing coastlines and shorelines into some type of order. The original classification of coasts proposed by Shepard in 1937 was revised in 1963 and then further refined in his most recent book *Our Changing Coastlines* (Shepard and Wanless 1971). In both the 1963 and 1971 groupings Shepard recognizes two major classes of coasts—primary and secondary. Primary or youthful coasts are shaped by nonmarine agencies. Their config-

uration is mainly determined by the sea coming to rest against a topography that previously had been shaped by terrestrial rather than marine processes. Included in this class are four groups or subtypes of coasts whose major features are determined by erosion, deposition, volcanism, or diastrophism (such as faulting and folding). Secondary or mature coasts are those whose major characteristics are determined by marine processes or marine organisms. This group includes three subtypes whose chief characteristics are determined by marine erosion, marine deposition, or the growth of marine organisms.

Shepard's classification is incomplete and he himself admits that several coastal types such as uplifted marine terraces should be added. Objections to the classification are that there is more concern for coasts rather than shorelines; that the system was devised largely from a study of coastal charts that give insufficient information for a proper classification; and that it does not give any idea of the evolutionary changes that shorelines undergo. Therefore the classification gives no indication of the stage of development of a coast.

Evidence shows that Pleistocene changes in sea level have been numerous and complex. The evolutionary changes shorelines undergo involve a number of factors that would be difficult to present in a book of this type. Realization of this emphasized all the more that the distinctions between shorelines of emergence and submergence can only be made by determining whether shore features reflect the dominant effect of submergence or emergence (Thornbury, 1969, pp. 437-442). Wooldridge and Morgan (1937) have emphasized that it is inexpedient and impracticable to keep coastline and shoreline features entirely separate. Along shorelines that are marked by submergence, geomorphic forms and geologic structures of the coast are bound to be dominant over less-developed shoreline features in determining the configuration of the shoreline, whereas along emergent shorelines the dominant features are those that result from marine processes. It may not be possible to develop a classification that satisfactorily separates features of coasts from those of shorelines.

Shepard's classification is very detailed (perhaps too detailed in most cases of general usage), but in this volume, because of the numerous photographic examples, the classification may not be detailed enough. One of the drawbacks of the Shepard classification is that it completely omits emergent coasts. Emergent coasts certainly do exist in tectonically active areas and in those regions that are still recovering from the load imposed on the earth's crust by the Pleistocene ice sheets. I have included emergent coasts under the category entitled "Evolution of Coasts Undergoing Vertical Movement," which is a broader division than Shepard's classification.

Although at first sight the Shepard classification appears to offer many more complications that the more simple groupings proposed by Johnson (1919) in his book *Shore Processes and Shoreline Development*, most shores can be classified satisfactorily from charts and aerial photographs. After some practice one can apply the groupings with considerable success. Thus the main coastal divisions in this book are based on Shepard's 1963 and 1971 classifications. Also included in Part I, however, is the phenomenology of waves, currents, and tides, which is descriptive (morphological), and the genetic classification of the shape and size of wave forms; wave refraction as waves move toward a coast; coastal currents, submarine forms created by waves and currents; and the effect of tidal conditions. Part II deals with primary or youthful coasts whose configuration is primarily the result of nonmarine agencies, for example, glacial eolian, and volcanic-type coasts.

Part III is concerned with secondary coasts that are shaped by marine agencies and marine organisms, for example, wave-cut cliff coasts and barrier island depositional coasts as well as mangrove coasts and marsh grass coasts. Part IV of the volume takes into account the effects of human beings on the coastal environment such as their settlement along the coasts; their pollution and modifications to normal coastal processes; and their engineering methods to control coastal processes. Part V portrays the overall changes of the coast in the past, present, and future bringing out the problems of sea-level rise and the effects of severe storm damage caused by hurricanes and typhoons, seismic waves, storm surges, and so forth. A book of this nature cannot cover all aspects of coastlines but the main characteristics of shorelines and coastlines is presented. A world map is included at the front and back of the book giving the location of all the photographs used.

Part I

Basic Concepts Concerning the Hydrodynamics of the Shore Zone

A large body of water is seldom completely quiet. Movement of the water goes on almost all the time near the surface and at depth. Minor oscillations occur because of the ebb and flow of tides, small breezes, or exchange of heat within a water body. In this book we are concerned with large-scale circulations, mainly at the surface; the interchange of water between the surface and depth is not our concern. Three types of movement are responsible for the changes taking place along a coast—waves, currents, and tides (tides are only rarely of geomorphic importance).

SHAPE AND SIZE OF WAVE FORMS

Wind is by far the most important but not the only cause of wave generation. Winds generate and affect wave motion through friction on the water surface, through the process of "push" against the rear of a wave, and "pull" at its front, along with suction over its crest, and compression in its trough. Figure 1 shows the various parts of a wave.

Wave length is the horizontal distance between adjacent crests or troughs, and wave height is the vertical distance that occurs between them. Wave period is the time elapsed as two consecutive crests or troughs pass a given point, and wave velocity is the speed at which the wave advances. Wave depth is the vertical distance from the still-water level to the bottom. It represents one-half the wave length. The size of a wave is related to the velocity of the generating wind and the length of time the wind is blowing. Maximum size is attained only in water that is deep enough so that the ocean bottom does not interfere with the undulatory movement of the water. The largest wave heights thus far accurately measured were about 16 meters (52 feet). However, on February 7, 1933, the navy tanker *U.S.S. Ramapo* encountered a prolonged weather disturbance and made several measurements of waves, one of which was at least 34 meters

(112 feet) high (Gross, 1972, pp. 253-254). Wave height is determined not only by wind velocity but also by the extent of water over which the wind can blow—the fetch. Very large waves develop only where the fetch is great, which explains why such waves cannot develop on lakes or enclosed arms of the sea. A fetch of at least 1,000 kilometers (621 miles) is required to produce the largest waves that have been observed (Kuenen, 1950).

Another factor that affects wave height is the duration of the wind. Studies made at Scripps Institution of Oceanography at La Jolla, California during World War II indicated that with wind velocity of 105 kilometers per hour (65 mph) and a fetch of 1,500 kilometers (931 miles), a wave height of 20 meters (65 feet) was theoretically possible, but the wind would need to blow continuously for at least fifty hours before it would be attained (Thornbury, 1969, p. 421).

Since we are mainly concerned with the shore and coastal zone, we should turn to the problem of how waves change as they move into shallow water. One of the first phenomena to be observed is the decrease in velocity with a consequent crowding together of the waves and the steepening of their fronts (Plate 1). Where the orbital velocity (speed) in the crest of the wave exceeds the rate at which the wave is moving forward, a curl develops in the top of the wave front that, lacking sufficient water to fill the cavity beneath it, lunges forward or breaks to form surf (Plate 2). The angle at which waves peak up and break is less than 120°. In breaking, waves of oscillation change into waves of translation, which rush forward onto the shore as swash. After the swash reaches its maximum forward position, the water runs back down the seaward slope as backwash. Whereas waves may wash up on the beach at an oblique angle, the backwash returns straight down the slope. The resulting zigzag motion of material being carried back and forth up and down a beach face results in slow longshore or littoral movement (Thornbury, 1969, p. 421).

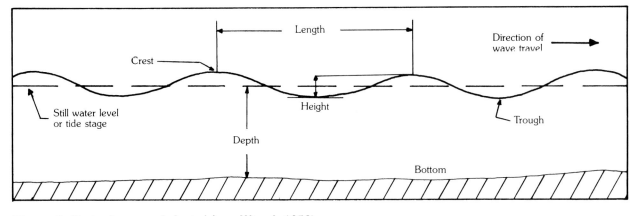

Figure 1. Parts of a wave (adapted from Wiegel, 1953).

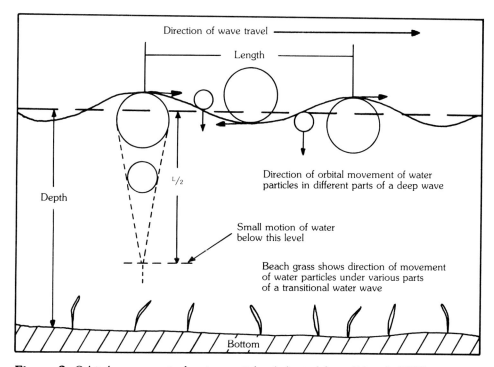

Figure 2. Orbital movement of water particles (adapted from Wiegel, 1953).

As a wave encounters very shallow water, wave height increases and wave length decreases. Several types of waves develop along the coast depending on the slope of the beach and the type of wave formation. Waves that develop in deep enough water to have free orbital movement are called waves of oscillation. In such a wave the main movement of water is roughly circular with the water moving forward on the crest, upward on the front, backward in the trough, and downward on the back. Figure 2 illustrates the orbital movement of waves in an open sea.

There is also a slow mass movement of water forward in the direction of wave propagation, mainly because water particles are moving forward at a greater velocity on the crest than in the trough. In higher waves this slightly forward movement of water is greater than in low waves (Thornbury, 1962, p. 428).

Oscillatory waves may exhibit two distinct phases of development. In one phase, their characteristics are directly under the control of the wind. These are called wind waves, forced waves, or sea waves (Plate 3). In the other phase, they are called swell or free waves. These waves have traveled beyond a storm area and are decreasing in height (Shepard, 1948). It is difficult to distinguish the two types, but swell waves are less complex than forced waves and display a kind of heaving motion of water with lower wave heights, longer wave lengths, and fewer breaking wave crests. It is the swell that accounts for strong wave action along coasts on days when the air is relatively calm (Plate 4).

During violent storms, waves break offshore, sometimes encountering water too shallow for their propagation several miles from the shoreline. Such waves begin cutting the seabottom, with part of the resulting debris being carried out to deeper water and another part being thrown upon the landward edge of the submarine cut, forming a submarine bar or ridge (Plate 5). These bars may, on occasion, be exposed during low tide but while they are partially submerged, they are a hazard to boats.

As mentioned earlier, as a wave encounters very shallow water, wave height increases and wave length decreases. With this situation, wave steepness increases and the wave becomes unstable when its height is about 8/10 of the water depth and in turn forms a breaker. A perfect oscillatory wave will form a plunging breaker where there is a moderately steep beach and periods of long, even swells (Figure 3). Plunging breakers tend to curl over and break with a crash (Plate 6). They usually develop where water depth is equal to wave height and they are accentuated during time of offshore winds. Energy is suspended almost instantly and the amount of energy is extreme. Thus, they can do a great deal of cutting when they break directly against objects. A 6.1 meter (20 foot) plunging breaker has been known to break a surfboard in half and to break the back of a surfer (Plate 7).

In contrast to waves of oscillation, in waves of translation, or solitary waves, the water moves in the direction of wave propagation without compensating backward motion. Also, unlike oscillatory waves that usually de-

PLUNGING BREAKER   SPILLING BREAKER

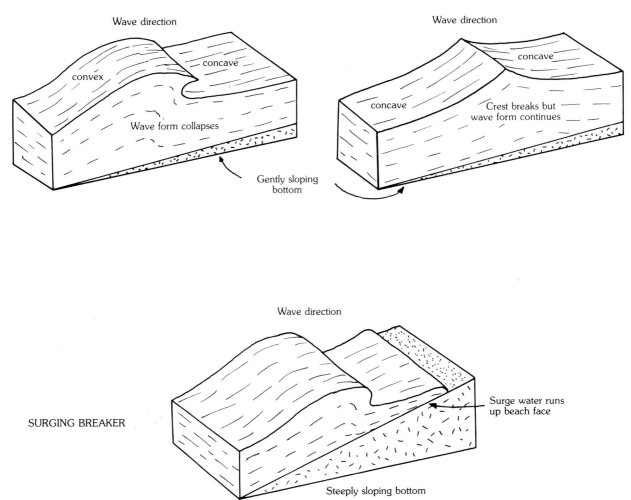

Figure 3. Types of breakers reaching a shore (adapted from Gross, 1972).

velop in chains, waves of translation are single and independent entities. Solitary waves may be generated at sea or in shallow water due to the breaking of oscillatory waves. They do not display the noticeable crests and troughs of oscillatory waves. Instead they look like welts separated by particularly flat water surfaces. A plunging breaker that begins as an oscillatory wave can change into a translatory wave and then re-form into an oscillatory wave once it returns to an orbital system. Solitary waves become two main types of breakers upon reaching shore—spilling breakers (Plate 8) and surging breakers. The spilling breakers are formed by wind waves or sea waves in contrast to swell waves. These waves develop best on a low sloping shelf and beach during local storms. They tend to run in with a foaming crest. Energy is spread out over a considerable distance so they are not as destructive as plunging breakers.

Surging breakers occur where a beach is very steep and there is a high tidal variation. Here a swell or wind wave peaks up to a crest and, instead of plunging or spilling, surges on the beach with a lot of foam (Plate 9). Spilling and surging breakers are both solitary waves. These breakers are more effective than oscillatory waves in moving material forward on the sea bottom and in erosion because all their energy is carried forward.

A fourth type is the collapsing breaker (Plate 10). These breakers occur on steep bottoms and may break over the lower half of the waves themselves with very little upward splash (Gross, 1972, p. 158).

The surf usually consists of a mixture of these different types of breakers, because of the different types of waves coming into the shore as well as the complex and uneven bottom topography offshore, which is changing because of tidal action.

WAVE REFRACTION

If a wave meets a barrier such as a vertical wall, it may be reflected and its energy transferred to another wave that travels in a different direction. Waves often approach a shore at an angle and then change direction on entering shallow water. We often see breakers nearly parallel to the coastline when they reach the beach, although they may have approached the coast from many different directions. This process, known as wave refraction, occurs because the part of the wave still in deeper water moves faster than the part that has entered more shallow water. This causes the crest to rotate into a position parallel to the depth contour of the bottom in the shallow water near shore (Plates 1 and 4). Because of wave refraction, there is a concentration of breakers and energy on headlands and spreading out, divergence,

and loss of energy in adjacent bays (Plate 11). The lines connecting wave crests are called orthogonals (Figure 4).

COASTAL CURRENTS

Currents differ from waves in that there is progressive forward movement of water. Currents may be created in several ways, but we shall discuss only those aspects that relate to coastal landforms. Winds are directly or indirectly responsible for the major surface ocean currents. Thus, currents are definitely related in direction to planetary wind belts, and are modified, in turn, by the deflective effect of the earth's rotation and the configuration of the continents.

Large planetary currents, such as the Gulf Stream and Humboldt Current, seldom affect continental shorelines

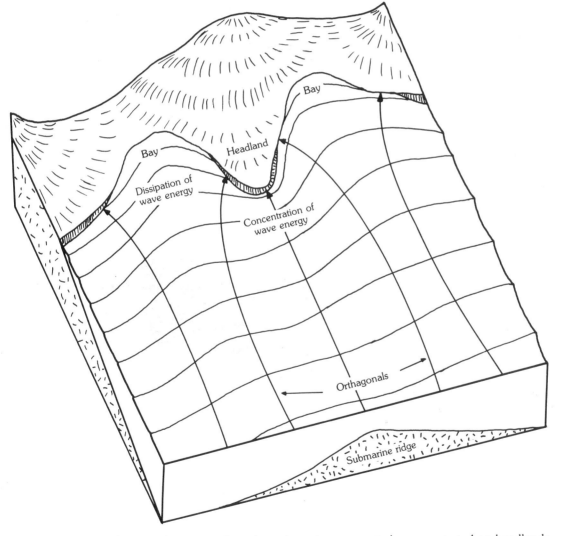

Figure 4. Wave refraction along an embayed coast causing energy to be concentrated on headlands (adapted from Strahler, 1971, and Gross, 1972).

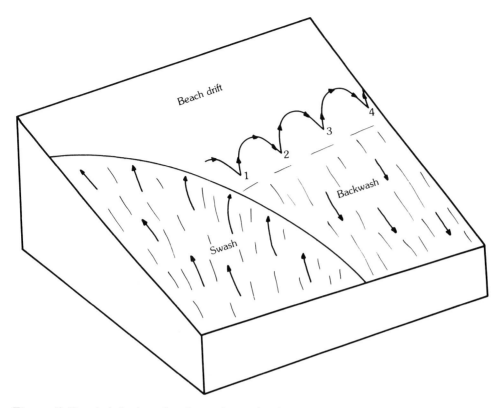

Figure 5. Beach drift of sand and gravel particles due to the swash and backwash of waves (adapted from Strahler, 1969).

because their main movement is too far offshore. However, the Gulf Stream does influence bottom conditions near several of the Bahama Islands, because its movement passes over several shallow shoals and reefs (Plate 12).

Where currents infringe on the land, they are forced to deviate in direction, this direction being determined to a large degree by the outlines of the continents. This is one of the reasons for longshore or littoral currents. Longshore currents are also generated when waves break obliquely against a shore. Longshore or wind-drift currents seldom affect water to depths in excess of 91 meters (298 feet). Their velocities are rarely great enough to produce significant erosion, but they can move material along the sea bottom, contributing to the development of depositional features along shorelines (Thornbury, 1969, p. 422). Numerous spits, bars, and barrier islands are built by longshore currents (see Plate 1).

Longshore movement of material that is the result of longshore drifting should not be confused with a different type of longshore transportation called beach drifting (Johnson, 1919, pp. 94-105). If a wave approaches a shore obliquely, its swash will run up on the shore in the direction of wave progradation, but its backwash will move down the steepest slope under the influence of gravity (see Plate 13). This movement is usually at a right angle to the shore; consequently particles being moved by the swash and backwash pursue parabolic paths that generally move them along the shore parallel to the front of the breaking waves (Figure 5). Where beach drifting coincides in direction with a longshore drift, pronounced movement of shore materials may result. If, however, beach drifting is in a direction opposite to a longshore current, the result will be that the finer beach material will travel in the direction of the longshore current and the coarser material will travel in the direction of beach drifting. It appears that beach drifting moves as much material along the shore as shore currents do and, if the sediments are coarse, beach drifting may be the more important mode of transport (Thornbury, 1969, p. 422).

It generally has been assumed that water carried landward by waves returns seaward mainly by a bottom flow called undertow. This is the current that draws a bather out to the next incoming wave. It often causes children to panic and in Hawaii, where large waves form, can be dangerous to body surfers. Some coastal geomorphologists (Shepard 1941) have claimed that rip currents are more important in returning water seaward than undertow. Rip currents consist of localized lanes or paths of water moving seaward through channels between barrier bars and across wave patterns in contrast to the nonlocalized flow of undertow (Plate 14). These currents are sometimes called rip tides, but this is a misnomer; they are in no way related to tides. Rip currents can be identified by brown streaks of sediment-laden water; streaks of agitated water; gaps in the lines of breakers; foam belts; seaward movement of floating objects; and streaks of green water resulting from the greater depth of water where a rip current forms. One can often find shallow channels on the seafloor that attest to their presence. Rip currents may represent a more significant method of carrying suspended sediments seaward than is generally realized.

EFFECT OF TIDAL CONDITIONS

Tidal currents maintain velocities sufficient to transport material but they are usually of minor geomorphic significance. In the Bay of Fundy, between New Brunswick and Nova Scotia, the tidal range varies from 9 to 15 meters (30 to 50 feet), and the flow of the tide is commonly marked by a front of advancing water known as a tidal bore that may be as much as 1.83 meters (6 feet) high (Plate 15). Similar tidal bores form in estuaries of rivers such as the Tsientan River in Chian (Kuenen, 1950) and the Severn and Trent rivers in southern England. A tidal bore 5 meters (16 feet) in height can be found in the Amazon River. Tidal bores do not appear to cause much erosion. Johnson (1925) concluded that there was more evidence of deposition than of erosion by tides in the Bay of Fundy. Tidal currents transport considerable debris and even carry on a scouring action. Water movement extends downward to greater depths than in wind-induced currents and may be marked by concentration of topographic features such as underwater canyons. Tides may be responsible for the most rapid constant flow of sea water known (Shepard, 1948). In Seymour Narrows, between the coast of British Columbia and Vancouver Island, tidal currents measuring 12 knots per hour (13.8 mph) have been recorded.

Part II

Primary or Youthful Coasts with Configuration Primarily the Result of Nonmarine Agencies

If you travel around the coasts of the world, you will notice that marine forces are operating at varying degrees from place to place. However, many land margins have scarcely been affected by marine processes, thus, they are essentially in the same condition as they were when the sea came to rest against them. These are called primary or youthful coasts. The shape of these shorelines, unmodified by the sea, depends on what happened to the area previously. Coasts that have been modified by the waves and currents along the shore are called secondary coasts (Shepard, 1963).

Nearly all coasts of the world have been submerged since the time of ancient civilizations. The reason for this is that prior to about 10,000 years ago, large parts of northern Europe and North America were covered by great ice sheets, similar to present day Antarctic and Greenland ice caps. As discussed earlier, the primary source for the ice was the ocean and, as a result, sea level dropped. When the ice caps melted, the water returned to the oceans and sea level rose on the order of 122 to 137 meters (400 to 450 feet) (Russell, 1967). Except where upward land movements have offset the effects, most coasts can be considered as submergent.

Some primary or youthful coasts are shaped by subaerial erosion and are partly drowned by sea level or downwarping, or they are inundated by an ice mass from a valley going into the sea. These are called land erosion coasts (Shepard, 1963).

SUBMARINE EROSION COASTS

Although this book is mainly concerned with coastal landforms near or above sea level, mention should be made of the numerous erosion features occurring beneath the surface of the water, especially near the edge of continental shelves.

Submarine canyons are the main form of erosion under the sea. These seafloor canyons include some of the most rugged topography on the face of the earth. Many of them have walls thousands of meters high. For example, Great Bahama Canyon, where it cuts the sea floor between Eleuthera and Great Abaco islands in the Bahamas, reaches a depth of 4,300 meters (14,104 feet), perhaps the highest canyon walls in the world—certainly far higher than those of the Grand Canyon of the Colorado River (Plates 5 and 12).

Submarine canyons are mostly winding, V-shaped gorges that extend all the way down continental slopes. Many reach great depths of the deep ocean floor. On the landward side, most of the canyons head near the coast, some of them so close that you can throw a stone from the beach into the canyon head. Others, however, head at or near the outer edge of the continental slope. This is

true of the east coast of the United States and along the outer rim of the wide Bering Sea shelf.

Many canyon walls have remarkably steep cliffs. Francis Shepard's dive in *Deep Star* showed the presence of an undercut cliff at a depth of 445 meters (1459 feet) in a canyon off the coast of La Jolla, California (Palmer, 1971). In another canyon off the La Jolla coast, there were numerous places where the walls were overhanging.

Most submarine canyons have been cut in rock. The type of rock varies from resistant materials such as granite and quartzite to soft sediments such as shales that are easily eroded. Another interesting aspect is that most of the well-surveyed submarine canyons have approximately as many tributaries as land canyons. Some, on the other hand, only have significant tributaries at their heads where they approach the shore (Shepard, 1972, pp. 1-12).

Although most submarine canyons and fans are formed by erosion, upbuilding may also take place. We usually think of a canyon as being the result of downcutting by erosion. Under the ocean, however, there may be a combination of downcutting of the canyon axis and upbuilding of the canyon walls. This possibility would explain the gigantic walls of Grand Bahama Canyon (Plate 12). It is now known that the Bahama Banks, associated with barrier reefs, have been growing upward as the entire platform sank. It could be that the canyon was maintained or even deepened as the walls of the canyon grew higher (Shepard, 1972, pp. 1-11).

One other aspect of submarine erosion that should be mentioned is the falls observed by a group of diving biologists in 1959 during an expedition to the submarine canyons off Baja California, Mexico. The so-called sand falls occurred where flowing sand spilled over abrupt dropoffs in the upper lip of the main channel of the canyon (Shepard and Dill, 1966; Fairbridge, 1966, pp. 763-764).

LAND EROSION COASTS

Ria Coasts (Drowned River Valleys)

The result of submergence, whether due to rising sea level or sinking land, is that river valleys become embayed. Their shape is due mainly to subaerial erosion. A classic example of the effect of drowning is the Chesapeake Bay with its many arms, looking very much like a giant maple leaf (Plate 16). Since the floors of river valleys slope outward and generally lack basins, the axes of the embayments due to drowning will also slope seaward unless they are later modified (Shepard and Wanless, 1971).

Richthofen (1886) proposed the term "ria" (Spanish) for a series of long, mountainous-sided estuaries in northwestern Spain that are not glaciated, thus not fjords, but are subaerially eroded. This type of coast is characteristically funnel-or trumpet-shaped in plan and not so deep as fjords. Other good examples of such coasts are found in southwest Ireland, China, the east coast of the United States—represented by Delaware Bay and Chesapeake Bay—and in such places where the structural texture of the rock is cut off obliquely by the trend of the coast. A special type parallel to the coast is the "Dalmation" type, from Yugoslavia (see below). Richthofen used the term "ria" in the strict sense, but others (Gulliver, 1889, Davis, 1915, and Johnson, 1919) applied it to all types of subaerially carved valleys. Most geomorphologists accept the more restricted term, which is used in this book.

One can usually recognize a ria coast by the relatively shallow water of the estuaries that indent the land. These coasts often have a barrier built across the estuary mouth. Two types are recognized: dendritic, resembling an oak leaf, which is usually found in horizontal beds or homogeneous material, and trellis, resembling fingers, which is found in inclined beds of unequal hardness. Dendritic coasts are found frequently around the world, but it is more difficult to find examples of trellis coasts. The Banks Peninsula of New Zealand (Plate 17) and sections of the coast of Burma are two of the few examples of trellis ria coasts.

Related Coastal Types

There are four related coastal types that are often associated with rias (Baulig, 1956). The first of these is the Cala (Balearic Islands) or Calanque (French coast of Provence) coasts consisting of narrow, short, drowned valleys with steep sides, characteristic of some limestone coasts and also similar to the sherm or cherm (Arabic) found on both coasts of the Red Sea (Schmidt, 1923). Sherms are special types of rias having long bays with narrow entrances. They are cut in low coastal plains and often have widening and branching within. Finding their origin is sometimes a problem because there is not always a wadi at the head of the main arm and they may be caused by structural control, that is to say, predetermined by geological structure. Sherms may be either of the tectonic or the ria type (Guilcher, 1958, pp. 156-157).

A second related coastal type is the Dalmatian from Dalmatia, Yugoslavia. It is a drowned mountainous coast consisting of parallel fold ranges, resulting in zigzag channels parallel and at right angles to the general coastal trend (Plate 18; Richthofen, 1886).

The third related ria coast is the Liman (Turkish for lagoon) that occurs along the Black Sea. These are broad valleys cut in a low, flat-lying coast, mostly cut off by baymouth bars or barriers. In the eastern United States and the Gulf of Mexico, where tides somewhat modify the pattern, coasts of this type are often called barrier island coasts.

Estuary is a name for embayments where rivers enter the sea, so that they are affected by tides and by salt and fresh water mixing (Fairbridge, 1980). Because of the low relief around Chesapeake Bay and Delaware Bay, some coastal geomorphologists feel they should be called estuary coasts rather than ria coasts (Plate 16).

Drowned karst topography is a fourth type of land-erosion coast in which the embayments are oval-shaped depressions indicative of drowned *sinkholes*. These coasts are rare. One exists along the east side of the Adriatic Sea (Plate 19), where bedrock consists of limestone or gypsum and erosion by rain and running water produces a very special type of local topography, because of rapid solution of these rock types. In such terrain, rivers only flow for short distances before running into caverns. The roofs of the caves are unstable and often collapse, developing the circular lakes or pits called sinkholes. Because of the prevalence of karst along the coast of Yugoslavia, the local topography has been given this name (in a broader view this is a Dalmatian type of coast seep.) The west coast of Florida, in the broad curve north of St. Petersburg, owes much of its form to drowning of a limestone karst area. Karst features also extend out into the sea along the north coast of Jamaica; also extensively in Greece and Turkey, as well as on the uplifted coral islands of the Pacific.

Drowned Glacial Erosion Coasts

Drowned glacial erosion coasts are easily recognized because they are deeply indented, due to fjords, and associated offshore with many islands. Marine charts show deep water (commonly over 50 to 100 fathoms) with the cross-section of the bays being U-shaped and with much greater depth within the bays than near the entrance (Plate 20). Hanging valleys and sides are commonly parallel and relatively straight as compared to rias. Almost all glaciated coasts fall into this category, which has several subdivisions.

Fjords (fiords) and fjards (fiards), like ria coasts, are fundamentally due to submergence since fjords are glacial valleys flooded by the sea. However, fjord coasts, like many glacial coasts, have undergone a postglacial isostatic uplift, which in certain places, such as the west coast of Norway, represent an emergent coast. But fjords are predominantly submergent in form, because the glaciers that occupied the present fjords were so thick that they did not float in the sea until they reached deep water (Plate 21). Great depths are found in certain fjords, for example, the Sogne Fjord, -1,244 meters (-4,080 feet), the Messier channel in Patagonia, -1,292 meters (-4,238 feet), and Scoresby Sound in Greenland, -1,300 meters (-4,264 feet).

There are true rias (drowned river valleys) in formerly glaciated areas. Examples can be found in Wales and southern Ireland, but there are no typical glacial erosion forms in these regions. Fjords, on the other hand, are not only deep glacial valleys but have steep mountain walls surrounding them, numerous waterfalls, and usually no large river flowing into them (Plate 22). These spectacular landforms develop as the ice pushes down valleys. The erosive action of ice is exerted sideways as well as downward and gouges out troughs with broad, flat floors and almost vertical sides. Tributary streams or glaciers join these valleys on top of the ice giving them little gradient and leaving numerous hanging valleys, many of which are occupied by spectacular waterfalls today. They are also characterized by closed depressions cut off by thresholds of solid rock and numerous islands usually occur offshore. A spectacular fjord on the South Island of New Zealand is Milford Sound (Plate 23). A youthful or rejuvenated relief is essential to the formation of a true fjord. For this reason, the submerged valleys of New England and Acadia are not fjords. Exceptions include Somes Sound on Mount Desert Island, which is the only true fjord in New England, and where the Hudson crosses the New York highlands in the Bear Mountain region, as well as downstream. At these locations deeply entrenched valleys were converted to glacial troughs that are now drowned (Johnson, 1919).

Fjards (fiards) are similar to fjords but are generally more irregular in shape and lack the high relief and U-shaped cross-sections of fiord coasts. By strict definition, a fjard is a rocky, irregular inlet of low relief, glacially scoured, and deeply drowned. There are lateral channels as well as radial channels. Fjards have some of the characteristics of true fjords (such as drowned glacial valleys), but they also fall into the class of glacial lowland coasts. Many of the Scottish firths are better characterized as fjards than fjords, as are many of the drowned rocky estuaries of Connecticut and Maine (Plate 24). Generally, fjord rock basins are much shallower than fjord rock basins and because of this can be separated from nonglacial coastal forms such as rias (Embleton and King, 1968, p. 245).

Glacial troughs have also been influenced by glaciation. These coastlines have deep estuaries with basin depressions of glacial origin (Plate 25). They differ from fjords and fjards by being broad indentations such as Cabot Strait and the Gulf of St. Lawrence or the Straits of Juan de Fuca. Other examples of such troughs include the Bay of Fundy, the Skageraak between Denmark and Norway, and the White Sea in the Soviet Union.

GLACIAL LOWLAND DEPOSITIONAL COASTS

These coasts may be emergent as in Sweden, where the postglacial isostatic rise still continues, or they may be submergent, where the relief, due to glaciation, has been drowned by the melting of the ice sheet and the resulting rise of the sea. In Sweden, submerged glacial topography is now in the process of emerging (see the discussion of emergent coasts on page 25).

These coasts, also called glacier plain coasts, are as intricate and are characterized by as many islands and arms as fjord coasts (Plate 26). They are much more varied morphologically because they have in juxtaposition so many glacial accumulation forms such as terminal moraines, drumlins, outwash plains, subglacial valleys, proglacial channels, eskers, kames, and kettleholes. Also, glaciation of a low-lying peneplain may produce subdued structural landforms. However, the relative dominance of each of these glacial accumulation forms gives a distinct appearance to the coast (Guilcher, 1958).

The development of glacial deposition coasts has reached a more advanced stage than that of fjord coasts, because the deposits are unconsolidated, easily attacked, and redistributed by the sea. In both North America and the Baltic, these coasts show rapid evolution and remarkable development of spits, bars, and beaches of all types (Plate 27).

Partially Submerged Moraines

These features are usually difficult to recognize without field study to indicate the glacial origin of the sediments constituting the coastal area, and such landforms are usually modified by marine erosion. Two terminal moraines parallel to the general trend of the coast in the Nantucket and Cape Cod regions have lagoons behind them. The moraines themselves are made up of glacial deposits and these often form cliffs along the coast as can be seen at the tip of Montauk Point, Long Island (Plate 28).

Partially Submerged Drumlins and Drumlinoids

A drumlin is an egg-shaped landform carved by a glacier. A drumlinoid is also often elliptical but has a bedrock core with a veneer of glacial deposits. The drumlins of Boston Harbor tend to give rise to oval islands and peninsulas, many of which have spits and several of which are connected by tombolos (Plate 29). Drumlins can also be found in Halifax Harbor, Nova Scotia, and Bantry Bay, Southwest Ireland.

Glaciofluvial Features Glaciofluvial features include a number of glacially related depositional landforms. I mention three of these features, because they can occasionally be found near coasts. Outwash plains are marked by broad fingers of water-laid deposits cut by old, slightly incised proglacial channels, that have been drowned by the sea in many areas. The south coast of Cape Cod is an example of an outwash plain. In Europe, glacial outwash coasts are called föhrden or förden coasts. These are often transgressed tunnel valleys produced by melt-water streams and therefore filled with glacial debris. Examples can be found along the Baltic coast of Germany and the eastern coast of Denmark. Unlike the coasts left by glacial erosion, those resulting from glacial deposition and outwash were quickly modified, partly because the materials were unconsolidated sediments and partly because in many places there was nothing to protect them from the wave attack of an open sea (Plate 30; Shepard and Wanless, 1971, p. 9).

Esker coasts are very difficult to locate because they are easily worked by the sea and usually are only recognized as material sources for beach ridges and beaches. At Billudden, north of Stockholm, Sweden, an esker coming out of the Baltic produces a small promontory, but the material and the form are reworked by the waves. Good esker features reaching the coast have not been found in Maine or Finland where inland eskers are quite numerous (T. Klemsdal, pers. comm.).

Kettleholes that are usually associated with moraines leave small depressions that are often filled with water. Some of the circular forms in tidal marshes in New England may well be former kettlehole depressions.

Although well-defined features are scarce, numerous glacial forms can be found on the east coast of Hudson Bay; north of the Labrador and Arctic regions of Canada; the Baltic region, especially Finland, Sweden, Poland, Germany, and Denmark; and, in the United States, the coast of New England has a great variety of glacial forms.

ICY, UNGLACIATED LOWLAND COASTS

Icy, unglaciated lowland coasts have received very little attention in the literature and represent a relatively new field among coastal geomorphologists. Included in this category are the coastal regions of the Arctic and Antarctic that are under the influence of ice and frozen ground—the ice pack and winter ice-flow depositional coasts. These coasts are affected by ice blocks, icebergs, and melt waters from glaciers. This is an important field and much research must still be done. Three examples are presented to illustrate how different these coastal areas can be.

Many areas under the influence of frozen ground are affected by a permafrost zone. The permafrost may be continuous where the climate is so severe that the ice close to the surface thaws only a few centimeters to several meters (Plate 31). The only unfrozen areas are those lying below certain deep and wide lakes, near flowing rivers, or beneath the sea. The Colville Delta of Alaska is an example of a river flowing through a region of permafrost with patterned ground occurring in the interfluves between the delta channels. Where discontinuous permafrost occurs, there are usually small scattered unfrozen areas. With sporadic permafrost, small islands of permafrost exist in a generally unfrozen area. Many of these frozen islands may be relics of a former colder climate; they are steadily diminishing in size. Continuous or discontinuous permafrost underlies as much as one-fifth of the earth's land areas, including 47 percent of the Soviet Union, as much as 50 percent of Canada and Alaska, and most of the nonglacial regions of Greenland and Antarctica. Because of the widespread occurrence of permafrost, more attention should be paid to this type of coast and a separate category should be included in any coastal discussion (Embleton and King, 1968, pp. 458-462).

Ice-shelf coasts and floating ice tongues are grouped together in this classification but they differ greatly in size. Ice shelves are more characteristic of the Antarctic, the Ross Ice Shelf being one of the best examples (Plate 32). The material of the shelf is partially derived from the outward flow of the inland glacial sheet but is mainly derived from the accumulation of snow on the upper shelf surface itself.

The bulk of the ice of the Ross Shelf is, therefore, made up of firn rather than true glacier ice. The floating ice mass is about 300 to 400 meters (984 to 1,312 feet) thick and covers an area of 550,000 square kilometers (212,000 square miles), more than the area of France.

The calving of the barrier, as the ice shelf is often called, produces very large tabular icebergs that only occur in the Southern Hemisphere, as ice shelves of this type are confined to Antarctica. Along large sections of the Antarctic coastline, ice sheets reach the sea in fairly high ice cliffs. This type of ice-lined coast needs to be mapped and studied in more detail.

Floating ice tongues represent an extension of a glacier that is projected seaward and usually afloat. When the tongue breaks apart numerous pieces of pack ice form, some of great size. The larger pieces of ice float to sea as icebergs. At the present time, floating ice tongues are restricted to high latitudes where glaciers reach sea level. The form that the floating ice takes depends on the surrounding coastal relief. Where a glacier is confined within a valley, the floating part of the glacier will be no wider than the grounded part and, if the bay or fjord contains quiet water, the pack ice will not move very far. However, where larger glaciers and ice masses enter the open ocean, the action of waves and currents can spread the pack ice over great distances and icebergs will drift far enough to threaten shipping lanes (Plate 33; Embleton and King, 1968, pp. 73-77).

SUBAERIAL DEPOSITION COASTS

Subaerial deposition coasts are largely formed by deposition by rivers that extend to the shoreline. Deltaic coasts will be considered first. Where rivers introduce more sediment into the sea than can be carried away by waves and currents, the land progrades in the form of deltas. Deltas are common at the heads of bays where waves are of minimal effect; but they also form in the open ocean where enormous quantities of sediment are introduced, such as at the mouth of the Mississippi, and are even found on a small scale as tidal deltas at the mouths of some bays. Since rivers develop distributaries at their mouths, the deltas are likely to have lobes separated by indentations, as in the Birdfoot delta of the Mississippi (Plate 34). Digitate is another name for fingerlike level extensions of the delta plain. This type is rare, however, the lower Mississippi Delta with fine silt deposition along the edge of the channels is one of the best examples. Another example can be found in the mudflats of the Colorado River Delta (Plate 35). In many places delta deposition is so general that only one broad arc develops. These deltas are classified according to their arcuate shape. The best examples of these arcs are the mouths of such large rivers as the Nile (Plate 36), the Niger, and the Yukon, but many small rivers also build out this type of delta. Arcuate deltas are rounded at their seaward edge indicating areas of active coastal currents (Plate 37). Another type of delta classified by shape is the cuspate form, which develops if there is only one main river channel, such as at the mouth of the Brazos in Texas or the Tiber near Rome, Italy. This type of delta represents concave crescents facing the sea. Marine erosion often plays an important role in their formation. A fourth type of delta shape is the lobate, which consists of convex lobes with position corresponding to the mouths of distributing streams. The western Mississippi Delta and Rhone Delta are examples.

Deltas are classified not only by their shape but also by where they form. There are many small river deltas of numerous shapes and forms whose formation depends on the relationship between the factors related to rivers (amount of sediment and rate of discharge) and marine factors (the depth of the in-shore zone, waves, currents, tides, surges, and long-shore drift). Tidal deltas often have a 90 to 180° fan of coarse-grained sediment extending out from either end of a tidal inlet and cut by its channel fans. The surface of the delta is usually composed of shifting bars and shoals with low—usually marshy—islands. On the seaward side, the inlet is flanked by low tidal levees or beach ridges. The mouth of the Santa Clara is an example of a river that has cut through a narrow barrier island and is building a small delta on the seaward side (Plate 38). Small deltas are often constructed in a lagoon in which the delta is partly or completely deposited in a shallow stretch of water that has been separated from the sea by a bar, spit, or reef. Direct wave influence is minimal except during severe storms. There are several locations where small deltas form, such as at the head of drowned estuaries of the Susquehanna Delta or the Colorado River Delta (Plate 39). Another location is at a bay head where rivers descend steeply from a mountain source and carry coarse waste to the sea. The Hutt River Delta and Wai-au River Delta (Plate 40) in New Zealand are prime examples. Still another location for small deltas is where glaciers enter the sea or at the heads of fjords where material is usually glacial outwash that has been carried and deposited by melt water distributaries (Plate 41).

Alluvial plain coasts are the second division under subaerial deposition coasts. These are relatively straight, gently sloping coasts being prograded by a group of braided streams, usually coming from a nearby mountain range. This type is typical along desert coasts that have a series of coalescing alluvial fans coming to the sea forming wide arcs. The coast of Baja California, particularly on the Gulf of California side, has excellent examples of this type of coast (Plate 42). Another good example in a humid region is the east coast of the South Island of New Zealand (Plate 43). Although the above examples are most common, volcanic coasts, where lava flows form depositional coastal plains with wide arcs, should also be included in this category.

Since alluvial coastal plains are widespread throughout the world, the limits of this definition could be stretched to include wide coastal belts covered by swamp or tropical forests in which there is a wide meander pattern and an almost featureless plain. An example of such a coastal region might be the eastern plains of Sumatra, which have the above characteristics plus a coastal zone that is filling in behind an advancing line of mangroves. Another, very different type of alluvial plain coast occurs along Arctic shores. Here, large winding rivers are carrying alluvium to the sea (Plate 44).

EOLIAN PROCESSES

Wind deposition coasts consist of dunes, fossil dunes, and sand flats (Shepard, 1963, pp. 159-161). The last two are not common features but coastal sand dunes are widespread around the world.

Active Dunes

Coastal dunes occur frequently where deposition of wind-blown sand is in excess of wave erosion. There must be a supply of sand from the beaches as well as the absence of obstacles in the sea that would hinder wind movement. Also, there must be an absence of most types of vegetation (a certain type of xerophytic scrub favors the formation of coastal dunes) in the part of the beach from which the sand is derived.

There are numerous types of sand dunes found along a coast, but only a few of the main types are included in this discussion. Smith (1954) devised a classification of coastal dunes that includes most of the main types:

Foredunes are mounds of sand up to 3.05 meters (10 feet) high adjacent and parallel to the beach. Plate 45 is an example of such small dunes along the Makrān coast of Pakistan.

U-shaped or **parabolic dunes** are arcuate sand ridges with the open end toward the beach. Vegetation traps the sand on the horns with blowouts between, creating U-shaped forms. An example can be found south of Point Sal in Southern California (Plate 46). Often these are relict dunes formed where vegetation has stabilized them and the wind forms blowouts (Plate 47).

Barchans or **crescentic dunes** have a steep, slip-off slope on the lee side facing away from the beach. These dunes usually form where there is unidirectional wind and lack of vegetation. They are quite numerous along barren desert coasts. Plate 48 depicts a half-mile-long barchan dune along the coast of Pakistan. Plate 49 shows sets of barchan dunes moving inland at Pismo Beach, California.

Transverse dune ridges are one of the most common coastal dune types. These dunes trend parallel or oblique to the shore and they are elongated perpendicular to the dominant winds. In perfect form, they are asymmetrical with a steep lee slope and a gentle windward slope. Plate 50 is an Apollo 9 space photograph of transverse dunes along the Namib coast of southwest Africa in Namibia.

Longitudinal dunes are elongated parallel to the wind direction and extend oblique or perpendicular to the shore. They are often symmetrical, but they are not a common dune form. A sand dune complex along the coast of Pakistan 81 kilometers (50 miles) west of Karāchi has characteristics of a longitudinal form but few of the individual dunes have the typical linear shape (Plate 51).

Blowouts often occur where vegetation exists or where the wind is channelled through dune masses. Blowouts are hollows or troughs cutting into dunes of the types mentioned above. Plate 30 depicts a series of blowouts along the coast near Aberdeen, Scotland.

Attached dunes depend on the existence of some obstacles around which sand accumulates. Plate 52 shows attached dunes along the north coast of Puerto Rico.

Whalebacks are heaps of sand of irregular shape and some of these large masses of sand cover several square kilometers. Such a large dune complex occurs near the outlet of the Santa Maria River in Southern California (Plate 53).

Stabilized or Fossil Dunes

These older sand deposits—called eolianite—are an unusual type found mainly in the tropics where calcareous sands have been lithified and, often, drowned by rising sea level. Eolianite is wind-deposited sand with calcium carbonate cement. It contains at least 5 percent carbonate (shell) grains. The cementing mineral, calcite, is similar to that of beach rock (see pp. 40-41). However, beach rock is primarily limited to the intertidal zone, but eolianite may be found at altitudes over 36 meters (118 feet) and at depths well below sea level. The degree of cementation appears to vary with age—older deposits tend to be better cemented than younger deposits.

An excellent example of eolianite (aeolianite or calcarenite) can be found along the coast of Oahu, Hawaii, around Waialeu Bay (Plate 54).

An eolianite shore that is exposed to strong wave action has a conspicuous terrace whose surface usually lies between mean-tide and high-tide level. Such tidal terraces or solution benches occur all along the eolianite shore of Puerto Rico (See Plates 99 and 194). Each step rises to successively higher elevations by increments. The outer edge of the tidal surface is a rim of eolianite, often thickly coated with crustose coralline algae and/or some growth of brown algae. Coralline algae thrive especially well in the intertidal zone on rocky shores that are exposed to strong wave action, which provides a continuous flow of aerated marine water. The algae protect the eolianite from being eroded away (Kaye, 1959, p. 90)

Another feature of eolianite is its pitted and honeycombed surface. This is especially true in the spray zone where numerous jagged pinnacles occur, often with knifelike septa and spikes that separate individual pits (see Plate 54). These pits vary in size. Outside of the spray zone, solution sinks are often large holes with rounded bottoms, quite often having eroding rock inside (Plate 92). Many of these holes resemble the typical solutional pit of limestones.

Sand Flats

The term "sand flat" is difficult to define. Zenkovich (1967, p. 660) states that sand flats are characterized by a smooth surface with a gradient of not more than 0.001, and that these flats are interesting from the dynamic standpoint since it is difficult to explain why waves should not transport sand shoreward and generate a normal profile to the bottom in the tidal zone. They form in front of advancing dunes, often in a zone of wind-blown sand.

Sand flats occur where the wave regime is weakened. They are found in the heads of open bays, behind islands, or at the inner margin of extensive shallows on which waves die out. A wide sandy bottom, similar in appearance and profile to mudflats (see p. 37), is often laid bare on shallow open coasts of nontidal seas during movement of water away from the shore. Plate 55 shows a sand flat at Plum Island, Massachusetts.

Generally, there are no minor relief forms on the sand flat surfaces except for ephemeral ripple marks and, sometimes, streams that flow during the ebb. If the material is coarse, small sand ridges may be present in front of the beach. This seems to indicate that shoreward movement of material may have occurred but for some unexplainable reason has ceased (Zenkovich, 1967, p. 661).

MASS WASTING ALONG COASTS

Coasts of this type are recognized by bulging earth masses at the coast and landslide topography on land. Undercutting by the sea often results in this type of topography. Numerous small earth movements such as slumping, soil creep, talus, and small rock falls might be included in this category, but the term "landslide" should be limited to larger unit movements that are perceptible downslope movements of rock, soil, or artificial fill. The motion may be that of a slide, flow, or fall acting singly or together. All are forms of slope failure arising from high shearing stress along a potential surface of rupture that exceeds the sheering resistance along that surface. The term "landslide" usually does not include creep or frozen ground phenomena (solifluction), which are undoubtedly present in coastal areas. Therefore, this type of coast should be referred to as mass wasting.

Landslides are important agents of denudation in tectonically active zones subject to earthquakes and regional tilting, in mountains in humid lands (notably the wet tropics), in semiarid landscapes, in cliffed coastal belts, and in those areas where new cycles of erosion are oversteepening the slopes.

Particular geologic conditions favor low shearing strength. Some sedimentaries may become very unstable, layered materials, for example, clays, shales, mudstones, as well as porous volcanics such as tuff and breccia. The deposition of strata is also an important consideration. The following conditions contribute to low shearing strength: rocks subject to much fine jointing, fissuring, and brecciation; interbedded permeable and impermeable strata; sediments dipping toward an unloaded face; and massive beds (jointed limestone overlying incompetents such as shale; D. S. Simonett in Fairbridge, 1968, pp. 639-641).

Different weathering states also greatly affect the degree of mass movement. Zenkovich (1967, pp. 296-316) discusses three different morphological types of landslides: stepped, cirquelike, and flowing.

Stepped Landslides   A stepped-landslide coast is most common in sedimentary rock where the blocks are sometimes arranged in a row, forming distinctive barriers parallel to the coast, and may become isolated as a result of the erosion of the unconsolidated strata. An example is the Point Fermin landslip along a fault at the Palos Verdes Hills of California. Plate 56 shows the coast in March 1924 and again in March 1941. The stepped nature of this landslide occurs as large blocks break off and slide downslope following periods of heavy rain. Although heavy rain may increase erosion, the largest cracks and slides take place after earthquakes. Plate 57 is a ground view that shows where movement was still taking place in 1977.

Cirquelike Landslides   In cirquelike landslides, whole rock masses subside toward the center of an amphitheater and then move toward the sea. The movement of these landslides is of the thrust type. Sections of the California coast erode in this cirquelike manner. Plate 58 depicts a section of coast near Gaviota Beach, California.

Flowing Landslides   This type of mass movement produces a distinctive rugged relief on the coast. Zenkovich (1967, p. 307) defines the characteristics of this type of coast:

Over a long period these earth flows erode their beds in the same way as glaciers do and carry to the sea all material they have accumulated in them. The upper layer of such a landslide, if protected by limestone fragments, is so little affected by surface water erosion that in some places, the relief of the foothill slope is apparently inverted. Temporary water courses form between the landslides, permanent streams excavate deep steepsided valleys and the landslide occupy the watershed between them.

In addition, large blocks are often carried by a flowing landslide and, being a stable coastal element, the slide gradually begins to stand out from the general coastline as a foreland-adjacent section, which is not protected and gradually recedes. A shoreline with excellent examples of mass wasting is the Baja California coast near Ensenada on the Pacific shore (Plate 59). Here, there is a slow continual movement of material to the sea. Another example is the east coast of Martha's Vineyard (Plate 60). Here, varicolored marls and clays of Tertiary age as well as glacial deposits are being undercut. Large glacial boulders are left on the beach and in the surf zone at the base of the cliff.

VOLCANIC COASTS

Because volcanoes are so widespread, there are many volcanic coasts. The landforms associated with volcanic eruptions are varied. The three main types presented here are broad categories; there are many possible subdivisions. All three types of volcanic coasts may and very often do occur in the same general area as is the case with the Hawaii chain. The identification of this coastal type is facilitated by such features as convexities of shoreline and conical slopes beginning on land and continuing under the water. Slopes of 10 to 30° are common above and below the water level (Shepard, 1963, p. 161).

Lava Flow Coasts

The most numerous volcanic coastal features are lava fans built into the sea with broad arcuate shapes (Plate 61). A coast of this type is characterized by a lava flow or a series of lava flows that have either terminated abruptly at the sea or have extended into the sea prior to cooling and solidification. Lava flows are recognized on coastal charts by land contours showing cones, by convexities of shoreline, or by conical slopes continuing from land out under the water. A coast of this type may also be produced by magma being extruded entirely underwater and layered after several successive stages of eruption until the structure is projected above sea level or raised by diastrophic movements. Islands such as those of the Hawaii chain are of this type.

The Flandrian Transgression or postglacial rise in sea level may be responsible for some present lava flow coasts. This type of coast is found on many oceanic islands (Pacific, Indian, Atlantic).

There are two main types of lava flow solidification. (The terms "pahoehoe" and "aa" are sometimes used to describe the types of lava, but these terms actually refer to the types of solidification.) Fluid lava is called pahoehoe or dermolithic lava. Pahoehoe solidification takes place when lava containing much entrapped gas spreads out in thin sheets. Such lava may be described as live lava. It typically exhibits a wrinkled, twisted, ropy, and tapestrylike surface. Its most distinguishing feature is a smooth, glistening skin (Thornbury, 1969, p. 475).

Clastolithic lava or "aa" is the second mode of solidification referred to when identifying lava. This lava typically displays a scoriaceous, clinkery, jagged, or blocky surface. The lava is dead in the sense that most of its gases have escaped and the vesicles are filled with air. The rapid cooling and greater viscosity of this type of lava is due to this loss of gas. The distinction between the two types of solidification is not as sharp as may be suggested, and one type may grade into the other within a single flow (Thornbury, 1969, p. 475). The active cones of Mauna Loa, Kilauwea, and Mauna Kea present some of the best examples of these types of lava. Plate 62 illustrates the 1973 lava flow in the Apura Point area of Hawaii.

Tephra Coasts

This term covers all clastic material ejected from a crater or some other type of vent and transported through the air. It includes volcanic dust, ash, cinders, lapilli, scoria, pumice, bombs, and blocks. Therefore, a tephra coast is characterized by fragmental volcanic materials and is often cliffed and generally convex. They may however, be concave and irregular depending on erosion. This fragmental material generally is more easily modified and eroded by waves than are lava flows. There are situations, however, where it is highly cemented and may stand as a very resistant barrier to marine erosion. There is a very good example of a tephra coast on the Kona coast of the large island of Hawaii where part of a prehistoric littoral cone stands. This cone is composed of glassy basaltic ash, lapilli, bombs, and blocks formed where lava from Mauna Loa flowed into the sea. Plate 63 depicts erosion of a tephra coast made up of ejected material—mainly ash and pumice—south of St. Pierre, Martinique, and Plate 64 shows a steep slope made up of ash in Baja California.

Volcanic Collapse (Subsidence) or Explosion Coasts

These coasts are characterized by craters, calderas, and volcano-tectonic depression structures that have been breached by wave erosion sometime after their formation. The term maar is also applied to this type of volcanic feature where no igneous ejection occurs but there is an explosion center.

Although quite common (especially on oceanic volcanic islands), these coasts are a local feature because of the scale involved. They are commonly recognized as embayments hemmed landward by slopes. The seaward edge is generally cliffed. In certain examples, such as Koko Head, Hawaii (Plate 65), a portion of a volcano many have been eroded back by waves.

Erosion of Volcanic Landforms

In many cases erosion of volcanic cones begins early due to a steep initial profile. Many coasts that are made up of ash are quickly reduced to shoals. The next three plates illustrate the erosion of volcanoes and lava flows in different stages of development. Plate 66 shows very slow rounding and smoothing of volcanic rocks on Santa Maria Island in the Azores. Very slow and long erosion of a volcanic plug near Mount Egmont on the North Island of New Zealand is depicted in Plate 67. After the volcanic material has been worn down by waves and currents, the resultant beaches usually consist of black sands, both coarse and fine (Plate 68).

The soils that develop from the breakdown of volcanic materials are often very rich as is the case on numerous volcanic islands such as Java, Bali, and the Azores. Plate 69 shows the beautiful terraced vineyards on the north side of Santa Maria Island in the Azores.

COASTS SHAPED BY DIASTROPHIC MOVEMENTS

Three broad categories of coasts fall under this heading: fault coasts; fold coasts; and sedimentary extrusions, which are not directly related to diastrophism but are concerned with earth movements.

Fault Coasts

The essential feature of a fault coast is a fault scarp that separates an uplifted block, forming the land from a subsided block that, after faulting, is depressed below sea level. The original surface may have been a smooth seafloor or it may have been a land surface with low, moderate, or strong relief. The vertical displacement on the fault may be great or small, but, if this prefaulting surface has strong relief, a continuous fault coast can be formed only by a vertical movement of hundreds, perhaps thousands of meters; that is, the movement must be sufficient to submerge the ridges of the downthrown block (Thrush, 1968). Typically, a fault coast is characterized by deep water resting against the fault scarp.

There are three main types of fault coasts: fault scarp coasts, fault trough coasts, and overthrust coasts. Fault scarp coasts are either straight (regular) or irregular, de-

pending on the type of faulting that has occurred. Faulting is either parallel to or transverse to the prior shoreline. A straight fault scarp shoreline is cliffed with deep waters resting against the scarp. Excellent examples of this type of coastline occur along the Makrān coast of Iran (Plate 70).

In an irregular fault scarp coast, faulting has occurred transverse to the coastal trend with headlands and embayments resulting. This type of coast is usually cliffed. Transcurrent fault coasts may be included with this type. Good examples of irregular fault scarp coasts are the South Pembroke Cliffs of England and sections of the New Zealand coast such as along the Kaikura Peninsula of the South Island.

Fault trough coasts are fault-formed valleys flooded by the sea. A fault trough is a sunken fault block that lies between two or more faults with approximately parallel strikes. The Gulf of California and the Red Sea are examples of this type of coast (Plate 71). The fault line valley coast might be thought of as a subtype of this category. These are valleys that follow the line of a fault, which may be strike-slip or downthrown. An example is where the San Andreas rift system goes off shore near Point Reyes, Tomales Bay, California (Plate 72).

An overthrust coast is one that corresponds to a thrust fault. This is a very complicated coast. Billings (1954, p. 184) defines an overthrust as "a thrust fault with an initial dip of 10 degrees or less and a net slip that is measured in miles." The overthrust sheet or overthrust block is the block above the fault plane. Although the initial dip is low, the overthrust may be folded to assume a steep dip, and it may even become overturned. In an overthrust coast the shore abuts against the hanging wall, but another type may exist—the underthrust coast—where the sea washes against the footwall. The difference between the hanging wall and the footwall is that the hanging wall is tectonically activated and the footwall moves. Evidence of slumping, landsliding, and block gliding are clues to overthrust coasts since very often the frontal portion of the overthrust sheet may be weakened, thereby initiating mass movement. Cliffs are generally present along these coasts. Underthrust coasts are difficult to recognize.

Fold Coasts

Fold coasts are difficult to identify on maps and charts but a few examples exist. On these coasts the shore abuts against a series of folds—representing undulations, or waves in the rocks of the earth. They are best displayed by stratified formations such as sedimentary and volcanic rocks or their metamorphosed equivalents (Billings, 1954, p. 33). Nomenclature of folds is based on the appearance in cross-section (anticlinal or synclinal) and on the attitude of the axial plane (where nomenclature is more detailed). The Zagros Mountains of Iran represent an excellent example of anticlinal folding that is being eroded at the coast.

Sedimentary Extrusion Coasts: Salt Domes, Mudlumps, and Mud Volcanoes

Salt domes are generally circular structures resulting from the upward movement of a salt mass. Oil and gas fields are commonly associated with them. They very often have minor surface expressions but can extend to great depths. Good examples are found in the Persian Gulf (Plate 73) and in the Gulf coastal plain of Texas and Louisiana.

Mudlumps are small islands that are formed by mud being upthrust in the vicinity of distributaries immediately seaward of a delta front (Plate 74). The loading of silt and sand onto prodelta marine clays can lead to the local "diapiric" upwelling of these domal structures, a phenomenon that is relatively common off the Mississippi Delta. The Indus Delta is thought to be another area of occurrence (Morgan et al., 1968, pp. 145-161).

Mud volcanoes are most closely related to salt domes, oil domes, or mineral springs, but they are cone- or dome-shaped like a volcano. A mud volcano is a high pressure gas seepage that carries with it water, mud, sand, fragments of rocks, and, occasionally, oil. Most mud volcanoes, especially the larger ones, are associated with anticlines, faults, or diapiric folds. Gas escapes under pressure and, as it rises, it mixes with the clay and goundwater to form a mud that erupts either steadily or spasmodically, depending on the local pressure conditions. Single cones or groups of cones may cover an area of several square kilometers and reach more than one thousand meters in height. However, they are more often measured in tens and hundreds of meters. The largest known mud volcanoes are found along the Makrān coast of Pakistan and Iran (Snead, 1964, 1970). Plate 75 shows one of these features. Although they occur on coastal plains, most mud volcanoes are not under attack by waves and currents. However, they do form mud islands off the Burma coast, which are easily destroyed by the sea.

Marine Terraces and Accumulated Forms (Emergent Coasts)

There is considerable debate concerning the tectonic movements along coasts in nonglaciated areas. Some authors, while recognizing the existence of eustatic movements, have considered tectonic movements to be more important in the Quaternary even in nonglacial regions (Guilcher, 1954, p. 49). Bourcart (1938) and Jessen (1943) believe that the edges of continents are in special positions in relation to the earth's crust; they are said to be subject to periodic expansion, the cause of which remains to be discovered. Much new evidence is coming forth with the new findings of continental drift, but much still needs to be done before marine terraces are fully understood.

Tectonic uplift can be found along a number of coasts, but few areas are as well understood and documented as the Palos Verdes Hills between San Pedro on the southeast, and Redondo Beach, on the northwest in southern California (Plate 76). During much of the Pleistocene, the Palos Verdes Hills area was an isolated island, probably slightly larger than the present hills, but similar to the southern California islands. The uplift of the hills was matched by subsidence of the Los Angeles basin to the north. During the later Pleistocene, a series of thirteen elevated marine terraces were developed to a maximum of 396 meters (1,300 feet) above sea level on all sides of the hills. There is no other place along the entire coast of the United States where the record of successive elevation of a land mass is better displayed (Shepard and Wanless, 1971, pp. 274-277). The most extensive terrace, which is also the latest and lowest, is bounded by sea cliffs 15 meters (50 feet) high on the south coast but rising to 91 meters (300 feet) on the northwest coast. Other sections of the California coast also show evidence of uplift.

Another region of uplifted marine coast occurs along the Makrān coast of Iran and Pakistan (Snead, 1967, 1969, 1970). Almost all of the coastline is undergoing folding, faulting, and gentle upwarping (see Plate 70). In some places the marine terraces rise from 3.05 meters (10 feet) to over 76 meters (250 feet). One of the highest terrace complexes is in the vicinity of Bris, Iran (Plate 70), with lower terraces to the west near Jask, Iran, and to the east near Karāchi, Pakistan. Correlation and dating of the terraces is extremely complex because of the uplifting as well as the downwarping and subsidence that has occurred.

Coastal terraces may also be due to other factors such as streams and subaerial erosion. Often the origin of such terraces is unclear. Along the coast of the Banks Peninsula in New Zealand, there are a series of gently sloping terraces with deep erosional valleys between (Plate 77). These are the result of running water cutting down through old lava flows. Such terraces appear to be of marine origin but no evidence of wave-cut scarps and nips can be found.

Orogenic regions, such as the margin of the Pacific basin, have domes or arches in the landscape over the crests of structural anticlines. Often warped coastal and river terraces are a common form of evidence. In New

Zealand, several active anticlines have warped a coastal-plain landscape into a number of terraces. One of the anticlines in the New Zealand group may have risen 170 meters (557 feet) in the last 20,000 years, at an average rate of 8.5 millimeters (0.33 inches) per year. Seismic surveys and the regional geologic setting suggest that active anticlines in both Japan and New Zealand (Ota, 1975) are surface manifestations of rising fault blocks of indurated basement rock. Each anticline is thought to drape over the highest edge of an upfaulted block beneath (Te Punga, 1957). The Kaikoura Peninsula on the northeast side of the South Island of New Zealand is such a region of uplift. Plate 78 shows uplifted terraces that rise to heights of over 80 meters (262 feet).

Another method of marine-terrace formation is through glacial isostasy. This special form of epeirogenic movement is of particular significance in the Quaternary period (Bloom, 1978, pp. 23-24). The theory of isostasy states that the pressure at the base of all vertical sections of the earth, above some deep level of compensation, is equal. An excellent example of this process is the alternate loading and unloading of large continental areas with ice sheets during Late Cenozoic time. Ocean water must evaporate and accumulate on land as ice in order for ice sheets to grow. Each glaciation involved the mass transfer of a layer of water as much as 100 meters (328 feet) in thickness from the 71 percent of the earth's surface that is ocean, and the concentration of that water mass as glacier ice averaging 2 to 3 meters (6 to 9 feet) in thickness on about 5 percent of the earth's surface. Since shorelines must initially have been horizontal, their present slope is a measure of the differential postglacial isostatic uplift. Uplift of 300 meters (984 feet) is known in areas on the eastern side of Hudson Bay, Canada, in less than 8,000 years. Postglacial isostatic uplift on the northern side of the Baltic Sea and around the Gulf of Bothnia totals more than 520 meters (1705 feet) and an estimated 210 meters (689 feet) of uplift still remains to be accomplished in order to compensate for the original deformation by ice loading (Flint, 1971, p. 352). Plate 79 shows raised coastal plains on the Beara Peninsula in southwest Ireland. At the head of the Gulf of Bothnia, the rate of increase is nearly 1 meter (3.28 feet) every hundred years. In the northern United States, Canada, and Scandinavia, the postglacial uplift is still in progress, although at a greatly reduced rate. Northern Sweden is presently emerging from the Baltic Sea at a rate of 9 millimeters (0.35 inches) per year, and Finland annually gains 7 square kilometers (2.70 square miles) of new land by the uplift.

Part III

Secondary Coasts Shaped by Marine Agencies or Marine Organisms

This section illustrates secondary coastal forms that result from marine modification. These types of coasts may or may not have been primary coasts before being shaped by the sea.

The term primary coast, according to Shepard (Shepard and Wanless, 1971), is somewhat deceptive since all coasts are secondary to the extent that the sea begins to act on a primary coast immediately after conditions stabilize. Where the waves are small, however, and where the rock is resistant to erosion (hard), the effects are slow to develop, so the coast continues to be primary in such cases for a long time. Most coastlines are a mixture of primary and secondary in varying degrees.

Although some coasts show little effect of marine processes since the sea approached its present level, most coastal regions show extensive indications of changes produced by waves and currents, even during the few thousand years since the sea ended its rapid rise from approximately -80 to -140 meters (-262 to -459 feet) (Bloom, 1978, p. 406). During that time, most coasts have been worn back by wave erosion, especially exposed points of the land. Some coasts, however, have been prograded by marine processes, producing advances of the same order as the deposition of deltas at the mouths of rivers.

SHORELINES SHAPED BY MARINE EROSION

The pounding of waves against the shore has produced large amounts of erosion in some places. The rate at which cliffs are worn back by waves, tides, and currents depends on several factors. Soft or less-resistant rocks and sediments are particularly vulnerable to waves. In those places where cliffs are receding as much as several meters a year, the materials of the cliffs are unconsolidated sands, clays, and gravels, or the type of rock that can be cut with pick or shovel. The rate of erosion is also related to the exposure of the cliffs to large waves. For this reason, the west coast of the United States has more cliff erosion than the east coast, due largely to the prevailing west winds. If the coast is deeply embayed, wave erosion is important only at the headlands that extend out between bays, because waves converge on these headlands.

Two main types of coast are produced by wave erosion. If the sea cliffs are of uniform material, the waves are likely to straighten them, but, if varying degrees of hardness exist in the coastal formation, the waves will cut indentations into the softer material, leaving the more resistant rocks protruding as points. There is a marked difference between an irregular wave-eroded coast and a drowned river-valley shoreline. The former does not have the extensive estuaries that the latter does and is

characterized by coves. If the prevailing trend of the rock structure is parallel to the coastal trend, wave erosion tends to make a coast straight, whereas, if the trend forms a large angle to the coast, erosion will ordinarily produce irregularities.

Wave-erosion coasts are being shaped by the sea according to one or a combination of several controlling factors listed below. Such coasts are commonly evidenced by cliffs or scarps.

Material Control Coasts

These coasts result where the type of material has a great deal of influence on the shape of the coast in areas of wave erosion.

Homogeneous material coasts result in shorelines being straightened cliffs. These coasts are generally bordered by a gently inclined seafloor in contrast to fault coasts where there is a much steeper escarpment. Good examples of this coastal type are found in sandstone, limestone, and uniform basalt. Such coasts are generally straight because they are under bedding control. Sections of the coast of Hawaii are straight because marine erosion has evened off the uniform basaltic lava. Such an example occurs in Plate 80, which shows sections of the coast of Hawaii. The few promontories that do exist are the result of either earlier or more resistant lava flows.

Sections of the California coast are straight because of fairly soft and, in places, uniform sandstones, conglomerates, and shales making up the cliffs (Plate 81). A gently inclined, uniform seafloor also allows the waves to reach the coast evenly. For miles along the Makrān coast of Iran and Pakistan there are long stretches of very straight coast cut into uniform shelly conglomerates, mudstones, and sandstones of Pliocene-Pleistocene age.

Heterogeneous material coasts generally result in very irregular shorelines. Coasts of this type usually have a variety of rock types and diverse bedding planes. Erosion takes place at the places of least resistance to wave attack. Such irregular coasts are widespread around the world. Europe has excellent examples such as the cliffs of Moher, in Claire County on the west coast of Ireland (Plate 82) and along Costa Brava in northeastern Spain. Another excellent example is along Sunset Cliffs, north of Cabrillo Peninsula in San Diego, California (Plate 83).

Structural Control Coasts

These coasts occur where erosion is influenced largely by bedding, dip-striking, jointing, or folding. Often a combination of these factors is involved. These are difficult coasts to identify but a few examples are given here. Along the coast of Portugal, near Peniche, steeply dipping limestone and sandstone rocks are under heavy attack by the Atlantic Ocean (Plate 84). Sea spray thrown against the rocks has removed the less-resistant layers accentuating the bedding planes. Changing of the dip and strike of bedding planes can cause differential erosion as is the case near Laguna Beach in southern California. Here the dip in bedding planes can change within a few meters. Another excellent example can be found along the Irish coast at Slea Head in Kerry County (Plate 85). Differential erosion can also occur where the rocks are severely jointed. Striking examples of this type of coast can be found around Housel Bay in Cornwall, England. In Plate 86, we see an entirely different type of jointing at the north end of the Gulf of California at Puerto Peñasco.

Where folding has taken place, waves may attack the less resistant rocks where the beds have been upturned or downbent. The coast of Portugal, west of the town of Sesimbra at a point called Cabode Espichel, presents just such an example (Plate 87).

Fault-Control Erosion Coasts

These coasts are often difficult to distinguish from fault coasts where the cliffs are actually due to faulting. Rather, these are fault-lined coasts that are definitely shaped by marine erosion. There are two subtypes: longitudinal faults or fault-line coasts and transverse fault coasts. Good examples of longitudinal faults are difficult to locate because sediments often cover the actual fault. They are most likely to be found where an old, eroded fault brings a hard layer to the surface allowing wave erosion to remove the soft material from one side, leaving a straight coast. The straight north coast of east Molokai, Hawaii, which is a wave-eroded cliff, largely formed prior to the volcanic building of the Kalaupapa Peninsula, is an example. The straightness is related to the faulting of the north margin. The fault scarp now appears to be 4.8 kilometers (3 miles) seaward off the coastline. The 4.8-kilometer (3-mile) shelf probably represents the retreat of the coast under wave attack after the formation of the fault scarp (Plate 88). Transverse fault coasts are even more difficult to identify, because wave erosion has removed most of the evidence of faulting. Plate 89 depicts an example near Cape Monze on the Makrān coast of Pakistan near Karāchi.

Erosional Remnant Features

This category differs from three previous categories under wave erosion coasts in that the erosional features are not usually the controlling factors. Often these are minor erosional features but many examples exist and

they usually are easily recognized.

Headlands and Promontories   Most irregular coastal regions of the world have headlands and promontories that jet into the sea. More resistant rocks usually result in these pronounced features, but sometimes the alignment of the coast or the prevailing direction of waves and currents will influence their existence and keep them from being eroded away. How long they are able to stand up to erosion depends on the amount of wave energy and the degree of rock resistance to wave attack. Lava rock often forms spectacular headlands as can be seen along the Oregon coast. More resistant granitic rock results in promontories jutting into the sea south of Sollar on the island of Mallorca (Plate 90). Another example of a beautiful coastline with headlands and promontories exists at Pt. Lobos in the vicinity of the Monterey Peninsula. Just north of Pt. Lobos is Carmel Bay, where a submarine canyon with arms comes into the indentations. Just off these bays the depth of water drops to over 305 meters (1,000 feet). Another section of the California coast that is very irregular with headlands and promontories is Laguna Beach. Here, conglomerate rocks, with greater resistance to erosion than less-resistant sandstones and limestones farther south, form many of the headlands and cliffs (Plate 91).

Minor Erosion Forms   These include a number of small, but often spectacular, features that occur where erosion is just beginning on the fringe of major wave attack. Included are such erosional forms as potholes cut out by stones and rocks eroded away by waves. Plate 92 shows the north coast of Puerto Rico where heavy storm waves are cutting into old cemented eolianite dunes. In addition to circular holes of all types, pounding waves and their accompanying spray often cut rocks into jagged pinnacles as has occurred near Marchiquita Bay in Puerto Rico and along the west coast of the South Island of New Zealand, near Greymouth (Plate 93).

Early cutting by waves often creates blowholes where water gets in between rocks and the pressure of incoming waves creates a concussion that forces air and water out under great pressure. Hawaii has excellent examples of spectacular blowholes called spouting horns (Plate 94). Other blowholes produce a great hissing sound as the air is forced out. Such an example can be found on the seaward side of Mount Desert Island in Maine (Plate 95). Unusual minor features occasionally found on wave-cut terraces and platforms are spheroidal balls or pedestal rocks consisting of all shapes and sizes. Plate 96 depicts such balls, called mushroom rocks, at Sunset Cliffs, San Diego, California. The largest of these concretion balls that I have ever seen is found north of Dunedin, New Zealand (Plate 97). Some of the balls are iron concretions; others, such as those in California, have a higher percentage of $CaCO_3$ than the sandstone concretions.

Figure 6. Stages in the development of a marine cliff (adapted from Strahler, 1971).

This enrichment imparts a hardness to the concretions that permits them to survive long after the less-indurated arkose material has been carved away (Palmer et al., 1965).

Wave-cut Benches, Terraces, and Abrasion Platforms An erosional coast often goes through a series of stages as it is being cut (see Figure 6). An initial stage is the so-called nip stage, a term used to describe the undercutting of a cliff at the wave level (Plate 98). This small notch, the nip, is slowly cut back to form a terrace or bench that grows as the sea cliff retreats (Strahler, 1971, pp. 678-679). These benches and terraces can take a number of shapes and sizes. Plate 99 depicts one of these small wave-cut benches that is being rapidly cut back, especially during high tides and storms.

The next stage is the formation of a larger abrasion platform that develops and grows as the detritus is swept seaward to accumulate as a shoreface terrace, often composed of gravel and coarse sand, and bearing much the same relation to the abrasion platform as an alluvial fan or talus cone does to a stream-carved ravine. Talus material can also build up at the base of the cliff waiting to be broken down and carried off by waves (Plate 100).

Sea Caves Inequalities in resistance of the bedrock result in narrow zones being more rapidly excavated, leading to the formation of crevices and sea caves (Figure 7). These features tend to be formed along lines of weakness such as nonresistant strata or along faults. The form of the caves depends on the dip of the beds or on the slope of the fault planes (Guilcher, 1958, pp. 62-64). Sea caves grow through roof collapse and with the help of compressed air trapped in them. A series of crevices, tunnels, and caves can be found along the south coast of Tasmania (Plate 101), and a large sea tunnel occurs on the west coast of the South Island of New Zealand. Sea caves and tunnels can also be found in softer Tertiary beds in southern Portugal (Plate 102). Some of the largest sea caves occur along the north coast of Puerto Rico (Plate 103).

Sea Arches Sea arches form when sea caves open up at both ends. Formed by differential erosion, arches are usually short-lived, because of possible wave attack from two sides and the growing weakness of the arches themselves. A small arch formed in 1946 at Sunset Cliffs, San Diego, California was completely gone by May of 1968. Only a small pedestal remained to mark the site of the arch. Although arches are fairly rare, they still can be found along most cliffed coasts, especially in bedded sandstones, shales, and limestones. They are less common in hard rocks such as granite or lavas, but they sometimes do occur as on the northeast side of Hanauma Bay in Hawaii, which is shown in Plate 104. Limestone-rock coasts have some excellent examples of sea arches. Oyster Rocks just off the shore at Beruit,

Lebanon, is an example of sea arches cut into white limestone (Plate 105).

Sea Stacks When isolated blocks of a cliff face are separated from the main rocky cliff, a sea stack remains. They also are formed when the roof of a sea arch collapses leaving remnants of all shapes and sizes. Like the other minor coastal erosional features, these picturesque sea stacks are due to differential erosion. More resistant rocks take longer to wear away. Less resistant rocks cut back faster. A sea stack that is slowly being separated from the main cliff occurs at Cabo de St. Vincent in southern Portugal. Composed of resistant limestone, it has stood for hundreds of years just at the extreme southwest point of Portugal (Plate 106). Farther west along the coast of Portugal, a soft sandstone is being cut away very rapidly, resulting in a spectacular coastline composed of caves, arches, sea stacks, and colorful cliffs. The popular resorts between Lagos and Faro present one of the most beautiful examples of cliff erosion in the world (Plate 107). Other areas where excellent sea stacks occur are the coast of California, especially along Big Sur, the coast of Oregon near Coos Bay, the northwest coast of Europe, especially the west coast of Ireland (Plate 108) and sections of the coast of England.

MARINE DEPOSITION COASTS

There are many different depositional features so only a few of the major types are illustrated in this volume.

Coasts change and prograde through the work of waves and currents. These are the agents of marine-formed landforms. The nature of these depositional features is a function of several constructional components, the most important of which include: type of material being moved; amount of material available; fetch or wave generation area; wave refraction; angle of wave approach, direction of prevailing winds; longshore movement; platform gradient; and tidal range.

Along many coasts the land has been extended seaward since sea level has slowed its rise. Unless offset by submergence, such shoreline extensions take place along coasts bordered by shallow water where so much bottom sediment is stirred up by waves that longshore currents are incapable of transporting all of it along the shore, and a considerable amount is piled up onto the adjacent beach.

The seaward growth of coasts results from waves causing accretion to the beaches, building out sand plains, or, breaking well out from shore, building up sand bars. The term "bar" may be used in a broad generic sense to include all the various types of submerged or slightly emerged embankments of sand and coarser materials, such as gravel, built on the seafloor by waves and

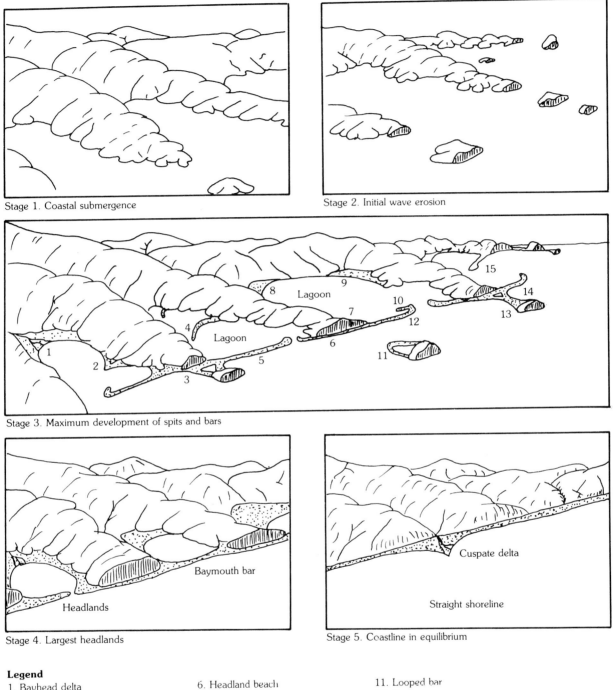

Stage 1. Coastal submergence

Stage 2. Initial wave erosion

Stage 3. Maximum development of spits and bars

Stage 4. Largest headlands

Stage 5. Coastline in equilibrium

Legend

1. Bayhead delta
2. Cuspate bar
3. Double tombolo
4. Midbay bar
5. Baymouth bar

6. Headland beach
7. Cliffed headland
8. Bayhead beach
9. Bayside beach
10. Complex spit

11. Looped bar
12. Spit
13. Tombolo
14. Recurved spit
15. Complex tombolo

Figure 7. Development of a submerged shoreline (adapted from Strahler, 1969).

currents. Specific names have been given to individual bars, depending on their form and position (Thornbury, 1969, p. 433). One of the most common types is a spit. Sand bars may become emergent and then, rather than being called bars, are called sand barriers or ridges. They often lie well out from the coast, enclosing lagoons on the inside (see Figure 8). These barriers are typical along the Atlantic and Gulf coasts of the United States where the continental shelf slopes much more gently than it does off the Pacific Coast.

Types of Barriers

The formation of barrier beaches and barrier islands is related to the deposition of material, mostly sand, on the seafloor by waves and currents. At low tide these features are exposed. At high tide many become partially submerged, but gradually sand driven by wind during low tide builds up the barriers so they remain exposed above water nearly all the time. For many years these formations were called offshore bars but, following Price (1951) and Shepard (1952), now they are called barrier beaches or barrier islands. The term "bar" seemed inappropriate since it was used originally to designate slightly submerged sand ridges. Barrier beaches, on the other hand, consist of elongated sand ridges, generally parallel to the shore, that rise slightly above high tide (Thornbury, 1969, p. 435). These sand barriers normally flank the mainland. If they consist of only one low ridge, they are called barrier beaches or barrier bars. However, if the barrier beaches include more than one ridge with intervening marshy flats, or, if the dunes are on the inside rising well above the beach, then they are called barrier islands. Plate 109 shows a barrier island at the mouth of the Indus River in Pakistan (Snead, 1969, pp. 45-50).

When barrier islands meet at a point they are called barrier spits. Nauset Beach is a barrier spit that extends into Nauset Inlet in Massachusetts. A series of islands that extend for miles along a coastline with numerous inlets

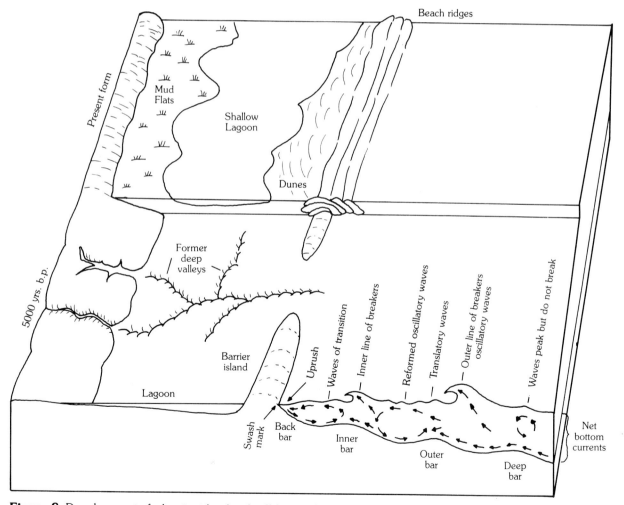

Figure 8. Development of a barrier island with offshore submerged bars (adapted from Wiegel, 1953, and Strahler, 1971).

between them are called barrier chains. From Cape Cod, Massachusetts, south along the Atlantic and Gulf coasts there are numerous barrier chains. Plate 110 is a space photograph showing the barrier chains along the coast of Long Island, New York. These islands grow smaller and more numerous as one goes southwest, because the source for most of this sand is Montauk Point at the tip of Long Island (see Plate 28).

A bay barrier is a coastal feature where material is carried across the mouth of a bay either completely closing it off or nearly doing so. There are three types of bay barriers. Baymouth barriers occur where waves and currents carry material across the mouth of a bay or estuary. Often an otherwise irregular shoreline will be straightened by the growth of such baymouth barriers. Plate 111 is an example of such barriers extending across several estuaries along the Rhode Island shore. When severe storms such as hurricanes hit this coastal region waves pass over or break through the sand barriers inundating the ponds with sea water.

Less common are the midbay barriers that occur half way into a bay. Due to greater wave and current energy, material is carried beyond the bay mouth and dropped farther into the bay or estuary. Such barriers are closely related to spits, and it is often difficult to distinguish between the two, except that a barrier would close off more of a bay area than a spit. Plate 112 is an example of a midbay barrier.

Bayhead barriers and spits are built in the innermost part of bays. A river carries material into the bay and currents redeposit it as a barrier or spit. A small lagoon, tidal marsh, or delta can sometimes be found behind the barrier (King, 1959, p. 373). An example of a bayhead barrier can be found at the extreme end of the Gaspé Peninsula, near the town of Douglestown, Quebec.

Types of Spits

In the early stages of development, short barrier beaches and barrier islands are predominately formed adjacent to stable land areas; these are referred to as spits. Evans (1942) defined a spit as "a ridge or embankment of sediment attached to the land at one end and terminating in open water at the other." Most often the axis of a spit will extend in a straight line parallel to the coast, but, where currents are deflected landward or unusually strong tides exist, growth of a spit may be deflected landward, with the resulting formation of a recurved spit or hook (Thornbury, 1969, pp. 433-434). Spits vary greatly in size and age; some are only a few meters long and may last only a few hours, others may be large and have a long life, such as Sandy Hook, New Jersey, or Cape Cod, Massachusetts (Evans, 1942, p.

847). Some of the best examples are found on the shores of landlocked seas, lakes, and coastal lagoons, where sand, gravel, and shingle are carried along the shoreline and deposited as spits. This is especially true where the orientation of the shoreline changes in relation to prevailing wave conditions (Bird, 1968, p. 112). There has been some controversy over the formation of spits. Their formation was formerly ascribed to longshore currents called wave currents. These currents are produced by both oscillatory and translatory waves meeting a shore obliquely (Johnson, 1919, pp. 287-300). Steers, (1964) believed that beach drifting, more than any other process, contributed to the movement of beach materials and the growth of spits. But more recent studies show that, although currents may contribute sediment to spits, they grow in the predominant direction of longshore sediment flow caused by waves, and their outlines are shaped mainly by wave action (Bird, 1968, p. 108). Lewis (1931) believed that spits were built as a result of spasmodic progradation by obliquely hitting waves at times of storms. Since there are many different types of spits all of the factors mentioned above probably come into play in their formation.

Spits take a number of different shapes. A simple spit is a single, long sand bar. Such a spit can be found at Cape Henlopen, Delaware (Plate 113). The axis of this spit extends generally in the direction of the coast. Spits that grow from two different shores at times nearly close off a bay and form a barrier bar (Plate 114). Often, however, where currents are deflected landward or where unusually strong tides exist, the growth of a spit may be deflected landward, resulting in a recurved spit or hook. Storm waves also influence these inward facing hooks. The southern end of Monomoy Island, Massachussetts, is a spit with recurved dune ridges indicating spit growth from left to right (Plate 115). Several stages of hook development lead to complex spits in which a complicated sequence of growth can be detected. A compound complex recurved spit or compound hook is one in which a spit has gone through a number of stages of growth and erosion. Sandy Hook, New Jersey, is a classic example of this type of spit but others can also be found. Along the coast of Pakistan 80 kilometers (50 miles) west of Karāchi, a beautiful compound complex recurved spit can be found (Plate 116; Snead, 1966, p. 59). Convergence of two spits offshore or the recurving of a simple or compound spit until it becomes attached to the shore at both ends produces a cuspate spit, an example of which can be found at the northeast end of Tiburon Island, Mexico (Plate 117). A small but nearly perfect cuspate spit can be seen in Plate 117. When variable or periodically shifting currents extend a spit first in one direction and then in another, a comparatively rare form called a serpentine spit results (Johnson,

1919, p. 291). Plate 118 shows a spit that has changed its form due to increased material being brought to the sea by the River Ythan north of Aberdeen, Scotland (Ritchie and Walton, 1972, pp. 12-14). This example is interesting because the sand extension into the sea becomes a submerged bar at high tide and a spit at low tide.

Winged Headlands

Winged headlands, whose occurrence is rare, are bordered on either side by bay bars or spits. Gulliver (1889) was the first to identify such a landform. He selected as his type example a very large winged headland at Long Branch on the New Jersey coast (Johnson, 1919, pp. 303-306). Grassy Hollow headland near the eastern end of Long Island is another typical example of this unusual form.

Cuspate Forelands

These forms have extensive forward building of the main shore into the water. Although there are a variety of shapes, the most common are more or less triangular with the apex of the triangle pointing out into the sea. The growth of cuspate forelands usually occurs during severe storms, when there is greater movement of material. When currents or waves from two different directions meet, the shore is aggraded on both sides so that fairly symmetrical lines of growth, consisting of beach ridges and swales, run parallel with both shores of the cusp, forming a simple cuspate foreland. Cuspate forelands are usually much larger than cuspate spits and consist of a number of growth stages. Plate 119 shows a cuspate foreland at Lacosta Island, along the coast of Florida, which was formed in an area protected by an offshore cuspate sand key.

When erosion attacks one side of a cusp to such an extent that no ridges or swales remain parallel to the shore, and the shoreline obliquely truncates these former lines of growth, a truncated cuspate foreland results. Cape Hatteras, North Carolina, is a well-known cuspate foreland with a nearly right-angle bend in shoreline (Plate 120). All the ridges and swales on the east side have been truncated by an erosion shoreline.

Occasionally, a truncated cusp is later prograded, forming new ridges and swales parallel to a new shoreline. This process of alternate retrograding and prograding may be repeated a number of times with constantly varying direction. The resulting feature will be a complex cuspate foreland. Classic examples of this feature are Dungeness, on the southeast coast of England, and Cape Canaveral, Florida, which has several distinct series of ridges and swales that have been successfully truncated (Johnson, 1919, p. 325).

Tombolos

Tombolos are bars that connect islands with mainlands or with other islands. The term "tombolo" refers to the connecting bar itself and not to the former island. As with other landforms, there are many different types of tombolos. The word is derived from Italian and the classic examples of this type of feature are found along the coast of Italy, with Monte Argentario the example used most often.

A single, simple bar connecting an island with the mainland or with another island is called a single tombolo. The sand bar connecting Morro Rock with the mainland at Morro Bay, California, is an excellent example (Plate 121). A very long, single tombolo occurs at Puerto Magdalena in Baja California (Plate 122), and another, wider, tombolo occurs at Palm Beach, north of Sydney, Australia. On the Massachusetts coast, Marblehead Neck is a single tombolo connecting Marblehead to the mainland.

In some places, two or three separate bars may be connected to an island in which case there is a double or even a triple tombolo. Monte Argentario in Italy almost forms a triple tombolo—an incomplete middle bar just escapes making it a very unusual coastal landform (Lobeck, 1958, p. 35; Johnson, 1919, p. 315). A few Y-shaped tombolos also exist but are difficult to locate. Morro del Puerto Santo in Venezuela is just such a tombolo. Complex tombolos result when several islands are united with one another and with the mainland by a complicated series of bars. One of the best examples of a complex tombolo is Big Nahant and Little Nahant on the Massachusetts coast, where the prograding of several sand bars has connected former islands with the mainland (Plate 123; Johnson, 1965, pp. 317-318; Lobeck, 1958, pp. 58-59).

Sand Cays

A sand cay or key is a low, small sandy bar or island, often situated on a coral-reef platform. The word is derived from the Spanish "cajo" meaning shoal. Generally, in the Pacific and Indian ocean reef areas it is spelled "cay" and so pronounced, but in the West Indies and in Florida the old English spelling "key" persists and the pronunciation is the same as the English word "key." The sand bank is usually composed of fine coral debris, often mixed with mollusk-shell material along with bryozoa, calcareous algae, and foraminifera. At first the bank is ephemeral and often moves to different positions during storms, but it eventually becomes fixed or semistabilized, especially if there is beachrock development. The cay will become covered with vegetation after the sand is built above high-water level. However, a single hurricane can remove completely both vegetation and sand, leaving only a coral formation. Sand cays occur on the platforms of the Great Barrier Reef in Australia, as well as in the East Indies, Florida, Jamaica, and other Caribbean locations (Fairbridge, 1968, pp. 972-973). Sand cays can be oval, lunate, or cuspate. Plate 124 shows lunate shaped sand cays at the north end of Eleuthera Island in the Bahamas.

Marine Bars

The term "marine bar" is used in a generic sense to include the various types of submerged deposits that extend along a coast. These submerged ridges of detrital sediments are larger and less regularly spaced than ripple marks. There has been considerable confusion over the word, because in time many bars become partially or wholly exposed during low tide and, when this occurs, they are really elevated beaches and islands (Stamp, 1961, pp. 47-48). Following Price (1951), the term "bar" is here confined to sand, gravel, and shingle shoals that are covered at least at high tide and the term "barrier" refers to the sand masses that extend along the coast and rise above high-tide level. A distinction is also made between marine bars along the coast and meander bars and delta bars associated with rivers. (Thornbury, 1969, pp. 165-166).

As with barriers and spits, there are many types of marine bars. They are formed in shallow epicontinental or shelf waters by waves and currents, and are found singly or together and are generally internally laminated. Longshore or longitudinal bars occur singly or in parallel series of two or three off sandy beaches. They form in the surf zone along the seaward flanks of plunge troughs excavated by the swirling motion of breaking waves. Longshore bars—straight or looped—are seldom built up above the stillwater (half-wave) level, because the breakers plunge on and over them, keeping their summits planed down. When they do build up above the high-water line, they are called barriers. Plate 125 shows longshore bars off Nauset Beach, Massachusetts. The dominant transport is from right to left.

Transverse bars extend approximately at right angles to shorelines. They are often confused with giant ripple marks that may extend across their surface, but the bars themselves are large, smooth, gently sloping features. Plate 126 shows an excellent example of transverse bars at Nauset Beach along the coast of Massachusetts.

Reticulated bars have a criss-cross pattern, with both sets of bars diagonal to the shoreline. Plate 127 shows criss-cross bars near Pleasant Bay Inlet on Cape Cod, Massachusetts. The white areas are swash bars formed by waves approaching from the lower right. The waves were generated by southwest winds blowing across Nantucket Sound.

Lunate bars are crescent shaped and are often found extending seaward of inlets and estuaries (Plate 128). There is a lunate bar off the coast of San Francisco and numerous examples can be found associated with sand cays in the Bahamas (see Plate 124). Another name for these lunate bars is tidal delta. Well-formed tidal deltas have a 90 to 180° fan of sand or coarse-grained sediment extending out from either end of a tidal inlet. Some of the larger lunate bars and tidal deltas may reach up to 11.3 kilometers (7 miles) out from the inlets.

Cuspate bars are similar to lunate bars, but they are not as cresent-shaped. Triangular-shaped cuspate bars are shown on Plate 129. These forms have been built into Lake Champlain at the delta of the Ausable River, south of Plattsburgh, New York.

Many submerged bars have no definite shape or pattern. These tidal current ridges are often longitudinal to the dominant current (Off, 1963), and can be classified under several broad categories, such as baymouth, inlet, or channel bars. Plate 130 depicts the many different forms these bars take in the Cape Hatteras region of North Carolina. On the seaward side of the tidal inlet, several cuspate bars are being built out into the ocean.

Sand bars vary greatly in types of material, shapes, and sizes. Huge calcareous sand bars can be found at shallow depth across the Bahama Banks. These are shaped like giant subaqueous barchans of calcareous sand and appear to be longitudinal to the dominant current.

Tidal Inlets

By definition, tidal inlets are short, narrow waterways with 90 to 180° terminal channel fans that connect a bay, lagoon, or similar body of water with a larger body of water such as a sea or ocean. They are maintained entirely or in part by tidal flow (Price, 1963). Many tidal inlets are no longer natural; they have been stabilized by dredging or have been extended between jetties seaward to deep water. Some of the factors controlling inlets are tidal range and regime; inlet flow volume; land runoff; currents; channel turbulence; wind-driven sheets of water and other marine floods; large waves; long-period wave energy; local rainfall and evaporation; seasonal ice; bottom sediment drift; and the lithology of bottom conditions, shores, and transported sediments as well as the volume of these sediments (Fairbridge, 1968, p. 1153).

Plate 131 is an excellent example of tidal inlets (as well as channel bars) at Pleasant Bay Inlet on Cape Cod, Massachusetts. (Well-formed tidal inlets as well as tidal channels can also be seen on Plate 130). These photographs show that flow through the inlet or gorge produces a local maximum of energy and velocity. During rising (flood) and falling (ebb) tides, water enters the inlet laterally at its then high-water end (the tidal drain) and emerges centrally from its low end (the tidal jet). The tidal drain is erosive and the tidal jet is partly depositional. Deposition is prominent at the turn of the tide. Jet and drain channels are partly separated by bars and shoals. The jet current typically flares at 20° (Albertson et al., 1950), characteristically bifurcating several diameters off the mouth at a crescentic bar or at an island (Bates, 1953).

Tidal Mud Flats

Tidal mud flats are common near river mouths in regions where there is a good supply of fine-grained silt and clay. They are usually seaward of the beach, have little vegetation, and are subject to rapid change during severe storms. Extensive mud flats occur along the Louisiana coast, east and west of the Mississippi Delta. They are also associated with mangrove swamps where these exist on the ocean side of the coast. A very soft mud flat extends across the mouth of the Ganges (Ganges-Brahmaputra) Delta seaward into the Bay of Bengal, covering miles of coast in the region called the Sundarbans (Plate 132). There are also mud flats east of the mouth of the Colorado River Delta near Puerto Peñasco, Mexico (Plate 132) and between the beaches and tombolos near Lynn and Little Nahant along the Massachusetts coast. Plate 133 shows mud flats in a bay near Abel Tasman National Park on the South Island of New Zealand.

Beaches

Beaches are accumulations of sediment deposited by waves and currents in the shore zone. Most beaches are composed of sand or coarse rock (shingle), but there are all types of beach materials from pure coral sands to black volcanic sands. As a rule, beach sediments are well sorted; the bulk of a sediment sample taken from a beach falls within a particular size grade (Bird, 1968, p. 81). Statistical parameters based on mechanical analysis indicate that the grain-size distribution of beach sediment is commonly asymmetrical and negatively skewed, the mean grain size being coarser than the median. It ap-

pears that the winnowing effect of wave action reduces the relative proportion of fine particles (Mason and Folk, 1958).

Types of Beach Material   Beach sediment is closely related to the material derived from the adjacent cliffs and foreshore or brought in from offshore or alongshore sources. The coarse material that makes up gravel or shingle beaches is found where coastal rock formations yield debris of suitable size, such as fragments broken from thin resistant layers in stratified sedimentary rocks, fragments eroded out of conglomerates or gravel deposits, or fragments derived from intricately fissured igneous formations. Much of the shingle on the beaches of southeast England has been derived, directly or indirectly, from flint nodules eroded out of the Chalk Cliffs. Plate 134 shows a coarse shingle beach on the Kaikoura Peninsula, South Island, New Zealand. This shingle is derived from coarse, layered bedrock and is piled up on the beach by high-energy waves. Plate 135 shows a gravel beach in Japan. Note how wave action has rounded the stones.

Coasts bordering regions that are, or have been, subject to glaciation and periglaciation have relatively abundant supplies of rock fragments derived from the erosion of rubble drift, gravelly moraines, or drumlins for the formation of shingle on beaches. In most other areas, sandy beaches are predominant unless a shingle source exists locally (Bird, 1968, p. 83). Plate 136 shows gravel on a beach in Portugal where coarse beach deposits are derived from sandstone and limestone outcrops.

Coral Beaches   Shingle (gravel) beaches are rare on tropical coasts, except where the coarse material is derived from coral or where torrential rivers deliver gravels to the shore. Plate 137 is a white coral sand beach in the Bahamas. Such calcareous sands, derived from shell fragments or coral debris, are common on oceanic islands and tropical coasts.

Sandy Beaches   Sandy beaches are supplied partly by material eroded from adjacent parts of the coast, partly by fluvial sediment, and partly by sand carried shoreward from the seafloor—the proportions being determined by local conditions. In addition, a considerable amount of sand may be blown from the land into the sea, particularly on a desert coast, and then delivered to the beach by waves.

Sand for small pocket beaches, such as at South Casa Beach, La Jolla, California, is derived from the arenaceous rock outcrops. At Tossa de Mar, Spain, sand for the pocket beach is derived from crystalline granitic rock (Plate 138). Near Bamburgh Castle on the coast of Northumberland, England, sand for a beach is supplied by several small rivers coming to the coast (Plate 139).

The sand for some large beaches appears to have been swept shoreward from the seafloor, during and possibly since the Holocene marine transgression. Bird (1968, p. 84) mentions that Ninety-Mile-Beach in Victoria, Australia, is not adjacent to eroding sandstone cliffs and no rivers are able to carry sediment to the shore, therefore, the source appears to be from offshore sand banks. When the wind is offshore, sand from the dunes is often carried out onto the beach or into a tidal channel where it may be carried to sea and then redeposited on beaches and spits. This is the case at the mouth of the Ythan River in Scotland (see Plate 118).

The most abundant mineral found in beach sands of terrigeneous origin is quartz and it is often accompanied by feldspars, mica, and varying amounts of heavy minerals. Sand supplied from erosion of nearby cliffs or brought down from river catchments reflect the mineral composition of the source areas. Calcareous sands occur where there are numerous shell fragments or coral debris. Shelly beaches are more often found near estuaries, lagoons, and bordering desert coasts, probably because the fluvial yield of terrigenous sediment has been meager.

On volcanic islands, such as Hawaii and Japan, black sand and gravel beaches occur, which consist mostly of basaltic fragments. Excellent black sand beaches can be found along the south coast of the island of Hawaii (Plate 140), and coarse black gravel can be found along many coastal sections in Japan (Plate 141). There are dark red beaches in Hawaii that are formed from burnt red ash deposits, and in Iceland you can find coastal sand bars that are reddish in color from red ash deposits (see Plate 41). Very white pumice beaches are also common (see Plate 63). Coasts adjacent to lumbering areas in Oregon, Washington, Western Canada, and Northern Russia are piled high with sawn timber or broken up logs. Plate 142 shows such a beach area in Olympic National Park near Kalaloch, Washington.

There are horizontal variations in the composition of beach material, particularly in the vicinity of eroding cliffs and headlands and near river mouths where a greater amount of fluvial sediment is likely to occur. Plate 136 shows coarse material dropping off rapidly toward the center at a small pocket beach in Portugal west of Sesimbra. Plate 143 shows the drastic changes that can occur in types of beach material along a beach at Camp Bay, on the south side of Lyttleton Harbor, New Zealand. Here, coarse material occurs near rock outcrops and near a small river mouth, with much finer quartzose sand occurring between.

Location of Beaches

Bayhead Beaches   Beach drifting, possibly aided by other types of longshore-current action, moves a considerable amount of unconsolidated material along the shores of bays toward the bayheads. Deposition occurs at bayheads because wave refraction reduces wave erosion to a minimum at these locations. Therefore, much of the debris eroded from headlands is built into bayhead beaches at the inner ends of adjacent bays (Plate 143).

Bayside Beaches   The material in transit along the sides of a bay may form bayside beaches, which when fully developed often connect the usually unimportant headland beaches with the more often well-developed bayhead beaches (Plate 144).

Pocket Beaches   These beaches, usually small, occur as a coastal re-entrant or can be found between two littoral barriers. They often occur near small river mouths but are most numerous where less resistant rock has been eroded away. They are numerous along rocky coasts because finer sands get carried into quieter coves and bays. Plate 145 shows very small pocket beaches along the south coast of New Zealand.

Uninterrupted Beaches   Long, straight beaches develop where there is an abundant supply of sand and no headlands to interrupt sand movement. Miles of straight beach exist along the east coast of the United States and Mexico from Cape Cod to Yucatan. Plate 146 shows a very straight beach west of Karāchi in Pakistan.

Beach Ridges (Accretion Ridges)   On a depositional shore, where the tidal range is sufficient to expose a broad foreshore at low tide, a system of ridges and troughs is often found parallel or at a slight angle to the shoreline. These beach ridges are also called ridge and runnel or low-and-ball coasts (Gresswell, 1953). This type of shoreline constitutes lines of growth of the beach plain and, when well preserved, makes it easy to trace the history of development with great accuracy. Beach ridges vary in size according to wave attack, but their length rarely exceeds 6 meters (20 feet). However, the distance between the ridges can be as much as 100 meters (328 feet). The number of ridges may vary from two or three to hundreds (see Plate 147). Depressions between the ridges are called swales.

Each beach ridge marks the position of a pre-existing shoreline. These beach forms are common constituents of prograding constructional shore features such as barrier beaches and cuspate forelands. The history of the ridges can be worked out through extrapolation of the older ridges. Radiocarbon dating may be obtained from beach shells found with the ridges or old vegetation, such as roots, buried in the swales. Although most beach ridges are postglacial in age, some have formed during the Pleistocene.

Beach ridges are most likely to form during storms when coarse sediment, sand, gravel, or shells may pile up just landward of the beach. Very similar ridges composed only of sand blown from the beach can form behind a beach. Since steeper beach faces occur with coarser material and higher waves, ridge building will be most favored by either of these two conditions (Savage, 1959). Multiple ridges apparently occur due to continued shallowing of the offshore profile, usually because of abundant sediment supply (Johnson, 1919). Shallowing of the offshore profile may also occur due to a fall in sea level. Radiocarbon dating suggests the association of some ridge systems with small, negative sea-level oscillations during the last five thousand years (Fairbridge, 1961; Schofield, 1961).

A succession of beach ridges can be clearly discerned at the southern end of the Banks Peninsula in New Zealand (Plate 147). Between twenty and thirty ridges have grown seaward in the last three hundred years. Vegetation on the swales, where there is more moisture, helps to identify the individual forms. In Pakistan and Iran beach ridge growth has been rapid in a number of locations along the Makrān coast. Where the ridges are perched on a muddy substratum, such as in deltaic environments, they are called "cheniers," Louisiana French for belts of oak trees that mark their distribution in the Mississippi Delta region (Plate 148).

Beach Plains and Coastal Plains Beach plains and wide coastal plains result from waves and currents carrying abundant material, usually sand, and depositing it seaward. Forward building of the shore apparently occurs because with a diverging current there is diminished current velocity. With diminished velocity, an accumulation of debris occurs on the face of the beach, carrying its entire profile seaward and producing by the expansion of its crest a tract of new-made land (Gilbert, 1885). If the supply of debris is fairly uniform and constant, the successive embankments will be closely spaced and will tend

to form a continuous plain, which may be called a beach plain or coastal plain. Such plains are rare, because it seldom happens that all forces operating at the shore are so uniform and continuous as to give a perfectly smooth plain surface. More often beach ridges will form, but smooth beach plains do exist. Plate 149 shows a wide beach plain at Konārak, Iran, near Chāh Bahār, and Plate 150 shows a sandy coastal plain along the north coast of Yucatan, Mexico, east of Progreso.

The Beach Profile

The beach profile depends on the height and width of the beach and also on the beach-face angle. Figure 9 shows the shore profile. If we ignore for the moment the effect of tidal range, the height to which a beach is built depends primarily on the height of the waves that built it. In the case of sandy beaches, the limit is set by the level reached by swash uprush, but on pebble and shingle beaches the limit is somewhat higher, because of the ability of waves to throw stones some distance past the swash limit. In this way storm ridges of pebbles may be built some distance beyond the swash limit. Plate 151, for example, shows pebbles 8 meters (26 feet) above the high-water mark at Dungeness, England. Therefore, the highest beaches are associated with big waves and coarse material, the lowest with small waves and sand (Davies, 1973, p. 119).

The width of a beach, if we again temporarily ignore the tidal range, is essentially a function of sediment supply. If more material is being added than subtracted, the beach will normally build out at the height and beach-

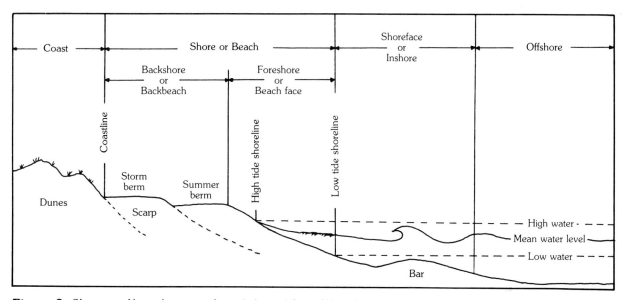

Figure 9. Shore profile with terminology (adapted from Wiegel, 1953, and Strahler, 1971).

face angle that apply in each particular case. In this way, the backshore zone is extended so that it may form a broad depositional platform (Plate 152). However, wave heights are never constant, so that, as the beach builds out, an unusually high uprush may carry material past the top of the normal beach face and deposit it on the outer edge of the backshore zone, forming a convex platform with the backshore sloping inland. Repetition of this process under conditions of continued aggradation appears to be one way in which ridging of the backshore zone is effected. The convex feature formed by progradation is called the beach berm (see Plate 151). Its surface is nearly always closer to the horizontal than that of the beach face, but it may slope seaward, be near to the horizontal, or slope landward in varying degrees (Davies, 1973, p. 120).

The beach-face angle is primarily a function of particle size and wave steepness; the coarser the beach material and the less steep the waves, the greater the beach-face angle will be (Inman and Bagnold, 1963).

Berms A berm is a low, nearly horizontal portion of the beach formed by material deposited by wave action. Some beaches have no berms, others may have one or more. In summer the berm is low and wide. (To the layman, it *is* the beach—the observable sand on which beachgoers sunbathe and play.) At that time, the underwater profile is likely to be smooth and barless. Plate 153 depicts the coast at Bethany Beach, Delaware, on an August day in 1963. Almost no berm can be detected. In winter or during severe storms, the berm is higher and narrower, as most of the sand is moved out off the beach to create underwater bars (Plate 153). The reason for the shift is the seasonal change in wave action. The large waves created by storms cut the berm back; the small waves of summer replace it again. If the amount of sand involved is constant, as it often is on a beach between two headlands, the entire beach motion is merely an exchange of sand between berm and bar (Bascom, 1963, pp. 188-189). Plate 153 shows Bethany Beach cut back and a new berm created after a hurricane hit the coast in 1963. The severe storm not only cut the beach back but also built a higher berm.

Beach cusps Cusps are interesting beach features, because they only form under certain conditions. They are evenly spaced, crescent-shaped depressions, concave to the sea, that are built by wave action on the seaward edge of the berm. Of all the curiosities of the shore, these are one of the most puzzling, and none of the dozens of explanations given for their formation is completely satisfying (Bascom, 1964, p. 208). Cusps are features of the upper beach and not the foreshore. They vary greatly in shape and have been seen on beaches of fine sand as well as of large cobbles, and they occur equally in protected bays and on exposed

beaches. Generally, coarser material is carried to the back and horns of the cusp, while finer sediment occupies the floor or bay of the depression between the horns. This separation of material can be seen clearly in Plate 154, which shows excellent cusps that formed on a beach near Dana Point, California. The building up of the horns is assisted by the refraction of the swash in the bays, which carries the coarser particles to the edge of the cusp (Kuenen, 1948). An important point is the effect the material has on the size and regularity of the cusps. Generally, it can be said that, all things being equal, cusps are longer and more regular on sand beaches than on shingle beaches and longer on shingle beaches than where seaweed is entangled in the upper beach, the reason being that sand is easier to move than gravel or shingle. Yet cusps occur less on sand beaches than on coarse material beaches, perhaps because a fairly steep slope is necessary for their formation and shingle beaches usually have steeper slopes than do sand beaches (Guilcher, 1954, pp. 80-81). Plate 154 shows poorly formed beach cusps that consist of large rocks on the horns and much finer particles in the bays on a steep beach north of Kaikoura Peninsula on the South Island of New Zealand. One of the unanswered questions is why there is such a sharp division in size and distribution of materials.

We now know that conditions are best for cusp formation if the waves approach the beach exactly parallel to the shore and are unconfused by local currents and winds. There must also be some original irregularity in the beach to start them forming. We also know that the spacing of the cusps is related to wave height. But the question of why cusps should form at all is still unanswered (Bascom, 1964, p. 210).

Beach rock Several other features besides beach rock are included under this heading such as incipient beach rock, lagoon rock, and coquina (although coquina has a different origin than beach rock). Beach rock is cemented beach material that crops out at about mean sea level in coastal areas of small tidal range, or at about high neap-tide level if the range is large (Plate 155). The interstitial-cemented aggregate may consist of quartz sand, black sand with a high content of heavy minerals, finer-grained coastal marsh or swamp sediments, or whatever else the beach may be composed of, including World War II cartridges shells on some Pacific Island beaches.

Several bands of beach rock usually occur, often separated by shallow strips of water. The bands may resemble pavements 9.14 meters (30 feet) or more wide, but ordinarily they are 3.05 meters (10 feet) wide or less. The oldest band of beach rock lies farthest seaward and the youngest continues inland, under the beach. Banding occurs because beach rock crops out only along retreating coasts. An inner band may be friable, in some cases so much so that it can be crumbled by hand, but outer bands are tough and durable (Plate 156; Russell, 1967, p. 118).

Beach rock is only visible where the shore has receded since it mainly forms under beach sands. Where shore retreat is slight, beach rock appears as a flat platform. Where the shore has completely retreated, beach rock may be left behind as an offshore reeflike ridge (Plate 157).

The origin of beach rock is not completely known, because there is probably more than one process of lithification that produces materials that are superficially similar. Beach rocks with calcite cement may be formed along the water table as a result of precipitation of calcite from groundwater. These beach rocks appear to be characteristic of high coasts where freshwater bodies are present. Beach rocks with aragonite cement, however, are likely to form as a result of deposition of aragonite from seawater and are characteristic of low-reef coasts and islands, where the presence of groundwater bodies are unlikely or impossible. The situation becomes even more complicated by the fact that aragonite recrystallizes to calcite after a lapse of time (Davies, 1973, p. 116). In addition to these physical processes, the possible role of beach microorganisms in precipitating the cement has been proposed by several authors (for example, Nesteroff, 1956). R. J. Russell at one time also thought that algae and algal crusts were responsible for cementation. Plate 158 shows that some beach-rock outcrops are covered with algae. But detailed investigations by two physiological algologists of eighty beaches on islands extending from Puerto Rico to Grenada refuted this concept of origin (Krauss, 1960; Russell, 1967, p. 125).

Climate probably influences beach-rock cementation through the availability of warm seawater or groundwater that is supersaturated with calcium carbonate derived largely from dissolved sea shells, and through high rates of evaporation and upward capillary movement through the sand. Beach rock is particularly characteristic of a tropical climate that has a well-marked dry season. These rocks are less likely to be found on coasts of free transport where there is a constant movement of sand along the shore. They are more likely to be found on coasts of impeded transport, particularly where shore retreat is occurring (Davies, 1973, pp. 116-117).

Several terms are used for different forms of cemented rock. For example, Russell (1967) talks about incipient beach rock as newly exposed water-table rock. In turn, water-table rock is at the beginning stages of cementation found at the edge of the water table. With further exposure it becomes indurated and forms true beach rock.

Beach rock may be closely associated with cemented dune sand called eolianite (see p. 21) and a variety of cemented swamp and aluvial deposits classified under lagoon rock (Plate 159), and, in many cases, it is difficult to distinguish among them. Some writers believe that cementation of all of the above results from the same process; others believe they each form in distinct and different ways. This disagreement indicates that the cementation process—at least of beach rock—is not yet clearly understood (Fairbridge, 1968, pp. 70-73).

Coquina looks very similar to some beach rock as Plate 160 indicates. But beach rock is primarily cemented sand, shells, corals, and other organic debris found on the beach, and coquina is a porous limestone composed of broken shells and corals found inland as bedrock. When coquina is exposed at the coast, as it is in Florida and Mexico, it is difficult to distinguish between the two.

Megaripples and Sand Waves   These are large, gentle ripplelike features composed of sand, which occur in nearshore marine situations usually formed by tidal currents. Some of these sand wave lengths may reach 100 meters (328 feet) and an amplitude of about 0.5 meter (1.64 feet) (Plate 161). This type is common in rivers and estuaries (Plate 162). The play of swash on a beach also can create transitory current ripple marks, megaripples, and sand waves. These often make picturesque beach patterns as Plate 163 shows. Megaripples have wave lengths between 0.61 and 6.10 meters, (2 and 20 feet), and sand waves have wave lengths greater than 6.1 meters (20 feet).

Minor Erosional Beach Forms

Ripple Marks   These minor shore features are found on the foreshore and not the upper beach. Numerous rills and ripples also are found at the bottoms of lakes, rivers, and seas, in some cases at great depths of 1,500 to 2,000 meters (4,921 to 6,561 feet) in restricted straits. There are several different types of sand ripples.

Oscillatory or wave ripples have symmetrical slopes, sharp crests, and usually rounded troughs (Plate 164). They result from the to-and-fro movement of the sea bottom produced by the passage and movement of waves. Their size varies with that of the waves and the depth of the water. Their height averages from 5 to 15 millimeters (0.20 to 0.59 inches) and wave length from 3 to 12 centimeters (1.2 to 4.7 inches). They form perpendicular to the direction of the waves.

Current ripples are asymmetrical and their crests are more rounded than oscillatory ripples (Plate 165). They are formed at right angles to the current, and their gentle slope faces the direction from which the current comes, the other slope being the angle of rest of the sand. These linear ripples occur when the current exceeds a critical speed, varying with depth of water and size of the sand grains, and they move in the direction of the current. If the current exceeds a second critical speed, they cease to form, because the sand is lifted and moves in suspension in the water instead of rolling on the bottom. If the speed increases further and reaches a third critical point, ripples again form but are displaced upstream by erosion on their downstream slopes and deposition on their upstream slopes. Gilbert (1885) called these symmetrical ripples antidunes (Plate 166). The passing of the third critical speed leads to the formation of broad, rounded, more irregular crests that move downstream with the current. These sometimes form cuspate ripples that look very much like wind-blown barchan-shaped sand and form best as current velocity decreases. As speed of the current decreases, they can change to current ripple marks of the first stage.

All the preceding ripple marks are features formed in sand or gravel. However, ripple marks also can occur in mud (Plate 167), but they are usually symmetrical and parallel to the direction of tidal current flow, unlike ripple marks of the neighboring sand banks that are perpendicular to the current and asymmetrical. Mud ripple marks disappear in very calm weather.

It is common to see oscillatory and current ripple marks combined as well as one or two sets of the same type crossing each other (Plate 168). These compound forms are more common than simple systems (Guilcher, 1958, pp. 80-83). The complexity of sand ripple marks is considerable; it is, in fact, far greater than can be dealt with in this discussion. Plate 169 shows an example of more complex ripple marks. Most of these forms are temporary, although they may be preserved in fossil form.

Rills   The water left in the sand of the upper part of the beach after the retreat of the tide or the dying down of storm waves often carves out tiny drainage channels as it flows back to the sea (Plate 170). These miniature river systems are known as rills. They do not form below sea level. The pattern often resembles that of branching plant stems, so much so that they have often been confused with small stream patterns in sedimentary rocks (Johnson, 1919, pp. 512-513). Rills and ripples are often closely associated as can be seen in Plate 171.

Rhomboidal or lozenge-shaped rill marks often form systems of marked regularity. The rhombs, whose diagonals follow the slope of the beach, are only a few centimeters long. They are formed at the time of the backwash. The flow of the film of water in rapid retreat is at first turbulent (see Plate 13). When it does not exceed approximately 2 centimeters (0.8 inch) in depth, a rhomboidal system is formed. But when the depth is no more than 1 centimeter (0.4 inch), small current rills and ripple marks are formed in the sand and everything becomes indistinct. After the backwash has passed, water

springs from the saturated sand and often forms small temporary cusps that are like small ditches concave toward the lower part of the beach. As the sand dries, a rhomboidal system of rills appears. All of this can happen in a matter of seconds (Plate 172).

Swash Marks   When a wave breaks at the foot of a gently inclined beach, part of the water glides up the slope in a thin sheet known as swash. After the retreat of the swash, the greatest advance of its irregular margin is often indicated by a thin, wavy line of fine sand, mica scales, bits of seaweed, or other debris. These are commonly referred to as wave marks, but since they are mainly formed by the swash a better term is swash marks (Johnson, 1919, p. 514). These are very small, delicate features and certainly don't attract very much attention on the modern shore (Plate 173).

Minor Depositional Forms   As a beach, spit, or barrier island is formed, bimodal crossbedding is often produced by flood and ebb waves and currents. This crossbedding consists of alternating coarse- and fine-grained layers as shown on a beach ridge at Crane Beach, Massachusetts (Plate 174). A cross-section of this bimodal crossbedding is shown on an intertidal sand flat on Cape Cod, Massachusetts (Plate 175).

Any obstacle can create a minor depositional form such as the isolated imbricated pebble with a current crescent on Nauset Beach, Massachusetts (Plate 176). Wind blowing across a beach can form sand shadows or sand ripples (Plate 177), or white wind-blown sand can emphasize former wave and current patterns by being deposited as a white veneer on top of existing sand.

And last, but far from least, are the many minor features created by animals such as foot patterns by birds, holes by mollusks and crabs, and even mounds by gastropods (Plate 178).

In winter, when snow and ice cover a coastal region, many different shapes and forms are created such as the ice wedges in the sand on Fire Island, Long Island, New York, on a March day in 1968 (Plate 179).

COASTS BUILT BY ORGANISMS

Coral Reef Coasts

A coral reef is defined as a complex organogenic framework of calcium carbonate (primarily of corals) that forms a rocky eminence on the sea floor and customarily grows upward to the tide limit. Thus coral reefs cause waves to break, and, consequently, the internal spaces in this branching framework are packed with fragments of broken reef material—broken up mollusca, coralline algae, echinoid debris, and foraminifera. The principal reef builders today are the *Madreporarian* (or *Scleracti-*

nian) colonial corals and the class Zoantharia, phylum Coelenterata. Calcareous algae often grow over and around the coral colonies, helping to hold them together and sometimes misleading observers into thinking they are the frame builders (Fairbridge, 1968, pp. 186-188). The corals themselves are animal organisms whose skeletons are formed from secretions of calcium carbonate. They live together with the algae in large colonies (Plate 180). As the corals die, new organisms grow on top of them, creating a reef made up of strongly cemented calcium carbonate skeletons.

Coral reef rock is usually very porous, having a large variety of clastic components that are principally organogenic, and is cemented with inorganic materials (Plate 181). Both the outer-reef periphery and the lagoon that often forms behind the reef are marked by loose clastic debris that has largely been wave-broken and washed off the reef. This detritus is known as bioclastic or coral sand when loose, or calcarenite when cemented. A special type of coral sand is found on many beaches that, after repeated concentrations of the interstitial seawater under the hot tropical sun over many low-tide periods, becomes cemented into beach rock, beach stone, or littoral calcarenite (Plates 155 to 160).

Temperature is the most important factor in the horizontal distribution of coral reefs. Although the outside limits are from about 16 to 36°C (61 to 97° F), the band of optimum growth is much narrower and may be 25 to 29°C (77 to 84°F). Therefore, most corals are found in warm-water areas generally between 30°N and 30°S of the equator, with a concentration in the western parts of oceans away from cold currents. Thus, there are two major provinces: an extensive Indo-Pacific province, stretching from east Africa to the Pacific, and a much less extensive Atlantic province, stretching from the Caribbean to west Africa.

Light is the most important factor in controlling vertical distribution of coral because of the extreme phototropism of the Zooxanthellae. Limits of toleration enable living coral to reach about 90 meters (295 feet) deep, but most growth ceases at about half this depth. Most vigorous coral growth occurs from 0 to 20 meters (0 to 65 feet) (Davies, 1973, pp. 68-73). Coral growth is inhibited by large rivers, which bring in fresh or muddy water, and by leeward locations, which lack moving water to bring food to the sedentary polyps, to prevent silting, and to provide a proper oxygen-carbon balance. Because of these factors, reef development is often more vigorous on the windward sides of islands. However, too much wave action may prohibit or inhibit reef formation by preventing establishment of polyp planules or by destroying established coral at too high a rate. Recent volcanic activity also prohibits their growth, as does the excessive turbidity often created by the many diatoms

found in the ocean waters of the eastern Pacific and eastern Atlantic.

Types of Reefs The simple breakdown into fringing reefs, barrier reefs, and atolls devised by Charles Darwin (1896) has stood the test of time very well, but his classical division needs to be amplified as a result of more modern work. For example, two more divisions—platform and patch reefs—need to be added. Certainly, other types could be added in view of the great variation in reef form but uniform agreement may be a long way off. The following classification is based on the one used by Fairbridge (1968, pp. 186-202).

Fringing Reefs According to Darwin, these are the basic reef types, which form a shallow veneer or shelf in shallow water at or near the shore of the mainland or around offshore islands. These reefs are usually attached to the shore. Heavy sedimentation and runoff make tropical mainland coasts less attractive for fringing reefs than offshore and oceanic islands. The nearshore surface of the reef often becomes covered by terrigenous sediments.

Plate 182 shows an excellent fringing coral reef around the north shore of Oahu, Hawaii, and Plate 183 shows a fringing reef around the crater of an old volcano at Hanauma Bay on this same island (see also Plate 65).

Platform and Patch Reefs These are usually rounded or ovoid; the large ones, over a kilometer or more, are called platforms and the smaller ones, patch reefs. They are also called "shelf," "bank," "table," and "hummock" reefs. These reefs are found in water of moderate depth, generally 20 to 40 meters (65 to 131 feet), on the continental shelves or midocean platforms, sometimes appearing as dots in a random manner. Malé Atoll in the Maldives has a rounded, almost ovoid, reef platform around it (Plate 184). Where these reefs are very small, they form simple rounded patches sometimes only 100 meters (328 feet) or so across. Many examples of the progression from a small patch reef to a big reef can be seen in the northern sector of the Great Barrier Reef of Queensland, Australia (Plate 185).

Barrier Reefs According to Darwin, tectonic (crustal) subsidence on a fringing reef, if carried out slowly, would cause the corals to grow upward, and, as the land behind gradually submerged, a lagoon would form between the land and the upgrowing barrier. The postglacial rise of sea level primarily caused the last submergence (Daly, 1915), although, in many parts of the world, tectonic movements and sea-level rise are contributing to lagoon formation. These lagoons range in width from 0.8 to 16 kilometers (0.5 to 10 miles) or more. The world's largest and finest example of a barrier reef extends along the northeastern Australian coast for 1,930 kilometers (1,200 miles), from the Gulf of Papua to the Tropic of Cancer. It is separated from the land by a lagoon 32 to 48 kilometers (20 to 30 miles) wide. Much of the Great Barrier Reef of Australia is actually a series of patch reefs (bank or hummock reefs) found on the continental shelf of Queensland, occurring inside the main barrier reef in the north and making up the whole system in the south.

Another large barrier reef occurs off the coast of Belize and Yucatan in the Caribbean. The Maldives, in the Indian Ocean south of India, are over 2,000 islands that form a long linear series of atolls and reefs (Plate 186). There is also a barrier reef along the Florida Keys. You can rent a boat at John Pennekamp Coral Reef State Park, off Key Largo, and go out to the reef and swim through one of the most luxurious coral reefs found anywhere in the world (Plate 186).

Barrier reefs are always asymmetric in plane and section, steep on the ocean side, often dropping abruptly away to 1,000 to 5,000 meters (3,280 to 16,404 feet), but grading off gently to the interior with a sediment-wedge often dotted by small reef patches, pinnacles, and coral heads. Depths in the lagoon may drop to 50 to 80 meters (164 to 262 feet) (Fairbridge, 1968, p. 189).

Atolls   These are ring-shaped reefs, very much like ribbon reefs that have been bent into circles, enclosing a lagoon. Charles Darwin suggested that during subsidence fringing reefs surrounding volcanic islands grew up gradually to develop ring-shaped barrier reefs and, as subsidence continued, eventually became center-island-free ring reefs. This may be the origin of some atolls, especially those of the Society Islands, but there are several other types of atolls (Agassiz, 1903; Fairbridge, 1950a; MacNeil, 1954).

Shelf atolls do not have volcanic foundations; they appear to grow up as open platform reefs or from earlier platform reefs. Off the northwest Australian coast several large atolls 400 to 500 meters (1,312 to 1,640 feet) rise from depressed outer sections of the shelf.

Compound atolls are barrier reefs and platform reefs that have grown upward in the same way as oceanic atolls where large continental crustal segments have slowly subsided. They can be found in the South China Sea, in sections of Indonesia, in the Maldives and Laccadives, and in the Coral Sea Plateau in the Australia region. Evidently, they grew up during subsidence, but they were exposed during the last glacial low-sea level to form a differentially weathered surface.

A third group of atolls is the true mid-Pacific type that rises in the deep ocean basins from isolated volcanic cones (seamounts or guyots), with up to 2000 meters (6,562 feet) of accumulated reef growth that may date back to the Cretaceous (Plate 187). These oceanic atolls often have U-shaped gashes, which are attributed to landslides down volcanic slopes, whereas shelf atolls are more often perfectly, smoothly rounded (Fairbridge, 1950b).

Reef Islands   Since the days of Captain James Cook, islands rising in the Pacific have been known as *high islands* and *low islands*. The high islands are continental or volcanic rocks such as those found off the Queensland coasts of Australia or the south coast of Puerto Rico (Plate 188). The low islands are strictly coral islands and fall into five categories (Fairbridge, 1950a, p. 348).

1. Simple sand cays (keys in the Caribbean) represent accumulations of loose coral sand and beach rock. They are generally situated on the lee side of a coral platform where intersecting waves have a minimum of energy and are likely to be washed over at high tide (Plate 189). Sand cays are also discussed in Part III under Marine Depositional Coasts (see Plate 124). I include them in this section, because their origin and makeup are related to coral reefs.

2. Vegetated sand cays are similar to simple sand cays but are larger, more mature, and covered with well-established flora, including large trees. Small dunes often can be found along their shores and their upper beaches offer sites for turtles to lay their eggs. Beach rock gives stability to these cays; otherwise they would be washed away during hurricanes.

3. Shingle cays are similar to sand cays in that they are accumulations of wave-tossed debris and dead coral heads, called "jetsam," thrown onto the reef by storms, but they are usually situated on the windward side of platform reefs. The coarse, heavy coral cobbles or shingle often are cemented into wave-resistant coral breccia or coral conglomerate (Plate 190).

4. Sand cays with shingle ramparts have more vegetation. On the protected lee side of the shingle rampart, there is an opportunity for floating mangrove seedlings to take root. Mangrove plays an important part in modifying the inner-reef environment, because it leads to the accumulation of organic debris, which causes bacterial decay to set in. Under these conditions, the coral sands and limestones rot and the interior of the reef flat literally becomes dissolved out. The lagoons thus formed become the site of flourishing mangrove swamps such as at La Cordillera Islands, off Puerto Rico (Plate 191).

5. On some of the better protected and more mature reefs, there are indications of older reefs at higher levels, some of which are of Pleistocene age. These emerged reef limestones form the foundations of many atoll islands across the Pacific and Indian oceans and at several locations in the Caribbean (Plate 192; Fairbridge, 1968, pp. 188-193).

Algal Reefs, Terraces, and Platforms   A number of marine algae produce encrustations or films of carbonate material, normally calcite that has a large amount of magnesium carbonate incorporated in it. A conspicuous and mainly tropical family of green algae—*Codiaceae*—produces lime around filaments. The *Codiaceae* are important geomorphically for the way in which they build calcareous banks in sheltered depressions such as those within annular reefs, but they are also found in sheltered lagoonal situations. Early explorers to the Pacific were often struck by the fact that coral reefs frequently possessed a slightly raised rim, or crestal ridge, especially on the seaward side that tended to protect the reef surface from the action of the surf and at low tide was often dry enough to walk on. These rims are built of calcareous algae, such as *Lithothamnion*, but, in other areas, the rim builders are predominately *Poralithon.* As a family, these algae have much wider temperature tolerances than hermatypic corals and are distributed from the Arctic Ocean to the Antarctic Ocean. They also are able to tolerate a wider range of salinity and turbidity and, as a result, are more persistant throughout the tropics. The biological and geomorphic importance of the algae rim is that it occurs where the waves habitually break.

1. Algal reefs are organic rocky structures found in the ocean and in certain carbonate-rich lakes. In warmer oceans, they contribute to the complex of coral reefs. They can occur as cabbagehead bioherms that form rocky hummocks 30 to 100 centimeters (12 to 39 inches) in height and are sometimes filled in with sediment to form a massive continuous reef. They can form algae mat platforms. They also form a thick veneer over the erosion surface of older limestones, helping to prevent further erosion and protecting the shore, or they can occur as algal rims or ridges on the exposed outer and upper parts of existing coral reefs (Plate 193). A large proportion of the intertidal surfaces of many modern coral reefs are covered by a thin veneer of encrusting algae.

2. In areas of heavy wave action, which in turn leads to constant heavy spray, the algae tend to build low-rimmed terraces analogous to the inorganic terraces of volcanic hot-spring areas (Plate 194). These corallinelike algae not only tolerate strong wave exposure but appear to be encouraged by it as long as the waves are not too effectively armed with abrasive material. In spite of their wide latitudinal distribution, calcareous algae are more important as constructional agents in the equatorial regions than elsewhere (see Plate 99). In high latitudes, sea-ice formation keeps them at depth. However, algae-covered shore platforms do reach north to Oregon (Plate 195) and south to the extreme southwest coast of Australia. The zone is wider than the coral-reef zone and approximates closely to that in which there is lithification of beaches and dunes (Davies, 1973, pp. 73-75).

3. Other reef builders include a variety of organic forms such as Serpula, Bryozoa, oyster *(Ostrea),* and mussel *(Mytilus).* Serpulid reefs are built out by the cementing of worm tubes onto the rocks and beaches along the shore. Such reefs are usually small structures covering limited areas but some may extend for kilometers. Serpulid (Plate 196) and bryozoa reefs are mostly found in the tropics, in some cases forming microatolls. Oyster and mussel reefs are more likely to be found in the middle and high latitudes, where they form banks or reefs, which in some places are now uplifted. In rare cases, even sponge banks form, which are made up of extensive deposits of siliceous spicules.

Among the organic reefs, those composed of geologically young oysters are now second in size and distribution to the coralline reefs. Oyster communities consist of scattered clusters, densely populated beds, elevated patch reefs, tubular bodies, and oval to linear reefs. The tops of the reefs range from the intertidal zone to depths, in some deep Atlantic Coast channels, of 12 meters (40 feet) below sea level. The Texas reefs seem to have steep sides and are based on sand or shell beds buried as deep as 24 meters (80 feet). Tertiary and Pleistocene oyster reefs are known, but only the post-Flandrian Holocene reefs extending from New Jersey to Texas have received detailed study (Fairbridge, 1968, pp. 799-803). I visited an oyster reef, possibly of Pleistocene age, on the shore of Bahia de los Muertos near the southern tip of Baja California (Plate 197).

Kelp, seaweed, and barnacles do not form reefs as such, but they are important in helping to protect a shore against heavy wave attack and kelp beds do slow down and reduce swells as they approach a coast (Plates 198 and 199).

MANGROVE COASTS

Mangrove swamps are submerged tidal woodlands and scrublands found along most alluvial coasts in humid tropical regions. Most mangroves are trees, although some shrubs are also classified as mangroves. All mangroves are salt-tolerant—holophytic—plants. The peculiar morphological adaptation of these plants to a saline environment, as well as the characteristic hydrology and landforms of the swamps they grow in, makes them one of the most distinctive of tropical vegetation types. In large mangrove swamps, trees reach heights of 30 to 36 meters (98 to 118 feet) and diameters of 0.61 to 0.91 meter (2 to 3 feet); however, most swamps are composed of smaller trees and low, scrubby forests.

Mangroves of the Western Hemisphere (Central and South America and the west coast of Africa) are composed of about six species that belong to four major genera; these include *Rhizophora* (red mangrove), *Avicennia* (black mangrove), *Laguncalaria* (white mangrove), and *Concocarpus* (buttonwood mangrove). In contrast, twenty species of mangrove are common to swamps of the Eastern Hemisphere (East Africa to the western Pacific), that, in size and maturity, attain their maximum development around southeast Asia. In this region, genera of *Rhizophora, Avicennia, Brugiera, Caropa, Ceriops,* and *Sonneratia* predominate.

Mangrove swamps only form in protected areas, such as tidal lagoons, or along open coastlines that are reached by waves of low energy. The southwest coast of Florida from Naples to Key Largo is such an area (Plate 200). They also only grow in shallow water areas, because the young trees cannot take root in water that is deeper than 0.61 meter (2 feet) at low tide (Plate 201). Mangroves thrive best in brackish water, although they can grow in fresh or hypersaline water. Thus, tidal estuaries, especially those served by mud-laden rivers, provide the optimum physical setting for the development of mangrove swamps along many coasts.

Along coasts where river-carried sediment is deposited in mud banks and mud flats, a coastwise or fringing mangrove swamp up to several kilometers wide may develop. Mangrove swamps often extend inland up to 32 to 64 kilometers (20 to 40 miles) where there are tidal rivers (Plate 202). In deltaic regions, the shape of the swamp is dictated by the shape of the delta itself. Along many coasts, mangroves develop best in lagoonal regions behind barrier bars and reefs. Therefore, the locations of tropical mangrove swamps are largely controlled by coastal geomorphology and by the pattern of coastal sedimentation.

Factors favoring the development of a broad fringing belt of coastal mangroves include: (1) tropical temperatures. (Well-developed mangroves are found where the average temperature of the coldest month exceeds 20°C [68°F], and where the seasonal temperature range does not exceed 5°C [9°F].); (2) a high tidal range; (3) a large supply of detrital sediments, especially fine-grained alluvium. (In some areas of the Caribbean, such as Jamaica, and in the western Pacific basin, mangroves occur on coral reefs, but such growth is stunted and can be considered abnormal.) (4) shores free from strong wave action, so-called low wave-energy coasts. Mangroves cannot tolerate strong wave action, either for the growth of seedlings or for the maintenance of mature forests.

Large mangrove swamps are seldom more than 1,295 square kilometers (500 square miles) in area. Some of the world's largest are found along the Pacific coast of Colombia, the southwest coast of Florida, the west coast of Malaya, the northern coast of Borneo and in the Guayaquil estuary of Ecuador. In the Philippines, mangrove forests occupy almost 5,180 square kilometers (2,000 square miles) of coastal area. About 25,899 square kilometers (10,000 square miles) of the earth's surface is covered by large mangrove swamps, which is

almost 1 percent of the area estimated to be covered by swamps of all types.

A distinctive characteristic of mangrove swamps is the entanglement of vegetation at and just above the floor of the forest. This is especially true of red mangrove (*Rhizophora*) forests (Plate 203). The red mangrove has prop roots that arch out from the base of the tree similar to the legs of a tarantula (see Plate 132). In addition, the upper branches drop aerial stilt-roots that reach to the ground and intermesh with the prop roots (Plate 204). Other genera, in particular *Avicennia* and *Laguncalaria,* have spikelike pneumatophores that project several centimeters to several meters above the mud and peat forest floor surrounding the trees (Plate 205). Many investigators believe this entanglement of roots and trunks serves as a sedimentary weir, promoting the seaward growth of the swamps through the entrapment of sediment (Plate 206). However, there is some debate over the ability of mangrove swamps to prograde coasts. It is now believed that sediment trapped within the forest may actually lead to a slowdown of coastal progradation as less sediment is thereby available for lateral or seaward accretion.

Mangrove swamps can be grouped into three principal types based on their most pronounced mode of sedimentation: (1) autochthonous swamps are those formed largely by *in situ* sedimentation, peat deposition or, more rarely, the precipitation of carbonate mud within the environmental framework of the swamp; (2) allochthonous swamps are those with dominant clastic sediments, such as those derived largely from outside the environmental framework of the swamp; and (3) a mixed type, which is a blend of the first two. For example, autochthonous peat swamps are found along the southwest coast of Florida (see Plate 200) and carbonate mud precipitation occurs along the western side of Andros Island, Bahama Islands. Allochthonous mangrove swamps are common along tropical coasts that receive an abundant supply of river-borne terrigenous (clastic) sediment, for example, the west coast of Malaya (Watson, 1928). There are several subtypes of allochthonous mangrove swamps: deltaic (Plates 132 and 204); estuarine (Plate 202); lagoon-barrier (Plate 201); and open coast (Plates 200 and 207). The mixed-type mangrove swamp develops in areas that have an intermediate to low supply of sediment with respect to the productivity of the mangrove forest. The extensive swamps fringing the Pacific coast of Colombia, South America, (Plate 206) are a good example (West, 1956).

Mangroves often are found in precarious environments. Not only do hurricanes and typhoons destroy them (Plate 207), but shifting tidal channels may cut away the silts and clays around the roots (Plate 208). Also, sand migrating across barrier spits and bars advance onto mangrove thickets from the landward side (Plate 209). Last, but certainly not least, the trees are cut for building material and fuel, and animals eat the leaves (Plate 210).

Because mangrove plants decay very rapidly in the heat of the muds and clays of the swamps, preservation does not appear to be very common. However, on the northeast shore of Key Biscayne, Florida, fossilized mangrove roots between 1,000 and 2,000 years old have been found. This is one of the first reported occurrences of the fossilization of mangrove roots (Plate 211). If mangrove plants were preserved in a region of rapid sedimentation, they would provide an excellent environment for the formation of coal.

Often associated with mangroves in tidal environments are other lower plants such as brackish-water ferns, low woody shrubs, and palms such as the nipa. Plate 212 shows nipa palms *(Nipa fruticans)* growing in the Sundarban swamps of Bangladesh. This thick junglelike vegetation lines the tidal channels (see Plates 132 and 204). Behind these palms are dense thickets of *Rhizophora* and *Avicennia* mangroves.

MARSH GRASS COASTS

Salt marshes are found between tide marks in quiet depositional environments, such as coastal inlets, estuaries behind barrier bars, and at bayheads. They also are found on the open shore, providing there is very little energy (zero energy) such as in northwest Florida (Tanner, 1960).

Most of these coasts also could be classified as mud flats or salt marshes. As in the case of mangroves, the geomorphic importance of salt marshes as agents of construction has probably been exaggerated in some of the literature. To a large extent, they must be thought of as taking advantage of locations where sedimentation is occurring because of ideal physical conditions. At the same time, there is no doubt that they do promote deposition (both organic and inorganic) and inhibit erosion. They also have an important effect on minor relief forms such as channel systems (Plate 213; Davies, 1973, pp. 59-61).

A major review of salt marshes in different parts of the world was prepared by Chapman (1960), who distinguished nine main groups. Some of the differences between the groups are due to factors related to historical plant geography. For example, the important genus *Spartina* has its largest concentration around the Atlantic Ocean from western Europe to northwest Africa and

from eastern Canada to Brazil (Plate 214). Outside of this area, it is of limited occurrence except where it has been introduced by humans. Other differences result from environmental factors such as climate, tidal range, and the substratum. Generally, the richest growth of grasses can be found on the muddy marshes of macrotidal, humid temperate coasts. In tropical areas, marshes are somewhat different. Soil erosion from deeply weathered catchments in the humid tropics has delivered vast amounts of mud to estuaries and coastal embayments, accelerating the progradation of mud flats (Bird, 1968, p. 154; Davies, 1973, p. 60).

Mud flats or salt marshes and marsh grass coasts should all be dealt with together, because of their intricate relationship. Guilcher (1958) defines these flats and marshes as drowned land areas covered by the rise of the sea level at the end of the last glaciation and later silted up. The history of marshes is complicated but can often be unraveled through the existance of datable deposits. Deposition gives marshes their present form. They occupy low tidal zones approximately at sea level. They are not always found at the mouths of rivers, but the majority of tidal marshes have small streams flowing into them.

Four types of marshes exist based on origin:

1. Those that are in the sheltered part of an estuary and are formed by silting at the sides of the estuary (Plate 215).

2. Those that form behind sand or shingle spits due to sediments being brought down by rivers (Plate 216).

3. Those that are formed at the head of a bay into which no large river flows and that is unprotected by a sand spit (Plate 217).

4. Those that develop on open, shallow-water coasts (Plate 218).

Marshes are widespread on many low coasts of the world. Deposition consisting of mud, sand, and salt or freshwater peat, begins at about 30 meters (98 feet) or less. The upper parts of marshes are nearly always muddy and often build up mud flats, but the lower parts are sandy, gravelly, or stony, reflecting more tidal scour. Vegetation begins to establish itself in the muddy areas. As time passes the vegetation catches more silt and a more permanent stable vegetation moves in—thus the marsh grows.

Features common to many salt marshes are residual enclosed depressions or ponds, many forming salt pans when dry (Plate 219). These remain unvegetated and retain water after the tide has fallen. In arid regions, high evaporation makes these areas hypersaline or dries them out forming salt flats (see Part V, Rapid Human-Induced Changes and Plate 247).

Part IV

Effects of Humans
on Coastal Environments

HUMAN SETTLEMENT ALONG
THE COAST

For millennia human beings have lived along the oceans, used their surfaces for travel, and drawn upon their marine life for food. Human beings have always revered and been in awe of the coast. Where land and water meet, humans have built ports and harbors. Trade carried on between settlements came from other regions by way of the sea. The ancient harbors usually were nearly landlocked or somewhat inland from the exposed shore, for early people respected the power of the sea. The nearby land, whether rock-lined or sandy, provided a zone of safety and a refuge from the fury of the powerful coastal elements. As more and more people lived along the shore, the number of structures increased rapidly.

Human invasion of the coastal corridor has accelerated most rapidly since World War II. This intrusion has taken many forms and includes greatly expanded urban sprawl, the ubiquitous spread of second-home coastal communities, and considerable industrial development (Plate 220).

An additional pressure for coastal real estate takes the form of recreational and sporting sites for leisure-time activities. For example, at Stone Harbor, New Jersey, until the Marshlands Act stopped the filling in of tidal marshes, numerous resort marinas were being built (Plate 221). Another example is near Sydney, Australia, where the coastline is being rapidly built up with sporting facilities. In winter the shoreline at New Kino Bay, Mexico, is lined with campers. The growth has been enormous. Nearly all the available land suitable for development has been built on along the east and west coasts of the United States. Most favorable European coastal stretches also have been built on. Plate 220 clearly shows this rapid growth in the Palos Verdes Hills of the California coast at two different time periods—September 1953 and October 1969. What were vacant hills with a few scattered structures in 1953 are now more than 60 percent covered by residential developments and shopping centers.

The population of shorelines is shown by the following demographic statistics. Although continental shelves and coastal waters comprise only about 5 percent of the world's surface, nearly two-thirds of the world's population lives near a coast. In the United States, about 90 percent of the population growth in the 1970s has been in the thirty states that border the shores of the oceans and Great Lakes. These thirty states contain nearly 75 percent of the total population and twelve of the thirteen largest cities, and nearly 50 percent of the people reside in coastal counties (D. R. Coates, pers. comm.).

Coastlines may seem impregnable, but they constitute some of the most fragile land on the surface of the earth. Humans often accelerate the degradation of this environment. An example of a fragile coast that is ever-changing is one bordered by sand dunes. Plate 222 shows just such a shoreline that was being changed rapidly in just four years. Large, stabilized sand dunes in 1924 were rapidly being covered with roads and structures by 1928. This construction alters the ecosystem of the area and greatly reduces the flora and fauna. To gain access to the beach, beach-cuts often are made in the duneline, which later may become the locus for overwash during storm surge. In many areas, it has been common practice for homeowners to build right on top of the dunes or to cut away the tops of the dunes so they will have an unobstructed view of the ocean (Plate 223).

There are innumerable examples of the use of coastal environments by humans. Only one example is presented here, because of the lack of space. For thousands of years, people have been collecting sea water into ponds where the salt is left after the water evaporates. This is one of the most ancient uses of the sea. The Phoenicians, who lived along the coast of Lebanon, collected salt in this way. Plate 224 shows the descendants of these Phoenician traders using windmills to pump the salt water into the collection ponds.

POLLUTION AND MODIFICATIONS TO
NORMAL COASTAL PROCESSES

One traditional use of ocean basins and coastal margins has been as a depository for the waste products of civilizations. The vastness of the oceans has given people a false sense of security. They seem to think that because the seas are so large they can sustain a never-ending amount of pollutants from an industrialized society. Most coastal communities, as well as a number of inland cities, are to blame for the ever-increasing amounts of pollution of all varieties that pour into or are placed into the coastal zone (D. R. Coates, pers. comm.). However, the current production of waste, particularly in the form of insecticides and municipal and industrial fallout and sewage, has surpassed the level at which it can be diluted, degraded, and dispersed by natural systems. The sea, like the other components of the hydrosphere, is showing the strain of such use. Oil slicks and floating debris may be encountered anywhere on the seas today, often far out in the ocean.

Sewage effluent amounts to about 2 percent of the discharge of all the world's rivers that end up in the oceans. Nearly 7 percent of the total solids in the rivers is human waste products. Solid waste now covers 210 square kilometers (81 square miles) in New York Harbor. Cities such as Venice, which releases untreated waste into the Adriatic Sea, and Miami, which discharges over fifty million tons of untreated sewage daily into the Atlantic Ocean, jeopardize the sensitivities as well as the health of tourists.

Oil spillage averages 2.4 million tons per year, and plastics are the ocean's most common flotsom, with 1,400 pieces per square mile. There is hardly any coast today that is completely free of the world's contaminants (Inman and Brush, 1973).

Two excellent examples of pollution in and near harbors are shown on Plates 225 and 226. Plate 225 shows a large oil slick on the seaward side of San Francisco Harbor, just outside the Golden Gate Bridge. This pollution occurred when a tanker leaked oil while entering San Francisco Bay. Plate 226 shows an oil spill discharged from a navy ship around a series of destroyers in San Diego Harbor. This image was one of several infrared photographs used by the city of San Diego in a legal suit against the U.S. Navy for contamination of the harbor. Many examples of pollution can be shown using remote-sensing techniques (Snead, 1978, p. 56). Evidence of oil spillage and pollution can be found on the beaches and rocks along many coasts. Plate 227 shows patches of oil and tar on the coast of California near Santa Barbara.

Still another example of pollution from industrial complexes is shown in Plate 228. At the Sparrows Point iron and steel plant near Baltimore, Maryland, waste products dumped off the end of a pier show up as dark wavy streaks, which then move out and become part of a larger circular pattern of pollution. Although serious efforts are being made to stop the dumping of waste materials into the sea, large industrial complexes find it extremely difficult and expensive to get rid of wastes by other methods.

Toxic substances, such as DDT, radioactive waste, mercury, and lead derived from gasoline, are found in alarming concentrations not only in the immediate coastal zone but far out to sea. The aerial distribution of DDT in 200 plankton is exhibited as hot spots along the California coast from north of San Francisco for more than 595 kilometers (370 miles) south to the Baja California coast of Mexico. Australia and Mexico are also having pollution problems from agricultural sources. The marshlands of New Jersey suffered greatly from these pollutants. Shellfish were completely depleted in some areas, and the marsh grass died leaving large, blighted areas around stagnant pools and isolated tidal marshes. Plate 229 shows such an area near Barnegat, New Jersey.

Pollution of the seas has had a serious impact on the fishing industry. Local studies have shown that production of marine plankton has been reduced as a consequence of small DDT and mercury concentrations. The

effects on the food chain, which is based on plankton, are not yet completely clear, but they can hardly be beneficial (Gabler et al., 1975, pp. 524-525). People have been killed by mercury poisoning in Japan. The incidence of hepatitis in coastal communities is linked to eating contaminated molluscs, and nitrates and phosphates contribute to the so-called red tides that are often seen along the coast. Great strides are now being taken to stop this pollution. If not greatly reduced, the entire food chain could be seriously affected by human waste products.

Another type of change in coastal waters is produced by power plants generating electricity. Fossil-fuel power plants require the mechanical equivalent of 1.4 watts of waste heat (coolant) for each watt of power generated and nuclear power plants need 2.1 watts. For example, the power needed by California in 1980 was 37,000 megawatts. The necessary coolant used was at a rate of about 1.2 calories per second, which is the equivalent of heating a flow of seawater 15,000m^3/sec. by 1°C (33.8°F). Such a flow would equal one-half the average flow of water over the California ocean shelf, or nearly 0.3 percent of the total flow of the California current. Such heat imbalances can produce ecological changes in sea life (D. R. Coates, pers. comm.).

ENGINEERING METHODS TO CONTROL COASTAL PROCESSES

Coastal engineering projects are undertaken in the nearshore zone to improve navigation, to remove material when it accumulates in an undesired area, and to diminish coastal erosion. Jetties and breakwaters are built for the protection of boats of all sizes and to aid navigation. Groins and the various types of seawalls, on the other hand, are constructed to prevent erosion of the coast. When changes are to be made, the coastal engineer should take every precaution to assure that: (1) the structure or structures being built are necessary and will accomplish their intended purpose; (2) construction is made at the optimum site and, in turn, will cause minimum environmental disturbance; and (3) planning and management have accounted for environmental feedback on contiguous lands and waters. In the past, these conditions have not always been met and the resulting consequences have been disastrous to the coast at times (U.S. Army Corps of Engineers, 1964).

Eroding beaches endanger nearshore structures, and this, in turn, reduces the recreational value of a locality. The shoreline stabilization concept is to maintain a constant beach with thorough erosion prevention, entrapment of material in the littoral zone, or by artificial nourishment of new materials. The technique chosen is determined by local hydraulic conditions, sediment supply, and the pressure of society (D. R. Coates, pers. comm.).

Most structures in the coastal zone are situated in the backshore area. The purpose of backshore protection is to shield the site from destruction by abnormal storm surge. The engineer may choose to protect the valued property by building structures, increasing the runup width of the beach with artificial nourishment, or encouraging the formation of sand dunes (U.S. Army Corps of Engineers, 1971a and b).

Jetties

Jetties are long, narrow, damlike structures that are built to prevent inlet migration, the shoaling of inlets or harbors, and the formation of subaqueous tidal deltas. A number of factors must be taken into consideration in designing the type, size, and placement of a jetty for maximum benefit. These structures are constructed singly or in pairs, usually perpendicular to the shore, and are made of steel, timber, concrete, or boulders. The angle the waves and littoral currents make with the shore and the amount of drift help determine jetty length and angle (Plate 230). Tidal flow must be sufficiently rapid to flush sediment from the inlet but the flow direction needs to be diverted from areas where erosion will damage valuable property (D. R. Coates, pers. comm.)

The plan is to stabilize the channel by preventing shoaling through littoral drift and to protect the channel entrance from storm waves. In order to prevent littoral drift from entering the channel, jetties generally extend through the entire nearshore to beyond the breaker zone. In doing so, they also act as a dam to the longshore drift of sand in the nearshore. Sand often moves along the shore under the natural processes of waves breaking obliquely to the shoreline (see Figure 5), and the drift must stop when it reaches an obstacle placed across the littoral zone. As a result, the sand accumulates on the updrift side of jetties and the shoreline advances. At the same time, on the downdrift side of jetties, the sand transport processes continue to operate and cause sand to drift away from the jetties. Erosion and shoreline retreat therefore occur on the downdrift side. This is shown very well in Plate 231 where the jetties at the entrance to Cape May Canal have caused a wide beach to be formed on the north side while coastal retreat is occurring on the south side of the jetty. The resort town of Cape May has been deprived of sand that would normally move along the shore. "South Cape May [New Jersey] has virtually disappeared during the past 50 years due to the jetties to the northeast and to the southerly current. Assateague Island has been eroded at least 457 meters (1,500 feet)

because of the Ocean City jetties" (Shepard and Wanless, 1971, p. 549).

McCormick (1973) has attributed increased erosion rates for part of the barrier beaches on Long Island to artificial inlet stabilization by means of jetties. The erosion rate of the barrier beach east of Fire Island was 0.46 meter (1.6 feet) per year prior to inlet stabilization and jumped to 2 meters (6.8 feet) per year after inlet stabilization. Most of the material lost, 12,000 meters³ (420,000 feet³) per year, accumulated in tidal deltas associated with inlets.

Thus, it can be seen that very serious coastal erosion has resulted, because the construction of jetties can interrupt the natural movement of sand along the beach and thereby cause erosion of adjacent beaches and coastal property (Komar, 1976, pp. 325–326). Jetties often have to be repaired because of storm damage or because the blocks of rock slowly sink into the sand. Many have to be extended when the coast progrades to their outer limits. One technique that might be used to help remedy the problem of jetties blocking sand is sand by-passing.

Breakwaters

These are structures that protect a portion of the shoreline by forming a shield to harbors and boat anchorages from the waves. These structures can be built in a variety of shapes and are generally attached to the coast at one or both ends, often with a gap for a boat entrance, and extend outward through the surf zone (Plate 232A). By constructing an offshore barrier the power of the waves is dampened. However, massive breakwaters are more costly to construct than onshore structures, so they are generally built only for navigation and harbor purposes.

One type—the detached breakwater—is built as a barrier parallel to the shore and, therefore, has no attachment with the coast (Plate 232B). Initially, the idea was to provide a protected area for boats, while at the same time allowing the sand to drift alongshore since these breakwaters provide no direct obstacle across the nearshore zone. However, it was found, that breakwaters diminish the wave energy at the shoreline and therefore reduce the capacity for waves to transport the sand alongshore. The result is deposition of littoral sands within the protected lee of the detached breakwater (Burton, et al., 1969, pp. 135–137). In some locations, such as Santa Barbara, California, and Ceara, Brazil, this has had adverse effects. The breakwater built in 1929 at Santa Barbara to protect the harbor contributed to erosion of downdrift beaches for a distance of 16 kilometers (10 miles) amounting to 75 meters (245 feet) in some areas (Wiegel, 1959, 1964; Carey, 1903; Johnson, 1957). Thus, breakwaters have both beneficial and detrimental effects on the shore. They can reduce or eliminate erosion, but by interrupting the free movement of sand they can starve downdrift beaches and cause shoaling in undesirable places.

Most breakwaters are constructed of concrete or riprap of giant rocks, forming a permanently emplaced structure. However, other less costly types of breakwaters are possible, such as flexible plastic bags or a variety of floating breakwaters. Concrete pontoons strapped together and floating tire breakwaters have been used successfully in Rhode Island, Massachusetts, and on Lake Erie (D. R. Coates, pers. comm.).

Seawalls, Bulkheads, and Revertments

These structures are built along the shoreline to prevent the erosion of property and other damage due to wave action. They are placed parallel, or nearly so, to the shoreline, separating the land from the wave action. They help to diminish slumping of the coastal sea cliffs, which they may front, and as protective devices these structures armor the shore in an attempt to deter direct wave attack on the beach or installations. They are erected when there is little or no beach as a last defense against ocean waves. Usually no attempt is made to modify coastal processes for, at best, such structures are only temporary expedients and should be combined with other types of protection whenever possible. They are not permanent solutions. I have personally watched bulkheads slowly erode away in Margate, New Jersey, for the last twenty years.

Seawalls, bulkheads, and revertments are somewhat similar structures, but they differ in function and shape. Seawalls generally are used to attenuate wave energy; therefore, they are larger and more massive than the others. They have three basic shapes: vertical, concave, and sloping. Vertical walls can be used as docking facilities, but are not very effective at stopping wave attack. There often is erosion at the tow of the wall since the wave energy is partly reflected, which leads to increased scour and, at times, wall failure. Sloping walls dissipate wave energy and allow easy access to the beach, but they can be easily overturned by wave action. Concave structures are used when high-energy waves are more common and structural strength is desired. Seawalls are made of solid or block concrete, steel sheets, timber or natural stone called riprap (Plate 233). Plate 234 shows a stepped seawall being repaired at Lynn, Massachusetts, in 1966. It should be noted that a seawall affords protection only to the land immediately shoreward and none to adjacent areas along the coast or to the beach fronting the seawall. Thus when built on an eroding shoreline,

the recession continues on the adjacent shores that are not protected (Komar, 1976, pp. 326-328).

Bulkheads do not require the structural bulk of seawalls, because they serve primarily as shoreline retainers of fill. They are vertical structures made of steel, timber, or concrete pilings. Bulkheads are highly susceptible to erosion, however, and can easily be undermined by waters that overtop them (D. R. Coates, pers. comm.).

Revertments conform to the contour of the shore and may be one of a variety of shapes. Although usually made of interlocking stone or concrete, they can be made from a variety of materials including wood piling. The armored slope dissipates wave energy with less damaging effect to the beach than waves striking vertical walls (Plate 235). They are most effective in retarding erosion by small waves and currents.

Groins (Groynes)

Groins are generally smaller than jetties but also extend from the foreshore into the breaker zone for the purpose of changing the character of the coastal process. They are rib-built approximately perpendicular to the shoreline to trap a portion of the littoral drift and, in turn, help to build out the beach. They are built to: (1) reduce the rate of littoral drift; (2) stabilize the beach; (3) widen the beach; (4) prevent accretion in downdrift areas; and (5) prevent loss of material from the beach. These structures help to prevent further erosion of an existing beach and, since the existence of a beach helps to protect the shoreward coastal property, groins also diminish erosion of sea cliffs (D. R. Coates, pers. comm.).

Groins are constructed of different materials, but their size specifications and orientation must be designed for the particular environmental setting. Groins are narrow in width and may vary in length from less than 10 meters (33 feet) to over 200 meters (656 feet). They appear similar to jetties in this regard, however, their function is very different. They have the same effect of damming the littoral drift so that the shoreline progrades on the updrift side and erodes on the downdrift side (Plate 236). To protect a stretch of coast from erosion, a series of groins—called a groin field—may be constructed to act together and cause deposition (Plate 237). This enables an extended section of beach to be built out and shifts the zone of erosion out of the immediate area to somewhere else down the coast (Komar, 1976, pp. 328-329).

One good feature of a groin is that once it is filled, it allows littoral drift to pass by its seaward end, so that it traps only a certain quantity of sand. Sometimes to prevent damage to adjacent areas of beach while groins fill, artificial beach nourishment is added behind the groin by trucking sand out onto the beach or by pumping it from a lagoon area out onto a beach (Plate 236).

Groins are temporary features, having a life span of about twenty years. Many groins slowly sink in the sand or are eroded away at the seaward ends.

Other Beach Protective Methods

A variety of other methods of beach protection have been tried with some success by local residents of coastal towns. Most of these efforts are soon removed by waves and currents. A very unstable wall of loose sand was built along the north end of Ocean City, New Jersey, in April 1979. At Sunset Cliffs in San Diego, California, rocks were dumped over a cliff in an attempt to keep waves busy eroding the loose rubble rather than expounding energy on the rock face (Plate 238). Both of these attempts are only temporary measures and the sea will quickly remove them.

As more of the Atlantic Coast of the United States is lined by structures such as groins, jetties, and breakwaters, less sand is available to fill the areas lost to continued erosion. It is now a policy of the U.S. Army Corps of Engineers to supply sand to a beach where necessary. There seems to be a growing realization that, in the long run, the best methods of beach growth must be as similar as possible to natural ones. To simulate this natural protection, dunes and beaches are rebuilt. Sand sources in the lagoons and marshes behind the beach are transported by pumping across the barrier islands onto the beach. Beaches have been built in this manner in a number of locations. Examples include Hampton Beach, New Hampshire; Sandy Hook, Cape May, and Ocean City, New Jersey; and Rehobeth Beach, Delaware (Plate 239). One problem with this type of beach nourishment is that a large percentage of muds and clays are in the lagoon sediments being pumped to the beach and these do not remain long, soon being carried offshore by waves and currents (Burton et al., 1969, pp. 133-137).

Land Stabilization

As we have sought to improve the outer defenses by groins and beach nourishment, we have belatedly recognized the need for protecting the inner defenses as well. Dunes come under the attack of wind, water, and, increasingly, the bulldozer. Efforts to restrict the activities of the bulldozer appear limited, but in the United States numerous state and federal projects are now underway to hold the sand on the barrier islands and to help sand dunes grow.

At a number of places along the east coast of the United States, sand fences have been erected to trap the sand as it blows from the beach. Cape Hatteras National Seashore, off the coast of North Carolina, is an area where dune building has been very successful (Nash, 1962, pp. 4-12). After the severe northeast storm of March, 1962, bulldozers pushed sand from the foreshore to the backbeach to form a line of high dunes. Fences were placed on top of these dunes to trap the sand. Plate 240 shows the 1.22 meter (4 foot) fences trapping sand around them at Cape Hatteras National Seashore. Sometimes an elaborate network of dunes is built by erecting several lines of fences (Plate 241) or a boxlike pattern of fences such as was done at Beach Haven, New Jersey.

Grasses such as American beach grass (Ammophila breviligulata) and sea oats (Uniola paniculata) often are planted on top of newly formed dunes. These grasses are usually planted by hand or machine, but the dunes can be seeded and fertilizd by plants as they were at Bethany Beach, Delaware. Local residents have planted grass by hand in front of their summer homes. A motel owner in Wildwood Crest told me he had put down bales of hay, covered it with sand, and planted dune grass on top. The grass is doing well because the hay held the moisture and protected the plants from wind erosion while they were young.

Part V

Overall Changes of the Coast

The geomorphological processes at work on coastal landforms are influenced by a number of environmental factors, such as geologic, climatic, biotic, and tidal, as well as oceanographic factors, such as salinity. As we have seen throughout this volume, these factors vary from one section of coast to another—the variation being zonal in terms of climatic regions and irregular in terms of geological outcrops (Bird, 1968, p. 2).

LONG-TERM COASTAL CHANGES

Landforms that relate to past conditions are found on many coasts. These include wave-cut scarps and benches, which developed when the sea stood higher relative to the land, and features related to submergence following relatively low sea-level phases. There are coastal landforms inherited from earlier episodes when the climate was warmer or cooler, wetter or drier, than it is now. The existing morphogenic systems were established only within the last few thousand years, during Recent (Holocene) times. However, the landform legacy of the preceding Pleistocene period, when marked variations of climate and sea level accompanied the waxing and waning of ice sheets over a period of at least a million and a half years, is still evident on many coasts (Plates 20 through 30).

Glacioeustatic changes of level between land and sea resulting from the melting of continental ice has raised the level of the oceans by some 137 meters (450 feet) during the Recent rise of sea level (Russell, 1964). This sea-level rise is responsible for drowning practically all sea coasts, so that they are almost universally submerged. That some coasts are smooth in outline, have barrier islands fronting linear lagoons, and display other features considered proof of emergence according to the classical theory of Johnson (1919) is really a demonstration of the efficacy of wave attack and related shore processes to wear away headlands and fill embayments, provided that the rocks under attack are unconsolidated (Russell, 1957). The classical shorelines of emergence occur only where the sea encounters Quaternary, Tertiary, or other rock that is poorly bound by cement or for one reason or another lacks induration. Where resistant, durable rock is exposed to wave impact, the forces of marine attack are almost powerless to change shorelines.

Some coasts change very slowly or almost not at all. The Atlantic wave and swell beat ineffectively against the high limestone cliff of Cabo de St. Vincent in southwestern Portugal (see Plate 106) and the crystalline rock in the vicinity of Rio de Janeiro without cutting an appreciable notch. These rugged, rockbound coasts retain practically unaltered evidence of drowning. Their rock is both indurated and durable (Russell 1967, p. 85; see also

Plate 90). At sections along the California coast there has been very little change in ten years (Plate 242; Shepard and Wanless, 1971, p. 276).

But erosion is a natural phenomenon and the power of the ocean is always working to create shoreline changes. Many coasts change seasonally with the addition of sand during the quieter summer months and removal of this sand during winter storms. An excellent example of these changes can be seen at a small beach near Scripps Oceanographic Institution at La Jolla, California (Plate 243).

Over a longer period of time there are more significant erosional changes, because sea level is constantly rising in most areas, which causes new lands to be inundated so that land erosion at new heights will be a continuing threat in the future.

In 1971 the U.S. Army Corps of Engineers completed an evaluation of the 151,000-kilometer (94,000-mile) coastline of the United States. Their study indicates that significant erosion is occurring along 32,900 kilometers (20,500 miles) of coasts, and 4,350 (2,700) of these kilometers (miles) are critical. Louisiana is losing coastal land at a rate of 41.4 square kilometers (16 square miles) per year and in the past one hundred years erosion at Cape Hatteras has been 914 meters (3,000 feet). Of the 4,828 kilometers (3,000 miles) of shoreline on the Virginia side of the Chesapeake Bay, erosion removed 85 square kilometers (33 square miles) of land during the period from 1850 to 1950.

RAPID COASTAL CHANGES

Coastal changes are particularly great when catastrophic waves are produced by big storms such as the three-day "northeasters" and the Atlantic and Gulf coast hurricanes. During these storms, in addition to the great heights of the pounding waves, the sea level is often raised as much as 3.05 meters (10 feet), and at times 6.10 meters (20 feet), above normal. When these storm surges come in at high tide, they often sweep over the low barrier islands and cause enormous damage (Shepard and Wanless, 1971, p. 17).

On March 4, 1962 the prevailing weather pattern over the eastern half of the United States gave no apparent cause for alarm. A small storm was developing along a cold front between Florida and Bermuda, but upper-air wind patterns indicated that it would move harmlessly out to sea. Simultaneously, another storm center sixteen hundred kilometers away over the Mississippi Valley was moving slowly northward and weakening. The weather forecasters viewed these as routine patterns and did not foresee what was to follow.

Both storms behaved in an unexpected manner. The

new Florida storm moved north along the east coast instead of moving east out to sea. The Mississippi Valley storm moved east instead of going north. The two met and coalesced over Cape Hatteras, gained strength and spawned the great Atlantic storm of March 6-7, 1962 (Stewart, 1962, pp. 117-120). An elongated and slowly shifting wind pattern developed with speeds up to 80 kilometers per hour (50 miles per hour) along a fetch of 1,930 kilometers (1,200 miles). This produced a storm surge of hurricane proportions in the normally less-dangerous month of March. Although the winds were less than hurricane force, the storm still had disastrous effects because it remained off the east coast during three succesive high tides. Offshore and man-made defenses survived the first high-tide period in many cases, but the repeated hard pounding during second and third high tides broke through in many places causing spectacular damage along Long Island, New York, and along many kilometers of the New Jersey shore, especially at Margate, Longport, Avalon, Wildwood, and Cape May (Plate 244). The battering and erosive action of high waves over such a prolonged period caused damage estimated at $190 million, with the greatest damage concentrated between New York and North Carolina but extending as far south as Florida. It is estimated that the storm caused the death of thirty-four people (Burton et al., 1969, pp. 1-5).

A much smaller "northeaster" hit the New Jersey shore three years later (March 1965) and did considerable damage to the inlet at Atlantic City, New Jersey.

Hurricanes and typhoons cause the most severe coastal damage and erosion. I studied damage to the northeastern Mexican coast from Hurricane Anita in January 1978 (Plate 245). Cape Hatteras, North Carolina, jutting east into the Atlantic Ocean, often is the victim of severe winds and waves from hurricanes.

Another type of catastrophic wave is caused by sudden movements of the ocean bottom, such as occur during faulting of the seafloor and its accompanying earthquakes. If the ocean floor drops, it carries water down to fill the void, thus initiating a series of waves of very long duration often lasting fifteen minutes or more. In turn, a sudden rise of the ocean floor causes a similar effect. These waves, called tsunamis or tidal waves (although they are not related to tides), are small in the open ocean but very quickly pile up along the shore, where they have been known to reach heights of 30 meters (90 feet). The Hawaiian Islands are directly in the path of these waves that are caused by faulting in the deep trenches off Japan, Alaska, and the west coast of South America.

A third type of catastrophic wave occurs from landslides. The classic example is in Lituya Bay, Alaska, where a very large mass of rock broke off the steep wall of a fjord and, falling into the bay, caused a surge on the opposite side that rose 518 meters (1,700 feet). Waves of this type are fortunately very rare and have caused little loss of life (Shepard and Wanless, 1971, p. 17).

RAPID HUMAN-INDUCED CHANGES

We have already seen in Part IV that people have been rapidly occupying the coastal zone all around the world. Innumerable examples could be given. Plate 246 sums up the whole rapid development of the coastal zone with a view of the yacht harbor at San Diego, California. Within just twenty years the entire coastal region of southern California has become one vast maze of man-made structures. In many areas this intense development has led to great ecological changes in the biotic environment. The use of large amounts of Colorado River water for irrigation has greatly increased the salinity in the lower Colorado River region. Plate 247 shows the extensive salt flats that have recently formed at the mouth of the river.

Plates

Plate 1. Here, a series of swells move into a bay and against the shore at Townsend's Inlet, north of Avalon, in southern New Jersey. Note how the larger swells, separated from each other by several hundred meters, begin to pile up and come much closer together as they approach the beach. A stone abutment has been erected (left center) to protect this section of coast from erosion. To the north the growth of the barrier island is almost reaching the draw bridge. Photograph by the author, October 20, 1964. (see p. 8).

Plate 2. Waves that have peaked, broken, and are moving forward as translatory foam waves are called surf. Out at sea under strong winds many swells have their caps taken off, forming small breaking waves. In this confused state surf can be created where there is enough agitation. Here, spilling breakers form surf as they move against the shore at San Juan, Puerto Rico. Note the considerable coastal erosion as waves cut away the protective barrier of rocks near the hotel Ponce de León. Photograph by the author, December 29, 1965 (see p. 8).

Plate 3. Wind waves, forced waves, or sea waves form when a storm creates a very agitated sea. We return to the north coast of Puerto Rico where we see strong northeast trade winds moving across the ocean, driving the waves against the seaward side of old Morro Castle at San Juan. Strong winds, especially during the hurricane season, make the entrance to San Juan harbor difficult for ships to navigate. Occasionally ships have been driven ashore. Photograph by the author, December 1965 (see p. 9).

Plate 4. Swell waves moving around flowing ebb current that is draining Hampton Harbor Estuary in New Hampshire are seen here. Note that the wave trains are approaching from two different directions. This wave refraction is the result of storm waves, shore currents, and estuary ebb currents all coming from different directions. The swell or free waves moving in against the shore on a relatively calm day have traveled beyond a storm area out in the Atlantic Ocean. Photograph by Miles O. Hayes (see p. 9).

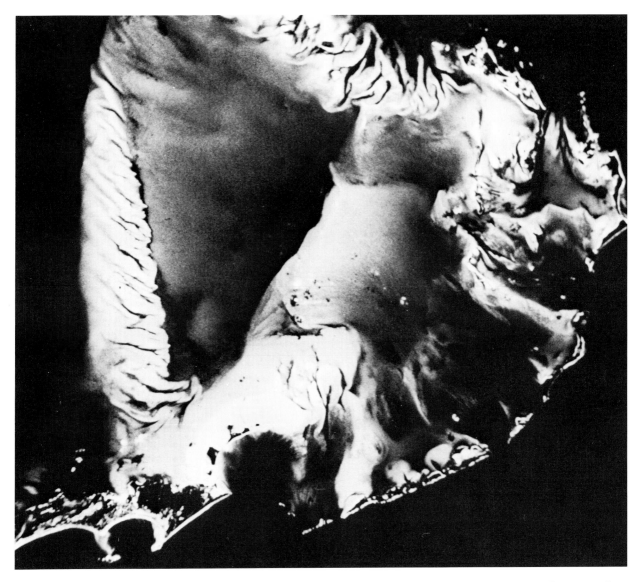

Plate 5. This NASA Gemini V space photograph of the Berry Islands in the Bahamas shows submarine bars extending to considerable depth below the surface of the ocean. You can detect the 40-kilometer (25-mile) wide sand shoal in the lee of the island chain. The depth of water is indicated by gray shade variations of water over the white sand background. The abrupt drop away from the cays or islands is typical of much of the Bahama Bank. This sand shoal lies between the Tongue of the Ocean (see Plate 12) and the Northwest Providence Channel. Photograph Courtesy of NASA (see p. 9).

A

B

C

D

Plate 6. These four photographs illustrate the stages of development and breaking of a plunging breaker at Birdlings Flat, south of the Banks Peninsula on the east side of South Island, New Zealand. The crashing of these large 4.57-meter (15-foot) waves and the backrush of gravel on the steep beach make a roaring noise. On this August day a large storm at sea had created this magnificant set of waves, although there was only a gentle breeze along the shore. Note in (B) how the curl of the wave leaves a considerable opening just under the crest. Photographs by the author, August 9, 1975 (see p. 9).

Plate 7. After plunging breakers plunge, they change into waves of translation and become spilling breakers with a forward motion. The storm waves shown here create a mass of foaming water at Fire Island, Long Island, New York. Note the teenage surfer with a wetsuit in the middle ground. He is having a difficult time in the cold water fighting the power of the spilling breakers. Photograph by the author, March 10, 1968, (see p. 9).

Plate 8. Standing on the cliffs overlooking the Mediterranean Sea just south of Netanya, Israel, you have a good view of spilling breakers moving in across a low-sloping, very gently inclined shelf. Several of the spilling breakers are created by swells passing over obstacles in the water. In the left background, detached breakwaters have been built off the coast. In the calm areas on the landward side, sand bars have created tombolos. A better view of these detached breakwaters and resulting tombolos is shown in Plate 232B. Photograph by the author, June 14, 1973 (see p. 10).

Plate 9. When the sea is deep just offshore, waves do not drag bottom and peak up until right against the shore. The swells, acting as solitary waves, can hit the coast with great force causing large sprays of water and much foam. Surging waves are shown here pounding against the south Oahu coast at Koko Head National Park, Hawaii. Photograph by the author, July 1968 (see p. 10).

Plate 10. The collapsing breaker looks like it may plunge, but, instead, it breaks on itself either at the crest, as shown here, or over the lower half of the wave with almost no upward splash. These waves usually break very close to shore as this one is doing on the north coast of Puerto Rico, near Punta Marchiquita, north of Manati. Photograph by the author, June 19, 1971 (see p. 10).

Plate 11. Waves and swells concentrate on headlands and diverge when entering bays. This bending of wave trains is due to the slowing down and piling up of swells as they approach a shore. At times, wave refraction can result in two different wave patterns crossing each other at almost right angles. An excellent example of these patterns often occurs at the tip of Cabrillo National Monument in San Diego, California, where there is a lighthouse and a Coast Guard station. Because of the location of this headland near the entrance to San Diego harbor, two or more wave trains cross or merge. Photograph by the author, July 1, 1972 (see p. 11).

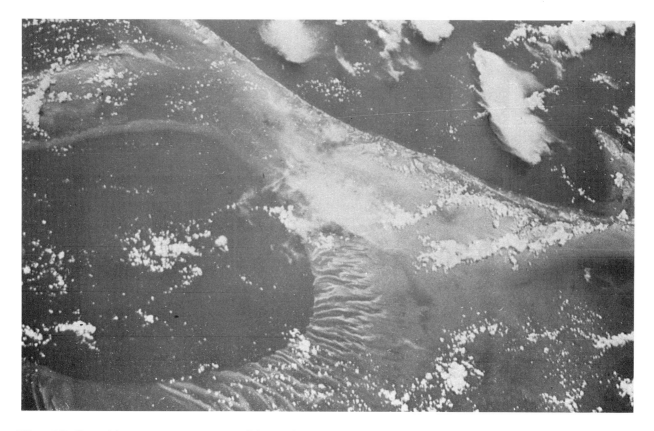

Plate 12. One of the great ocean currents of the world is the north flowing Gulf Stream east of Florida through the Bahama Islands. Although the flow is not very swift, it does move soft marls and coral sands across the Bahama platform. In this space photograph large sand ripples can be seen on the flanks of a very deep depression called the Tongue of the Ocean, which is, as its name implies, a channel as deep as 2,400 meters (7,874 feet) penetrating the bank. Slowly moving currents shift the very fine sediments across the bottom, building shoals and reefs where islands and barriers exist (see Plate 5). Carbonate sedimentation has continued in the Bahamas since at least Cretaceous times, so more than 4,600 meters (15,000 feet) of limestone and dolomite have accumulated. The long barrier is Great Exuma Island. Photograph courtesy of NASA (see p. 12).

Plate 13. Backwash and surf on a coarse volcanic cobble beach in front of Kealakoma lava delta at Apua Point on the large island of Hawaii. Faint ripple marks can be detected as the water rushes back down the beach. Photograph by R. T. Holcomb, 1973 (see p. 12).

Plate 14. Localized lanes or paths of water moving seaward through underwater barrier bars or across waves and swell patterns are called rip currents. Rip currents, seen here as foam belts, are moving out toward beds of dark kelp. Fans of sediment are carried along with the moving water along the Big Sur coast of California, south of Monterey. Photograph by the author, March 11, 1979 (see p. 12).

Plate 15. Twice a day a large tidal bore moves in and out of the Bay of Fundy, between New Brunswick and Nova Scotia, Canada. With a tidal range greater than 12 meters (40 feet), this is the largest in the world. Because of such a range, the tidal bore moves in as a wave. Shown here is the 0.31-to-0.61-meter (1-to-2-foot) wave at Moncton, New Brunswick. Photograph courtesy of New Brunswick Department of Tourism, Fredericton, New Brunswick, Canada (see p. 13).

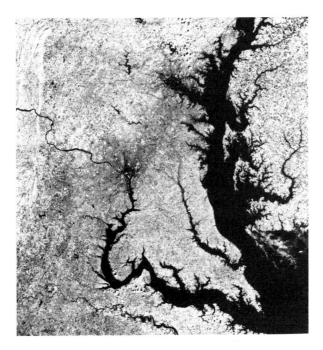

Plate 16. This NASA space photograph shows Chesapeake Bay with its many branching arms. This is a classic example of a ria coast. The arms can be followed inland where they merge with rivers, but many of these rivers are so small that they cannot be easily seen on the space photograph. This pattern of ria coast is called dendritic, which resembles an oak leaf. The horizontal beds help to contribute to this leaflike pattern. Photograph courtesy of NASA (see p. 16).

Plate 17. Examples of a trellis ria coastal pattern are rare, but one appears to be the long drowned fingers around the Banks Peninsula on the South Island of New Zealand, south of Christchurch. This magnificent region consists of several old volcanic cones that have been eroded along inclined beds of unequal hardness resulting in a series of rock fingers separated by drowned estuaries. The view here is looking south across Lyttleton Harbor toward the highest peaks of the eroded volcanoes that reach elevations of 960 meters (3,150 feet). Photograph by the author, August 9, 1975 (see p. 17).

Plate 18. Much of the coast of Yugoslavia represents a submergent coast of solutional limestone. This type of ria coast consists of long, mountainous-sided estuaries that are not glaciated. This coast has been subaerially eroded with former river valleys being drowned by postglacial sea level rise. The hills consist of parallel folded ridges made up of resistant limestone. This drowned section of coast shows Kornat Island, near the town of Zadar. Photograph courtesy of the Yugoslavia State Tourist Office (see p. 17).

Plate 19. We return again to the coast of Yugoslavia when discussing examples of drowned karst topography. Along the east side of the Adriatic Sea, where the bedrock consists of limestone or gypsum, there are a series of oval-shaped depressions across a marsh-covered plain indicative of drowned sinkholes. This picture was taken north of Dubrovnik, Yugoslavia, at the entrance to the Neretva River estuary. Photograph by the author, August 21, 1968 (see p. 17).

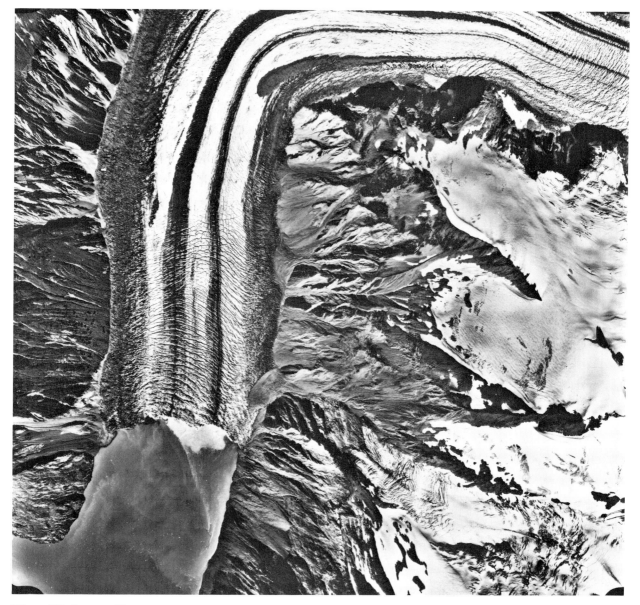

Plate 20. Lituya Glacier, a mountain glacier, is seen here feeding into Lituya Bay. This glacier is probably not as thick as some of the Pleistocene glaciers, therefore, its terminal end is a tidal glacier where the terminal ice is floating. Near the end of the glacier, the crevasse pattern consists of bunched-up and jagged masses of ice. The tidal rise and fall of the sea helps to create this situation. Note the width of the glacier and the channel. Dark bands in the ice are moraines composed of debris carried along by the glacier. The two medial moraines are less thick and darker than the two lateral moraines (the outer stripes). Due to the steep channel walls, material might have slid down on the ice, adding to the lateral moraine. Photograph courtesy of U.S. Geological Survey (see p. 17).

Plate 21. In Glacier Bay, Alaska, large and small boats move very close to the glaciers calving off into the bays. This closeup view is from the small boat *Glacier Bay* as it moves along the ice edge of Margarie Glacier. Photograph by the author, July 29, 1979 (see p. 18).

Plate 22. Some of the largest and most famous fiords in the world are found along the west coast of Norway. A fjord (fiord) is a Norwegian term for a long arm of the sea characterized by more or less straight trends, steep mountainous sides, and very great depth. Fjords are found along coasts of high relief marked by severe Pleistocene glaciation. Geiranger fjord is located in the north-central part of the Norweigan fjords, near the town of Geiranger. Photograph courtesy of the Royal Norweigan Embassy Information Service (see p. 18).

Plate 23. One of the most beautiful, but isolated, fjord regions of the world is along the southwest side of South Island, New Zealand. Behind the fjords are the Southern Alps, the main mountain range of New Zealand. Accessibility to this region is difficult with only one road leading to Milford Sound, one of the largest fiords in this area. This is an aerial view looking toward the head of Milford Sound in winter. Because of heavy rains and much cloudiness, a clear day with no clouds is rare. Photograph by Robert Kirk (see p. 18).

Plate 24. The Connecticut coast represents a fjard coast rather than a fjord coast, because of the low, rocky relief around the inlets. Although glacially scoured and, at times, deeply drowned, this shoreline does not have the spectacular mountains and glaciers behind it. This fjard coast, near Stamford, was cut by continental glaciers rather than mountain glaciers. Note the lineation of the islands and glacially cut inlets. With the rise of sea level, the coast was drowned. Where rivers enter the bays, the shoreline has more of the characteristics of a ria than a fjard coast, especially where the inlet does not have a rock bottom. Some controversy exists as to what the Connecticut coast should be called since it has characteristics of both ria and fjard coasts. Photograph by the author, December 1, 1967 (see p. 18).

Plate 25. The Hood Canal on the Olympic Peninsula of Washington represents an excellent example of a glacial trough that has been deepened and straightened by glacial ice. At its southern end, the canal takes a sharp turn to the east, forming a hook-shaped estuary. When the glacier receded, the sea invaded the trough creating a fjardlike feature. Mt. Rainier can be seen very faintly in the distance. Photograph by D. J. Easterbrook (see p. 18).

Plate 26. This group of islands is in Yakutat Bay, off of Phipps Peninsula, Alaska. The islands are the northwestern corner of a large shore deposit of unconsolidated glacial and fluvial deposits derived from the highlands 32 kilometers (20 miles) to the northeast. The area has undergone some recent tectonic uplift, as much as 14 meters (46 feet) locally. The bottom of Yakutat Bay is constantly changing due to the soft sediments and strong currents. This activity and the soft nature of the island material is causing the dissection and slumping that can be detected on the left side of the photo. The town of Yakutat, seen near the bottom of the photo, is located in an unsuitable area in terms of earthquake survival. Photograph courtesy of Department of Geography, University of California, Los Angeles (see p. 18).

Plate 27. The surface of Cape Cod, Massachusetts, is dotted with numerous kettleholes—lakes formed by the melting of the continental glaciers. Large ice blocks remained as the ice melted away. As these blocks disappeared, depressions were left that formed numerous lakes of all sizes and shapes—most tending to approach circularity. Some of the larger kettles are now connected to the sea, because rising sea levels at the end of the Pleistocene moved inland to fill valley bottoms and drown low glacial plains. In the last few thousand years, waves have straightened sections of the coast by cutting back the morainic cliffs and carrying the material west along the shore to form spits and bars. Thus, the ocean-facing coast has been partially shaped by marine agencies, and the shoreline around inner bays and lagoons has been shaped by subaerial glacial deposition. Kames and kettles are associated with the morainal topography of Cape Cod. As the ice dropped material, it formed a very irregular surface. Photograph courtesy of U.S. Geological Survey, November 21, 1938 (see p. 18).

Plate 28. At Montauk Point, near the tip of Long Island, New York, a glacial terminal moraine is exposed to coastal erosion. The large blocks lying on the beach are left as the till is removed. The finer sands, silts, and clays are carried offshore or along the shore to build the barrier islands of Long Island. During severe storms, retreat can be as much as 0.91 or 1.22 meters (3 or 4 feet) and over a year as much as 1.83 to 2.44 meters (6 to 8 feet) of coast has been cut away. Photograph by the author, August 1963 (see p. 18).

Plate 29. Boston Bay, Massachusetts, offers an excellent example of drumlin and drumlinoid islands that are partially submerged or drowned due to the rise of sea level. A drumlinoid differs from a true drumlin by having a hard bedrock core with a thin veneer of glacial till on top. Some of the islands in Boston Bay have been partially removed and others are a few meters below sea level. Materials gathered by shore currents from marine erosion have accumulated as spits, bars, and tombolos. A number of the islands have been cut off by the waves so that their elliptical drumlin shape is not complete. Most of the cliffs face east, toward the open ocean, where the strongest waves come. Photograph courtesy of U.S. Geological Survey, September 1959 (see p. 18-19).

Plate 30. A number of coastal, eolian, and glacial features are shown north of Aberdeen on the coast of Scotland. The high-tide line is clearly distinguishable as a nearly straight line. Landward of this tidal zone are large sand dunes, some nearly 61 meters (200 feet) high. A large pinnacle occurs just inland from the beach. Vegetation has stabilized most of this white sand but in places strong winds have created large blowouts. One such V-shaped blowout is in the left center portion of this photograph. Farther inland, sand has moved across a mottled glaciated surface. Kames and kettleholes are associated with this deglaciated surface (upper right portion of the photo), and sand and gravel deposits comprise the light gray areas. The unconsolidated glacial deposits are quickly modified by storm waves and currents. Photograph courtesy of the Department of Geography, University of Aberdeen, Scotland, October 1967 (see p. 19).

Plate 31. The Colville Delta shown here flows into the Beaufort Sea on Alaska's Arctic slope. The river flows continuously into the sea, which is frozen over during eight months of the year. The outstanding feature on this photograph is the tundra polygons that have been developed on permafrost by ice wedging. There are a series of barrier channels and sand bars along the Colville tributaries. The picture was taken in early June after river breakup but before ice had melted from the large lakes. Photograph by Harley J. Walker, June 9, 1974 (see p. 19).

Plate 32. A tabular iceberg, 402 kilometers (250 miles) west of McMurdo Sound at the edge of the Ross Ice Shelf, is shown here. In the foreground, rough shelf ice has recently been frozen over and covered with a light snowfall. The large iceberg is slowly moving to the edge of the shelf where it will drift to sea. But this ice mass may be stuck on a submarine end moraine that runs across the mouth of the Ross Sea. Photograph by Steve Frishman (see p. 19).

Plate 33. Crevasses in the floating tongue of Koettlitz Glacier, at the head of McMurdo Sound, Antarctica, are shown here. Koettlitz Glacier, which originates within the Royal Society Range, floats on the waters of McMurdo Sound from Heald Island to foreground. The surface of the ice is extremely rough because of ablation that is aggravated by windblown dust (dark areas) that accumulates on the surface. Etching by ablation accentuates a rectilinear crevasse pattern, which is typical of floating ice tongues and tidal action. Photograph courtesy of U.S. Navy, December 19, 1957 (see p. 20).

Plate 34. This unusual NASA space photograph shows sediment moving out into the Gulf of Mexico from the Mississippi River. Note the pattern of sediment being carried to the southwest as large sediment fingers. The birds-foot pattern of the delta can be faintly seen through the very white sediment deposits. Photograph courtesy of NASA (see p. 20).

Plate 35. The delta of the Colorado River, as it enters the Gulf of California, has a number of interesting characteristics (see Plate 39). Because of the high tidal range in this area, as much as 6.1 meters (20 feet), the delta of the river becomes a drowned estuary at high tide. At low tide, vast mud flats become exposed and are crossed by branches of the river spreading out in a digitate pattern as the water sinks into the fine muds and clays. Such a pattern looks very much like a deciduous tree with branching limbs in winter. The very short, first-order streams create a pinnate form that usually indicates very fine uniform materials. Photograph courtesy of the Department of Geography. University of California, Riverside (see p. 20).

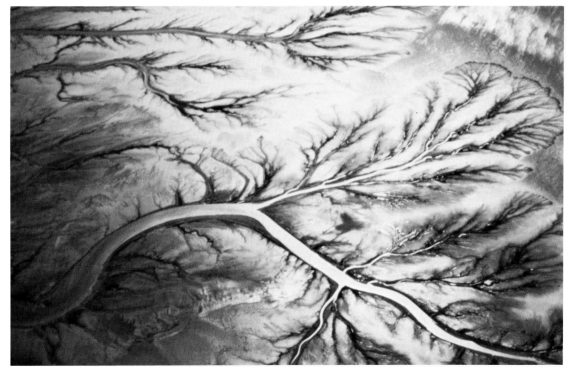

Plate 36. This Gemini space photograph of the Nile Delta shows clearly a coastline shaped by subaerial deposition. The Nile Delta is a classic example of river deposition extending into the sea. The two main tributaries of the Nile—Raiyah el Beheira to the west and Raiyah el Taufigi to the east—are building large deltaic extensions into the Mediterranean Sea. Earlier tributaries have built the arcuate delta form for which the Nile is so famous. The building of the Aswan Dam has changed the entire profile of the Nile Delta, because, instead of seasonal flooding with sediment being carried to the sea, the rich river deposits are being left in Lake Nasser, which extends into the Sudan. With deposition lessened, waves and currents are actively redistributing the river deposits, forming more sand bars and spits. Wind already has moved some material inland, forming a band of white sand dunes along the delta shore. Photograph courtesy of NASA (see p. 20).

Plate 37. The mouth of the Clarence River on the northeast coast of South Island, New Zealand, has built a small arcuate delta into the sea. The shifting channels can be seen clearly as the river shifts around material dropped in its braided channel. River changes are numerous due to the low gradient across a nearly level coastal plain and also due to the large volume of water the river carries from snow melt in the Southern Alps of New Zealand. Active coastal currents quickly smooth out the river deposits leaving a very gentle, arcuate form. Photograph by Robert Kirk, (see p. 20).

Plate 38. In January 1969, the Santa Clara River in southern California was actively building a delta seaward of the barrier beaches. Heavy rains in the coastal mountains created the higher than normal discharge. Note how the river is building an arcuate delta into the sea. However, waves and currents will quickly disperse the coarser material along the shore and carry the finer material out to sea. When the flow ceases, the small delta will be destroyed and the sea will again enter the inlet. Photograph courtesy of Ventura Port District (see p. 20).

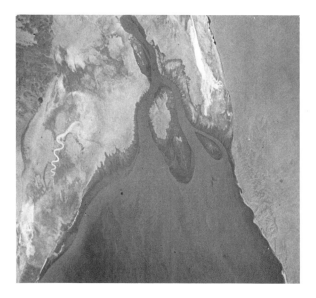

Plate 39. The Colorado River, where it enters the Gulf of California, has no true delta form because the lower part of the river is drowned, forming an estuary that greatly changes shape and size between high and low tides (see Plate 35). The Gulf of California is a tectonic depression that is continuing to sink. Imperial Valley, to the north of the Colorado River Delta, is below sea level and would fill with sea water, as it has in the past, if it were not for this delta forming a type of dam across the northern end of the Gulf. Because of all the man-made dams on the Colorado River, much less alluvium now reaches the Gulf of California. Therefore, the delta is not growing as fast as it did at one time. Photograph courtesy of NASA (see p. 20).

Plate 40. The Wai-au River at the southern end of South Island, New Zealand, is an excellent example of a small river descending steeply from the high mountains of the Southern Alps and carrying coarse waste into Te Waewae Bay. The river is confined in its course by spurs of the mountains. This area is tectonically active and has a number of uplifted terraces and faults along this section of coast. Photograph by Robert Kirk, (see p. 20).

Plate 41. In southeastern Iceland, where the Vatnajö-kull ice cap is entering the sea, glacial outwash deposits consist of red volcanic ash left as delta deposits. The small bay behind these glaciofluvial deposits contains scattered pack ice and small icebergs. Tides moving across the delta deposits separate and redeposit the assorted glacial material. Photograph by the author, July 10, 1964 (see p. 20).

Plate 42. Point San Fermin is located on the east coast of the Baja Peninsula, Mexico, about 145 kilometers (90 miles) south of the U.S. border. This coast is being built by alluvial fans from the mountains to the west. The climate is arid with only occasional rainfall to transport material, but there is very little coastal energy to erode this aggrading coast. Note the slightly southerly long-shore drift removing material from the mouths of the arroyos. The source of material is the Cenozoic volcanic rock that forms the mountains in the background. Photograph courtesy of Department of Geography, University of California, Los Angeles (see p. 20).

Plate 43. The Canterbury Plain on the east side of South Island, New Zealand, is an example of an alluvial coastal plain in a humid region. Several rivers (one of the largest being the Rangitati) cross this plain, depositing a layer of rich alluvium. Photograph by Robert Kirk (see p. 20).

Plate 44. The Mackenzie River Delta enters the Arctic Ocean in a series of tidal channels and meandering tributaries. This large alluvial-plain coast is covered with forested swamps and elongate/oval oriented lakes adjacent to and within the Mackenzie Delta. Photograph by Warren Hamilton (see p. 20).

Plate 45. Low foredunes have formed around clumps of vegetation along the Makrān coastal plain of Pakistan. The vegetation is usually a salt-tolerant shrub, such as *Prunus amyadalus,* or grasses, such as *Aerua lavanica* and *Aristida nutahilis.* The mounds of sand are in most cases sand shadows no more than 0.91 to 1.52 meters high (3 to 5 feet). Where no vegetation occurs, small barchan sand dunes form that feed larger barchan dunes as they move inland. Where there is a large mass of sand, the dune fields will become much more extensive, forming whalebacks of irregular shape. Photograph by the author, October 10, 1960 (see p. 21).

Plate 46. A parabolic-dune pattern south of Point Sal in southern California is shown here. Plants play an important role in controlling sand dunes; the roots in a complex system bind the sand together. There is a definite order of colonization by plants on developing dunes. The most important dune builders are the grasses that flourish in loose sand. The dunes in this picture are predominately U-shaped (called parabolic). Note that the dunes are elongate in the direction of the prevailing wind. These dunes are still active. Active young grass-covered dunes extend up to an elevation of 37 meters (120 feet) and older dunes to nearly 122 meters (400 feet). Photograph courtesy of Department of Geography, University of California, Los Angeles (see p. 21).

Plate 47. At the edge of the Las Bela Valley, 64.4 kilometers (40 miles) west of Karachi, there are a series of parabolic-shaped Pleistocene dunes. Vegetation, mostly grasses and euphorbia shrubs, now cover their surface, stabilizing the sands. Photograph by the author, October 12, 1960 (see p. 21).

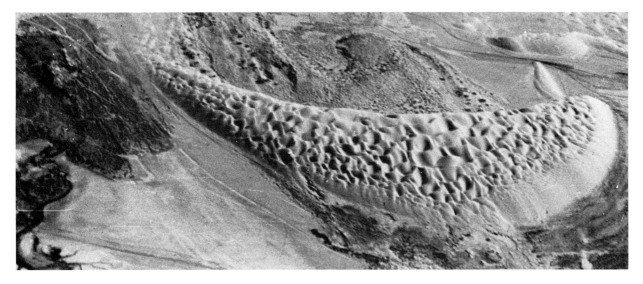

Plate 48. One of the largest barchan dune forms I have ever observed occurs in the Las Bela Valley of Pakistan, 81 kilometers (50 miles) west of Karachi. This large dune mass is nearly 0.8 kilometer (0.5 mile) long and rises to a height of 31 meters (102 feet). On top of this crescentic-shaped dune are a whole series of small barchan forms moving across its surface and down the slip slope. Photograph by the author, October 12, 1960 (see p. 21).

Plate 49. A set of transverse barchan dunes moving inland at Pismo Beach in southern California is shown here. Fairly uniform coastal breezes and a lack of vegetation enables these dune forms to develop. Note how the sand from the horns of one dune feed the slip face of the dune form inland of it. Photograph courtesy of Department of Geography, University of California, Los Angeles (see p. 21).

Plate 50. In August 1965, as the Apollo 9 spacecraft was crossing the Namib Desert of Southwest Africa, this magnificant photograph was taken by Gordon Cooper. This very dry stretch of coast has great sand accumulations migrating inland in the form of long transverse dune ridges. Note how the coastal dunes are light while those farther inland are darker shades of gray. This difference in coloration is believed to be the result of the greater age of the inland dunes, which has allowed greater oxidation of the iron components within the sand. Photograph courtesy of NASA (see p. 21).

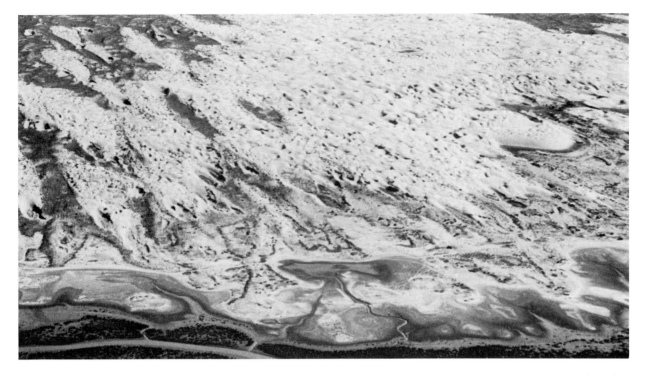

Plate 51. Where strong winds move inland and change direction from one season to another, as they do across the Las Bela coastal plain of Pakistan, barchan dune forms change into longitudinal forms parallel with wind direction. In the summer, southwest monsoon winds blow inland, but in the winter the winds are more variable, sometimes coming from the west or northwest. These changeable winds extend the horns of barchan dunes and cause them to become much more linear. The sand over much of this region has become compacted and stabilized with the active dunes mainly around the margins. Photograph by the author, October 12, 1960 (see p. 21).

Plate 52. Along the north shore of Puerto Rico, east of Arecibo, sand is held in place by vegetation on the leeward side of a high dune ridge. Sand in this area quickly becomes cemented into rock called eolianite, because of rapid oxidation and calcification in the humid climate. These dunes are stabilized by vegetation and by the underlying indurated sand. Photograph by the author, January 11, 1974 (see p. 21).

Plate 53. Near the outlet of the Santa Maria River in Santa Barbara County, California, large masses of sand, called whalebacks, have formed over thousands of years. The source for most of the sand is the Santa Maria River itself, which over long periods of time has carried considerable quantities of sand to the shore. Today, the rivers of southern California are so controlled by human beings that very little sand reaches the coast and the shape and size of the dunes has been greatly altered. Photograph courtesy of Department of Geography, University of California, Los Angeles, 1937 (see p. 21).

Plate 54. Eolianite (aeolianite) is common along tropical coasts becauce the calcium carbonate that makes up shells in coastal dunes dissolves rapidly with the percolation of water. This calcium carbonate later cements the quartz sand grains together. In time a very resistant rock (eolianite) is created. This outcrop of eolianite occurs around Waialua Bay on the island of Oahu, Hawaii. Photograph by the author, July 17, 1965 (see p. 21).

Plate 55. The sand flats on Plum Island, Massachusetts, represent a ridge-and-runnel intertidal system where waves and currents erode and deposit fine-grained materials. Here waves are weakened as they enter a tidal inlet. This loss of energy enables the sand to be deposited in the shallows. Often where sand flats are created, such as tidal inlets and lagoons, sand is removed from other coastal locations. Many beaches on the east coast of the United States are starved of sand because it is trapped at another location. Photograph by Miles O. Hayes (see p. 22).

A

B

Plate 56. These two photographs show coastal changes of the Palos Verdes Hills in Los Angeles through mass wasting at two different time periods. The first photograph (A) was taken in March, 1924, the second (B) in March, 1941. Within this sixteen-year timespan, whole sections of the shoreline have been breaking away and falling into the sea at Point Fermin. The stepped nature of these landslides occurs as large blocks break off and slide downslope following periods of heavy rain. Earthquakes also help to create the large cracks, which can be seen on the landward side of the street in Plate 57. Photograph courtesy of Department of Geography, University of California, Los Angeles (see p. 22).

Plate 57. This ground photograph shows landslide damage and the stepped nature of mass wasting at Point Firmin, Palos Verdes Hills, California. By 1977 the coast highway was falling into the sea. Some of the cliffs in this area are over 183 meters (600 feet) high and are made up of volcanic tuffs, altered to bentonite, and interbedded with other sediments. Bentonic clays greatly swell when moisture is added and the bedding surfaces become soft and plastic. Because the tuff beds slope seaward, this area is particularly subject to mass wasting on a rapid scale. Photograph by the author, March 18, 1976 (see p. 22).

Plate 58. Slump scars can be seen along the cliffs to the west of Santa Barbara, near Gaviota Beach, California. The cirquelike features result when rock masses subside toward the center of an amphitheater and the debris is removed by the sea. Earthquakes, such as the one in July 1968 with an intensity of 5.3 on the Richter scale, help loosen the rock, especially along fault and fracture zones. Photograph by the author, April 8, 1967 (see p. 22).

Plate 59. Flowing landslides occur along the coast of Baja California, north of Ensenada, Mexico, indicating rapid marine erosion. The cap rock of this region is Rosarito Beach basalts, but underlying this layer are 152 to 213 meters (500 to 700 feet) of weak sediments composed of sandstones, conglomerates, and shales. Flowing rubble slides occur from the basalt cap, but rotational slumps are more common from the weaker sediments So much movement is taking place along this coast that any building construction is difficult. Photograph by the author, July 2, 1972 (see p. 23).

Plate 60. At the western end of Martha's Vineyard, Massachusetts, at the point called Gay Head, several cliffs consisting of soft Tertiary formations are exposed to erosion. The retreat of the cliffs has been irregular, because of the extensive creeping slides that are still occurring. The average recession of the cliff tops has been approximately 1.52 meters (5 feet) per year. Where glacial till occurs, large boulders are found on the cliffs and along the beaches as well as some distance out from shore. Photograph by the author, July 5, 1963 (see p. 23).

Plate 61. This view is southwestward across the very dark lava flow of 1969 toward the actively forming Apua Point lava delta of 1973 on the large island of Hawaii. Apua Point is at the left, and the active pahoehoe flow comprises the lighter gray area. There is a steam cloud at the shoreline. Note how the delta extends laterally along the shoreline to form horns. Caption and photograph by R. T. Holcomb, (see p. 23).

Plate 62. A small lobe of pahoehoe lava at Apua Point, Hawaii, is at the subaerial front of a lava delta, that is built by extrusions from a distributary tube. The man is cringing from the heat of the lava toes in front of him, which are flowing over the front of the lobe and trickling into the water. Caption and photograph by R. T. Holcomb, (see p. 23).

Plate 63. The erosion of a tephra coast made up predominately of ash and pumice is shown here. The picture was taken near the town of St. Pierre, Martinique, and the ejected material is from an eruption of Mount Pelee in 1902, which sent an enormous volume of ash and poisonous gases, both fiery hot, across the town of St. Pierre. The indurated pyroclastics shown in this picture were formed during this eruption. The pumice eroded from the cliffs makes the beach very white in color, very light in weight, and very coarse in texture. Photograph by the author, June 24, 1971 (see p. 23).

Plate 64. A small ash cone in the Gulf of California, south of Isla Angel de la Guarda, Mexico, illustrates a steep volcanic slope almost completely lacking in vegetation. The angle of rest of this ash slope is about 26:5°. Note how the slopes descend almost directly into the sea with very little beach or shelf. Photograph by Leonard Bowden (see p. 23).

Plate 65. Near Koko Head, on the southeast corner of the island of Oahu, Hawaii, there is a breached volcanic crater that has been partially indurated with the rise of sea level. Hanauma Bay, on the inner side of the crater, is a beautiful circular bay with a fringing coral reef (see Plate 183). A second volcano, Koko Crater, is located to the northeast. Photograph by E. A. Wingert, January 14, 1963 (see p. 24).

Plate 66. Tidal pools provide small swimming holes for children on Santa Maria Island in the Azores. Because of their massiveness and hardness, these volcanic rocks are very slow to erode; most are rounded over long periods of time by waves splashing against their surfaces and small stones (lower left) washing against them during storms. Photograph by the author, May 31, 1973 (see p. 24).

Plate 67. This spectacular view shows an old volcanic plug at New Plymouth on North Island, New Zealand. The snowcapped volcano, Egmont, can be seen in the distance. Like the volcanic rocks on Santa Maria (Plate 66), this volcanic mass has very resistant rock and is slow to erode. The limit of wave splash can be seen clearly at the vegetation line near the base of the volcanic rocks. Photograph by Robert Kirk, (see p. 24).

Plate 68. Many volcanic coasts have black sand beaches, such as the one shown here near Apua Point on the large island of Hawaii. Cracks extend across the black sand beach atop the front of the active delta. Several of the cracks are potholes. The front of the lava flow is very unstable and is collapsing as it is undercut by the surface. An earthquake centered about 60 kilometers (37 miles) away, with a magnitude of 6.2, had occurred about one hour before this picture was taken. Caption and photograph by R. T. Holcomb, 1973 (see p. 24).

Plate 69. Well-kept terraced vineyards can be found on the steep volcanic cliffs on the west coast of Santa Maria Island in the Azores. The volcanic material on these islands, in places, has broken down to form excellent soil that is rich in minerals. Photograph by the author, May 31, 1973 (see p. 24).

Plate 70. Recent tectonic movements along the Makrān coast of Iran, east of Chāh Bahār, are shown here. The fault is transverse to the shoreline, resulting in cliffed promontories and very sharp-angled rock-lined embay- ments. The small sailboat in the foreground gives a scale for these 46 meter (150-foot) cliffs. Photograph by the author, October 12, 1968 (see p. 24).

Plate 71. The Gulf of California represents a trough that lies between two faults. Actually, there are a series of faults with approximately parallel strikes. Baja Peninsula is slowly moving north and has been for millions of years. The islands in the Gulf are pulled away from the main- land by these transcurrent faults. Note how the large island of Tiburon has been pulled away and rotated clockwise from its former attachment to the Sonoran coast. Photograph courtesy of NASA (see p. 24).

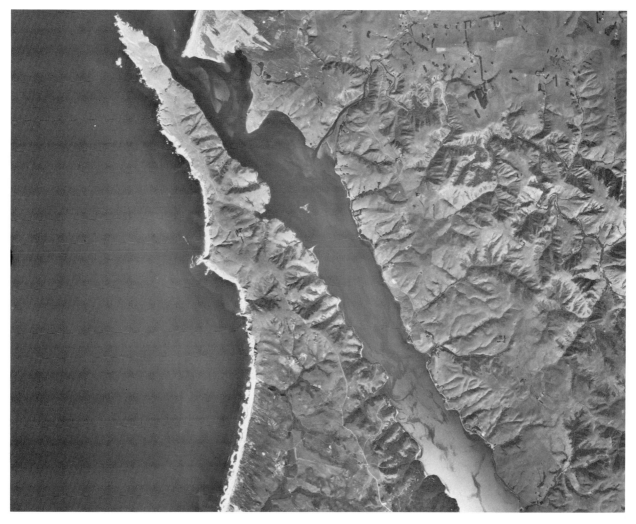

Plate 72. This aerial view of Tomales Bay, California, shows the fault alignment of the San Andreas rift system as it extends northwest into the Pacific Ocean. Photograph courtesy of U.S. Geological Survey (see p. 24).

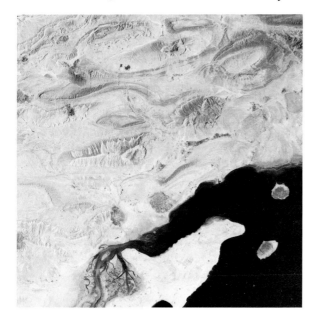

Plate 73. In southwestern Iran, there are a number of large salt domes, which occur as dark, rounded mounds and islands off the coast in the Strait of Hormuz. One of these larger salt dome islands, just off the coast, is called Hormuz. This island represents a large salt plug with a magnificent series of circular ridges, some of them 91 meters (300 feet) high. The island is about 7.6 kilometers (4.5 miles) long and 8.8 kilometers (5.5 miles) wide. Photograph courtesy of NASA (see p. 25).

Plate 74. Mudlump islands are surface manifestations of intrusive clay masses that result from depositional processes at the mouths of major Mississippi River dis- tributaries. This photograph shows the overall distribu tion of mudlumps at the Southeast Pass mouth. Photo- graph by James P. Morgan (*see* p. 25).

Plate 75. Four mud volcanoes are situated in the mid- dle of a large, featureless coastal plain approximately 10.5 kilometers (6.5 miles) inland from the coast and 13.7 kilometers (8.5 miles) northeast of the settlement of Tang, Iran. This is in the Makrān region of Iran, bordering on the Arabian Sea. Napag, the largest of the cones, raises 73 meters (240 feet) above the plain. These cones are not true volcanoes, rather they are formed by liquid mud flowing out of a central vent. Their formation is due to pressure along a zone of weakness in the Miocene and Pliocene silts and clays. Photograph by the author, Octo- ber 12, 1968 (*see* p. 25).

Plate 76. One of the most spectacular regions in which to view uplifted marine terraces is the Palos Verdes Hills, near Los Angeles, California. There are thirteen recognized terraces, ranging from about 30 meters (100 feet) to nearly 396 meters (1,300 feet) above sea level. Nine of these thirteen terraces have been identified through fossil shells. There is no place along the entire coast of the United States where the record of successive elevation of a land mass is better displayed and more carefully studied. Caption drawn from F. P. Shepard and H. R. Wanless (1971); photograph courtesy of the Department of Geography, University of California, Los Angeles, September 28, 1921 (see p. 25).

Plate 77. What appears to be a series of marine terraces are really stream and subaerial erosional terraces on the outer edge of the Banks Peninsula on South Island, New Zealand. It is often difficult to determine the origin of such terraces. No evidence of former wave-cut scarps or nips can be found on the slopes, and there is greater evidence of subsidence of the cluster of old volcanoes than uplift of the region. Photograph by Robert Kirk (see p. 25).

Plate 78. Kaikoura Peninsula on South Island, New Zealand, is a complicated uplifted terrace region. It is a fault-bounded block that has been dragged up marginal to the seaward Kaikoura Ranges. It is still rising, with as much as 2 meters (6.56 feet) of uplift in the last 10,000 years. There are three elevated marine terraces, each of which is capped by reworked loess and hillslope deposits of various types. Caption and photograph by Robert Kirk (see p. 26).

Plate 79. An area of postgalcial isostatic uplift occurs in southwest Ireland, near Eyeries on the Beara Peninsula in the County of Cork. At this location there are a series of marine terraces. Photograph courtesy of Irish Tourist Board (see p. 26).

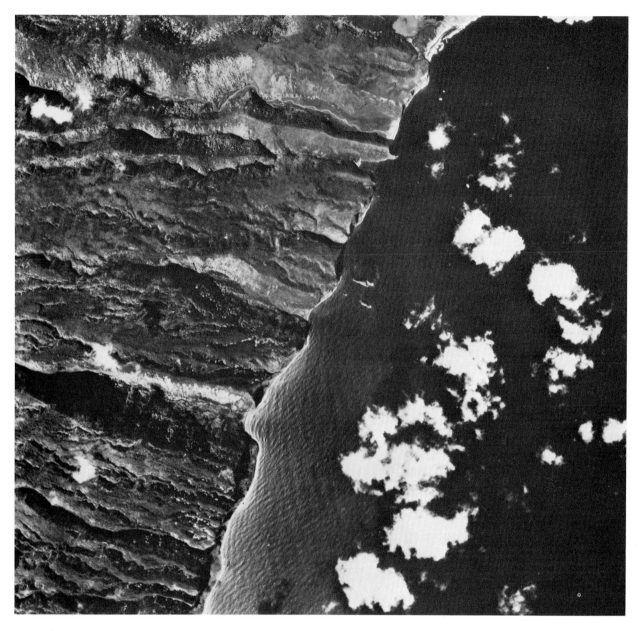

Plate 80. On the northeast coast of the large island of Hawaii, at the base of the Kohala Mountains, there is a nearly straight stretch of coast where the lava has been cut back uniformly. A few indentations and small bays exist where active streams have cut down steepsided valleys and entered the sea. The rainfall on the 1,828-meter (6,000-foot) volcanoes exceeds 1,016 centimeters (400 inches) per year. Photograph courtesy of U.S. Geological Survey, October 14, 1954 (see p. 28).

Plate 81. Along the coast of southern California there are stretches of straight coast with marine erosion cutting away fairly soft cliffs. This straight stretch of coast occurs for 29 kilometers (18 miles) in the Redondo Beach–Santa Monica area, where there are numerous beach resorts and where the area is densely populated. When this photo was taken, however, back around 1930, there was very little settlement along this stretch of coast. Caption and photograph by F. P. Shepard (see p. 28).

Plate 82. An excellent coastal region with a variety of rock types and diverse bedding planes occurs along the cliffs of Moher, in County Clare, on the coast of Ireland. These cliffs are made up of sedimentary shales, sandstones, and limestones. Photograph courtesy of Irish Tourist Board (see p. 28).

Plate 83. Sunset Cliffs, north of Cabrillo Peninsula in San Diego, California, presents an irregular coastline made up of small coves and bays cut by waves attacking rocks of unequal resistance. The shaly parts of Sunset Cliffs are being undermined, causing occasional slides. Where sandstone cliffs occur, only minor changes appear to be taking place. Such uneven erosion is characteristic of the entire west coast of the United States. Caption by F. P. Shepard; photograph by the author, November 25, 1967 (see p. 28).

Plate 84. On the coast of Portugal, near the town of Peniche, steeply dipping limestone and sandstone rocks are under heavy attack from the Atlantic Ocean. The irregular, jagged nature of this coastline results from the steeply dipping beds of rock. Sea spray thrown against the cliffs has removed the less resistant layers accentuating the bedding planes. Rapid erosion can take place under these conditions. Photograph by the author, August 7, 1964 (see p. 29).

Plate 85. The excellent rocky coast near Slea Head, County Kerry in southwest Ireland is shown here. The bedding planes are slanting away from the shoreline, and this direction of dip results in much less erosion, because the waves wash up against a more uniform sur- face, therefore, undercutting is less severe. Compare this photograph with Plate 84 where the bedding planes are toward the oncoming waves. Photograph courtesy of the Irish Tourist Board (see p. 29).

Plate 86. Nearly vertical jointing and fracturing of white granitic rock occurs at Puerto Peñasco, Mexico, at the southern end of the Gulf of California. Photograph by the author, November 23, 1972 (see p. 29).

Plate 87. The coast of Portugal, west of the town of Sesimbra at a headland called Cobode Espichel, is an example of folded rocks extending to the coast. The more-resistant conglomerate and sandstone layers stand up longer than the less-resistant shale and softer limestone rocks. Photograph by the author, June 1973 (see p. 29).

Plate 88. The nearly straight, fault-lined coast of Molokai, Hawaii, is shown here. This wave-eroded cliff has been cut back nearly 4.8 kilometers (3 miles). Photograph by the author, July 31, 1975 (see p. 29).

Plate 89. Just to the west of the fishing village of Khori Khod in the Cape Monze region of Pakistan, west of Karāchi, a transverse fault extends into the sea. The fault-line scarp stands out well at the base of the small headland. This is where the Kirthar Mountain Ranges, running in a northeast to southwest direction, extend into the Arabian Sea eventually becoming the Murray Submarine Ridge. Photograph by the author, October 12, 1960 (see p. 29).

Plate 90. A granitic rock promontory extends into the sea on the west side of the island of Mallorca in the western Mediterranean. These headlands are just to the south of the town of Sóller. Photograph by the author, June 8, 1973 (see p. 29).

Plate 91. We return to Laguna Beach, California, for an aerial view of rocky headlands and promontories with pocket beaches between. This spectacular coastal region is now densely populated, but this 1932 photograph shows only scattered settlement on the promontories. This is an excellent example of how fast a coastal region can be developed. Photograph courtesy of Department of Geography, University of California, Los Angeles, September 18, 1932 (see p. 29).

Plate 92. Large rocks, churned by waves, bore large potholes into the indurated eolianite dunes along the north coast of Puerto Rico. This picture was taken near Punta Marchiquita, north of Manati. This is a high-energy coast, especially during severe storms such as hurricanes. Photograph by the author, June 17, 1971 (see p. 29).

Plate 93. Jagged pinnacles are often cut by waves and sea spray in different rock types, especially sandstones, limestones, and shales. These pinnacles are cut in layered shale on the west coast of South Island, New Zealand, north of Greymouth. Photograph by the author, August 3, 1975 (see p. 29).

Plate 94. Hawaii has several spectacular spouting horns, as can be seen here on the south coast of Kauai, Hawaii, near Kukuiula Harbor. Another large spouting horn can be found at Koko Head, on the island of Oahu. Photograph by the author, July 24, 1965 (see p. 29).

Plate 95. A large blowhole occurs in Acadia National Park at a location called Thunder Hole on the southeastern side of Mount Desert Island, Maine. As the waves rush into the large cavity, a thunderous hissing sound can be heard as the water becomes trapped. Because of the resistance of the massive granitic rock, erosion is very slow. Such blowholes may last for years before finally being eroded away. Photograph by the author, May 11, 1968 (see p. 29).

Plate 96. Numerous minor erosional features can be found on coastal terraces at Sunset Cliffs in San Diego, California. Here, spheroidal balls are left when less resistant sandstones are cut away by pounding waves. The iron and manganese concretions form in the bedded deposits and remain as isolated, resistant features because of their much greater hardness. These features are sometimes called mushroom or hoodoo rocks. Snails, crabs, and mussels bore holes in the surface of the rock. Photograph by the author, November 1967 (see p. 29).

Plate 97. North of Dunedin on South Island, New Zealand, there are a group of very large boulders spread across the beach and in the cliffs. These are called the Moraki boulders. They consist of massive iron and man-ganese concretions found in less indurated sandstones and siltstones. These may well be the largest boulders of this type in the world. Photograph by the author, October 3, 1975 (see p. 29).

Plate 98. On the east coast of Yucatan, Mexico, at the Mayan archaeological site of Tulum, there is a small nip being cut in the limestone rock. This nip is the initial stage of undercutting of cliffs at the wave level. This small notch will slowly be cut back to form a small terrace. Photograph by the author, January 11, 1973 (see p. 31).

Plate 99. The next coastal form to develop after the nip stage (see Plate 98) is usually a small coastal terrace. These vary in size and height depending on the power of the waves and the rise and fall of sea level. Here, a small terrace is being cut into eolianite rock on the north coast of Puerto Rico, north of Manati. Photograph by the author, June 17, 1971 (see p. 31).

Plate 100. With the retreat of a rocky coast, an abrasion platform often forms after the terrace stage, (see Plate 99). This view is along the south coast of Australia, near Melbourne. It is an excellent example of a platform of rock cut by waves at the wave-abrasion level. Small piles of talus rock often form at the base of the cliffs, which are later broken down and carried off when waves are able to cross the nearly level platform and reach the cliffs. Photograph by the author, October 9, 1975 (see p. 31).

Plate 101. A large arch and sea cave occurs southeast of Hobart, Tasmania, near Port Arthur. Because of the bedding and fault planes of the rock, this sea tunnel is nearly rectangular. Nearly all the caves and tunnels in this area have formed along zones of weakness in the rock. Photograph by the author, October 10, 1975 (see p. 31).

Plate 102. In poorly consolidated rocks, such as the marls and limestones shown in this photo, the sea quickly eats into the material making an intricate series of tunnels and caves. This photo was taken near the town of Albuferia, on the south coast of Portugal. This type of cliffed coast is made less regular by marine erosion. Between the high- and low-tide line, chemical and organic activity has turned the rock to a darker, weathered state. These weathering agents help to erode the rock and form caves. The fact that caves are forming on the landward-facing side, away from the mechanical abrasion by waves, shows that considerable erosion does take place by chemical and biological forces in a wet-dry environment. Photograph by the author, July 1974 (see p. 31).

Plate 103. Very large sea caves occur along the north coast of Puerto Rico in the old, cemented eolianite dunes (see Plate 99). One of the largest, Cave of the Indian, is located about 8 kilometers (5 miles) east of Arecibo. The entrance of the cave is shown here, a sea arch can be seen in the background. Photograph by the author, January 11, 1974 (see p. 31).

Plate 104. Sea arches are less common in massive rocks, such as granite or lavas, than in weaker sedimentary rocks, but they do occur as can be seen here. This sea arch is located on the northeast side of Hanauma Bay, Oahu, Hawaii. Photograph by the author, July 22, 1975 (see p. 31).

Plate 105. Sea arches are more common in sedimentary rocks such as limestones, sandstones, and shales. This photo depicts several excellent arches in very white limestone rock at Beirut, Lebanon. These are called Oyster Rocks. They occur directly in front of a series of large hotels and apartment houses in the modern district of Beirut. Photograph by the author, February 25, 1972 (see p. 31).

Plate 106. The sea stack at Cabo de St. Vincent has stood for many years at the extreme southwest point of Portugal. It is composed of very resistant limestone. Photograph by the author, August 1964 (see p. 31).

Plate 107. Between Lagos and Faro, Portugal, nearly horizontal limestone beds have been eroded into vertical cliffs, sea stacks, and sea caves. A fairly resistant layer of white calcareous limestone caps the less resistant Faro limestone undernearth. Under wave attack, the limestone erodes quite easily, forming one of the most spectacular erosion coasts in the world. Photograph by the author, August 1964 (see p. 31).

Plate 108. Sea stacks are found in more resistant, massive Precambrian rocks along the southwest coast of Ireland. This view is at Ballybunion, in County Kerry. Photograph courtesy of the Irish Tourist Board (see p. 31).

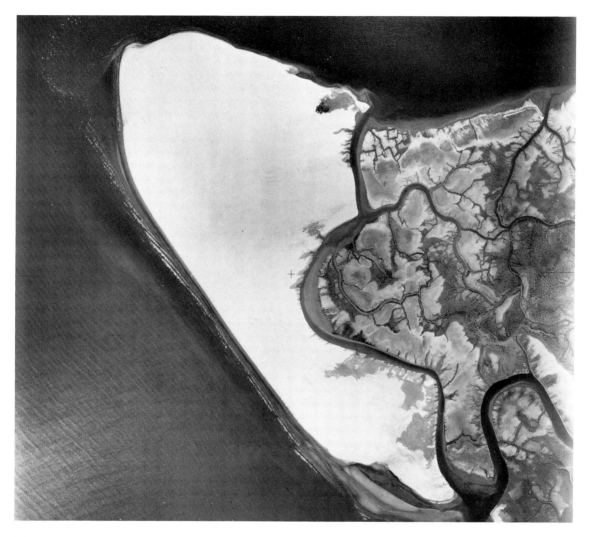

Plate 109. Sand barrier islands occur at the mouth of the Indus River, southeast of Karāchi, Pakistan. Most of these sand barriers have very little vegetation, because of the aridity of the region, their consistantly shifting nature, and the severe storms and tides that quite frequently cross their low surface. They are true barriers, however, for they protect the mud flats and tidal vegetation behind them. Photograph courtesy of U.S. Geological Survey, 1953 (see p. 33).

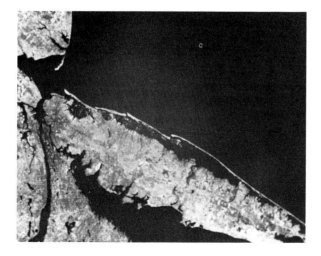

Plate 110. The offshore islands of Long Island, New York, present an excellent example of a barrier chain-fringed shoreline. The source for most of the sand making up these barrier islands comes from the tip of Long Island, near Montauk Point, where glacial morainic deposits are being eroded. Traveling southwest, the islands become smaller with a larger number of inlets between them, because there is less sand source. Brooklyn and Queens, the two boroughs on Long Island, are shown in the extreme southwest portion of the photograph. Photograph courtesy of NASA (see p. 34).

Plate 111. Baymouth bars extending across tidal lagoons in the Charlestown coastal region of Rhode Island are shown here. The baymouth bars and barrier beaches connect headlands. The lack of surface runoff due to the permeability of the glacial material has allowed the baymouth bars to seal off the bays called ponds. The central and upper portions of this photograph show a segment of the Charlestown moraine and its outwash plain. Photograph courtesy of U.S. Geological Survey, October 12, 1951 (see p. 34).

Plate 112. Near the mouth of the Hab River in Pakistan, 48 kilometers (30 miles) west of Karāchi, midbay barriers have formed in a large tidal estuary. Although the Hab River is not large, it does bring considerable sediment to the coast when monsoonlike floods occur in July and August. This increased volume of water during the summer keeps the barriers from sealing off the middle part of the estuary. Photograph by the author, October 12, 1960 (see p. 34).

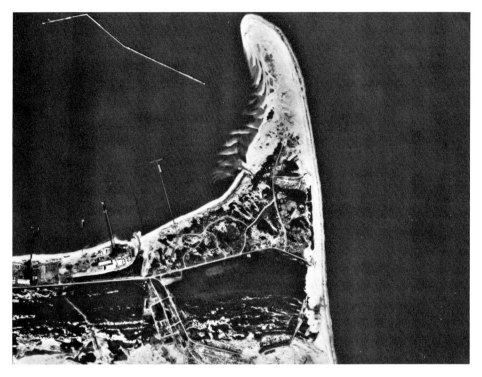

Plate 113. Cape Henlopen, a simple spit at the mouth of Delaware Bay opposite Cape May, New Jersey, has grown northward more than 1.6 kilometers (1 mile) since the area was first surveyed about two hundred years ago. Most of the spit is covered with dune ridges. A large breakwater was built to protect the docking facilities from wave attack. Photograph courtesy of U.S. Geological Survey, March 15, 1962 (see p. 34).

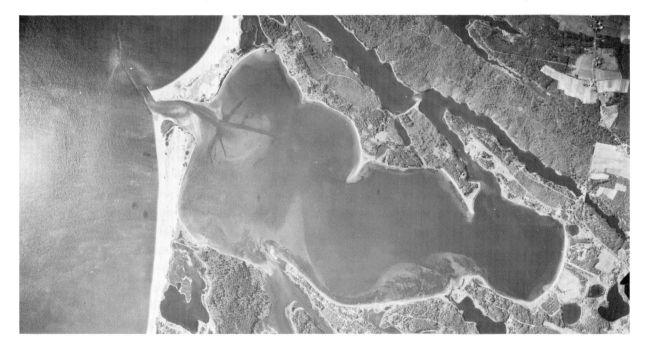

Plate 114. On the south coast of Cape Cod, Massachusetts, south of the village of Waquoit, two spits, growing from two different directions, nearly close off Waquoit Bay. The inlet is kept open by the extension of two jetties. Note the small tidal delta on the inner side of the spits. The lineation of the ponds represents glacial outwash channels from the Cape Cod moraine (see Plate 111). Photograph courtesy of U.S. Geological Survey, November 21, 1938 (see p. 34).

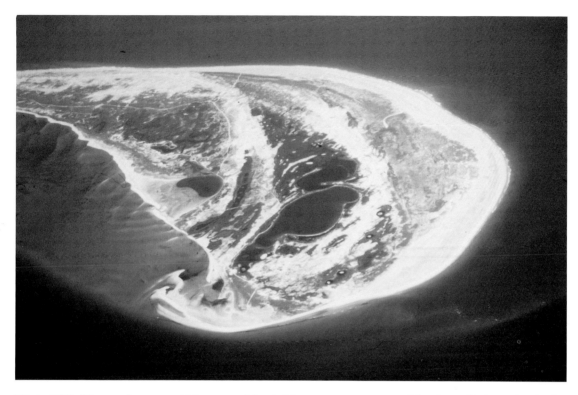

Plate 115. The southern tip of Monomoy Island, Massachusetts, is a recurved spit. The recurved dune ridges indicate the growth of the spit from left to right. This spit extends 11.3 kilometers (7 miles) south from the south- east corner of the Cape Cod mainland. This is one of the best studied spits in the United States, with changes noted as far back as 1899. Photograph by Miles O. Hayes, 1971 (see p. 34).

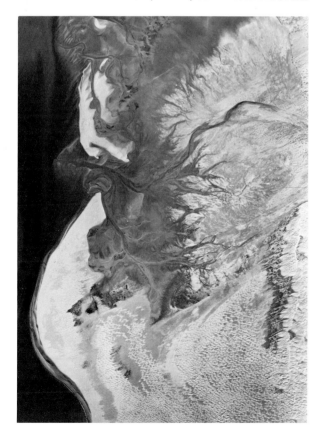

Plate 116. Compound complex spits and hooks develop through a series of growth and erosion stages. Old remnants of Sonmiāni spit, left as islands, occur north of the present main spit. Note the successive stages of growth of the spit (lower, right-hand corner). This spit is at the entrance to Sonmiāni Lagoon 80 kilometers (50 miles) west of Karāchi, Pakistan. Photograph courtesy of U.S. Geological Survey, 1953 (see p. 34).

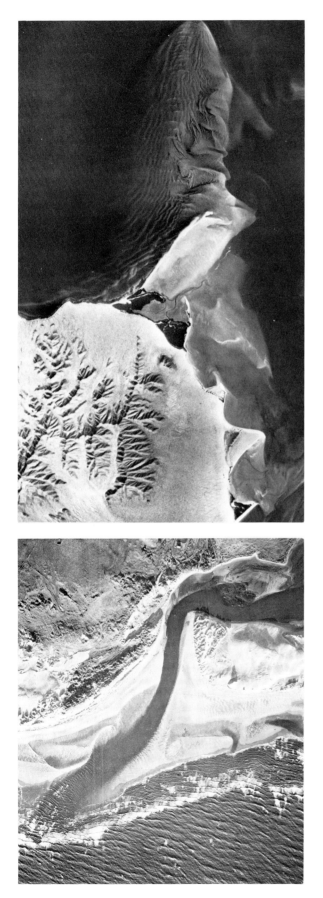

Plate 117. The Gulf of California is a splendid area to see all types of spits and bars as yet unaffected by human habitation. Because of the high tidal range, large sections of the coastal shelves are covered and uncovered by Gulf waters twice a day. A series of cuspate spits and a large simple spit occur on the northeast side of Tiburon Island, Mexico. Photograph courtesy of U.S. Geological Survey (see p. 34).

Plate 118. Serpentine spits are unusual in that they change their form due to increased material brought to the sea by a river. The River Ythan, north of Aberdeen, Scotland, is a good example of such a spit. Instead of having a hook curving inland, as it once did (see the inner shoreline with dunes), increased material has built a spit that now grows seaward leaving extensive sand flats at the mouth of the river. Photograph courtesy of the Department of Geography, University of Aberdeen, Scotland, October 21, 1967 (see p. 35).

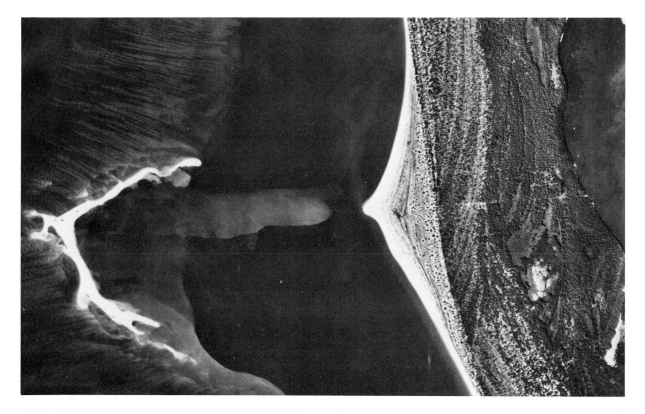

Plate 119. A cuspate foreland is a spit that has grown seaward in a series of stages. Lacosta Island, on the west coast of Florida, north of Sanibel Island, is a good example of this coastal feature. Note how an offshore cuspate sand key has resulted in currents from two directions building out a pointed sand spit from the island. Sediment deposited in the quieter, protected water results in an underwater sand bar extending toward the cuspate foreland. Photograph courtesy of U.S. Geological Survey, February 17, 1944 (see p. 35).

Plate 120. A truncated cuspate foreland occurs at the tip of Cape Hatteras, North Carolina. Projecting more than 48 kilometers (30 miles) out from the mainland, this is the northernmost of the series of cuspate forelands found along the southeast coast of the United States. Offshore of this point is called the graveyard of the Atlantic, with old ship wrecks still visible along the outer shore. The long, nearly straight beach ridges are truncated on the south side of this large foreland. Photograph courtesy of U.S. Geological Survey, August 16, 1959 (see p. 35).

Plate 121. An excellent single tombolo occurs in California, connecting Morro Rock with the mainland. Originally an island lying a short distance offshore, the northward-flowing countercurrent deposited a sand spit along the coast, which resulted in the rock being connected to the shore, creating a tombolo. Dunes 15 meters (50 feet) or more in height developed on the spit and the onshore winds have created a steep front on the spit toward the lagoon. Photograph by Antony R. Orme, September 22, 1936 (see p. 35).

Plate 122. A 11.3-kilometer (7-mile) tombolo connects the island of Magdalena with the mainland just south of Bahia Santa Maria on the Pacific side of Baja California, Mexico. Most of the sand spit making up the tombolo is completely devoid of vegetation. A small pocket of mangroves can be seen in the extreme lower right. Photograph by Leonard Bowden, (see p. 35).

Plate 123. The sand and gravel beaches that have tied Big Nahant and Little Nahant, Massachusetts, to the mainland are tombolos. Complex tombolos result when several islands are united with one another and with the mainland by a complicated series of bars. Photograph courtesy of U.S. Geological Survey, April 1, 1977 (see p. 35).

Plate 124. At the northern end of Eleuthera Island in the Bahamas is a large lunate-shaped sand bar called a cay. This shoal is formed by water passing through an inlet and depositing sand on the quieter lagoon side. Unless stabilized by vegetation or beach rock, these features are usually ephemeral, continually changing their shape and size, especially during hurricanes. Photograph by the author, January 8, 1979 (see p. 36).

Plate 125. Sand bars and channel bars at the southern end of Nauset Beach spit, Massachusetts, are shown here. The main ebb channel is shown at the left. The channel between the depositional lobe of the tidal delta (lower left) and the main body of the spit is a flood channel. Note the strong tendency for sediment to be transported landward. Caption and photograph by Miles O. Hayes, 1971 (see p. 36).

Plate 126. Transverse bars off the spit at Nauset Beach, Massachusetts, show up very well in this photograph. The dominant transport of material is from right to left. Caption and photograph by Miles O. Hayes, 1971 (see p. 36).

Plate 127. Closeup of the western margin of a flood-tidal delta shows reticulated bars at Pleasant Bay Inlet, Cape Cod, Massachusetts. The white areas are swash bars formed by waves approaching from the lower right. The waves were generated by southwest winds blowing across Nantucket Sound. Caption and photograph by Miles O. Hayes, 1971 (see p. 36).

Plate 128. An excellent example of a lunate bar that takes on a crescent shape occurs off the mouth of the Jagin River, along the south coast of Iran. The fine sediments carried through the inlet by tidal currents are deposited on the narrow shelf that borders this Makrān coastal region. Photograph by the author, October 28, 1968 (see p. 36).

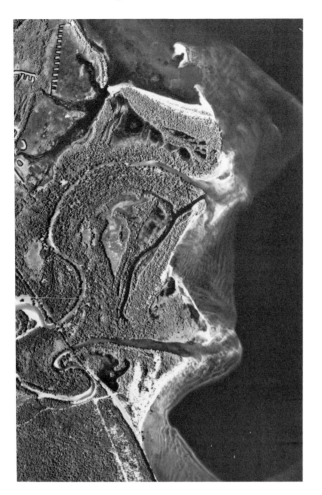

Plate 129. This photograph shows beaches, spits, and underwater features near the mouths of two distributaries of the Ausable River Delta flowing into Lake Champlain on the New York State side. At least two, and possibly three, triangular-shaped cuspate bars are being built at the mouth of the river delta. Former channels of the delta can often be detected through a remnant cuspate bar. Photograph courtesy of U.S. Geological Survey, July 28, 1962 (see p. 36).

Plate 130. Hatteras Inlet, near Cape Hatteras, North Carolina, and the lagoons behind it show the many different forms the submerged and partially submerged bars can take. On the seaward side of the inlet, the faint pattern of several cuspate bars can be detected. Photograph courtesy of U.S. Geological Survey, August 16, 1959 (see p. 36).

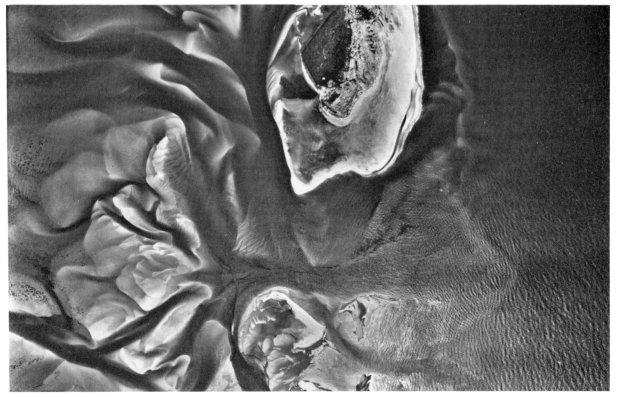

Plate 131. This excellent photograph shows a flood-tidal delta with channel bars at Pleasant Bay Inlet, Massachusetts. Note the modification of the margin of the tidal delta (lower foreground) by waves approaching from the bottom of the photograph. The spit at the top of the photo is the same one as shown in Plate 125. Photograph by Miles O. Hayes, 1971 (see p. 37).

A

B

Plate 132. Where the Ganges and Brahmaputra rivers join and then enter the Bay of Bengal, there are extensive mudflats (A). Here, the rivers are depositing huge amounts of silts and clays, especially during the monsoon season when floodwaters move to the bay from the nearby mountains. Because of the severe Bay of Bengal cyclones and tidal bores, the silts and clays are continually shifting. Such an active delta makes it difficult for vegetation, such as mangroves, to grow and also very difficult for navigation. Extensive tidal mud flats can be found at Cholla Bay, north of Puerto Peñasco, Mexico (B). The view is seaward to the mouth of the bay. A tidal range of from 3.05 to 6.10 meters (10 to 20 feet) exists at the northern end of the Gulf of California. Photographs by the author, December 1957 and November 24, 1972 (see p. 37).

Plate 133. Tidal mudflats extend across a small bay at Abel Tasman National Park on South Island, New Zealand. At high tide most of these mudflats are covered. Photograph by the author, August 17, 1975 (*see* p. 37).

Plate 134. A very steep cobble beach occurs on Kaikoura Peninsula, South Island, New Zealand. This high-energy coast receives the full force of storm waves moving across the Pacific Ocean. Many of these boulders have not yet been worn into more rounded shapes as those shown in Plate 135. On shingle beaches, the stones are usually flattened and often fit together almost like desert pavement. Photograph by the author, September 19, 1975 (see p. 37).

Plate 135. Very rounded gravels and boulders were found on a beach north of Miyazaki, Japan, on the island of Kyushu. Photograph by the author, October 1960 (*see* p. 37).

Plate 136. A gravel and sand pocket beach at Cabo de Espichel, Portugal, is shown here. The rock for the beach is derived from sedimentary sandstone and limestone headlands that extend to the sea. Note how an area of fines occurs in the middle of the beach where wave energy is much less. Photograph by the author, June 2, 1973 (see p. 37).

Plate 137. White coral sand beaches are common on many tropical coasts. This view shows a coral sand beach with scattered coquina rock on the south side of Grand Bahama Island. Photograph by the author, January 6, 1979 (see p. 37).

Plate 138. Small pocket beaches between headlands nearly always have their source of sand from nearby rocky headlands. Quartz sand for the pocket beach at Tossa de Mar, Spain, comes from the very old crystalline granitic rocks that make up the headlands along the Costa Brava (see Plate 136). Photograph by the author, June 3, 1973 (see p. 37).

Plate 139. Two small rivers feed the coast with sand of terrigenous origin near Bamburgh Castle on the coast of Northumberland, England. The finer quartz grains are carried inland by winds to form low, vegetated dunes. Photograph courtesy of the British Tourist Authority (see p. 37).

Plate 140. Black sand basalt beaches are common along the south coast of the large island of Hawaii. This view is of a beach near Kalapana Park. Photograph by the author, July 1965 (see p. 38).

Plate 141. Light pumice beaches and dark volcanic beaches can often be found along the coast of Japan. This view shows coarse volcanic material being brought to the shore south of Choshi on Honshu Island, Japan. Photograph by the author, November 1968 (see p. 38).

Plate 142. Where large forests grow on coasts or active lumbering operations take place, coasts get piled high with sawn timber or broken-up logs. Such is the case along the beach at Kalaloch, Washington. Photograph by the author, August 1965 (see p. 38).

Plate 143. On the south side of Lyttleton Harbor, New Zealand, a small bayhead beach occurs at Camp Bay. The interesting feature at this site is that the river has brought coarse material to the shore and this has left a zone of gravels in the middle of the beach, with fines occurring on either side. If there were more energy in the bay, it would rearrange these deposits. Photograph by the author, September 13, 1975 (see p. 38).

Plate 144. A poorly developed bayside beach occurs along the north shore of Kaikoura Peninsula, South Island, New Zealand. This beach is connected with a series of uplifted low marine platforms that occur around the peninsula (see Plate 78). Photograph by the author, September 19, 1975 (see p. 38).

Plate 145. Small pocket beaches can often be found along irregular rocky coasts. Finer sands get carried into the more quiet waters of the coves and bays. This picture shows small pocket beaches along the west coast of South Island, New Zealand, south of Charleston. Photograph by the author, August 3, 1975 (see p. 38).

Plate 146. Miles and miles of long, straight beaches occur around the world, such as the Makrān coast of Pakistan and Iran. The view shown here is west of Karāchi, Pakistan. An excellent series of beach ridges can be found here. Photograph courtesy of U.S. Geological Survey, 1953 (see p. 38).

Plate 147. South of the Banks Peninsula at Birdlings Flat, South Island, New Zealand, a series of accretion (beach) ridges have been developing as the coast progrades. Abundant sediment brought down from the nearby Southern Alps has helped this coast to grow rapidly. Note how the large lagoon, Lake Ellesmere, has been closed off by the growth of the beach ridges. The eroded hills of the Banks Peninsula are in the distance (see Plate 77). Photograph by Robert Kirk (see p. 38).

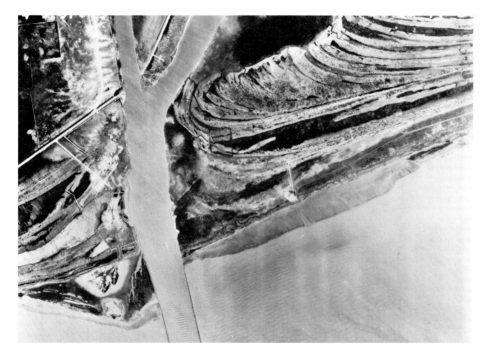

Plate 148. A series of beach ridges called cheniers are found on top of a muddy substratum in coastal Louisiana at Cameron. They record progressive changes in the configuration of the shoreline as it advanced seaward during the last 3,000 years. Photograph courtesy of U.S. Geological Survey, April 5, 1957 (see p. 39).

Plate 149. Beach plains and wide coastal plains are the result of waves and currents carrying abundant material, usually sand, and depositing it in low-energy areas such as behind headlands and terraces. This view shows a very wide coastal plain behind an uplifted terrace at Konārak, Iran. The distance across this marine-deposited plain is nearly 14.5 kilometers (9 miles). Photograph by the author, October 12, 1968 (see p. 39).

Plate 150. Along the north coast of Yucatan, east of Progreso, there is a wide sandy beach plain. Much of the sand on this beach is derived from shells and small pieces of coral; the beach contains more calcareous sand than terrigenous. Photograph by the author, January 9, 1973 (see p. 39).

Plate 151. During storms, waves have the ability to throw stones higher up on a beach, beyond the swash limit. This photograph shows the very coarse gravel beach and berm at Dungeness, England. Because this cuspate foreland jets a considerable distance into the sea, it is a high-energy coast. Photograph by the author, December 6, 1975 (see p. 39).

Plate 152. A broad depositional platform can be found along the north shore of the Gaspé Peninsula at Mont. St. Pierre, Canada. Erosion from the cliffs in the background has contributed material to this beach. Note that the beach has a convex profile, because high uprush carries material past the top of the normal beach face and deposits it on the outer edge of the backshore zone. Photograph by the author, August 13, 1972 (see p. 40).

A

B

Plate 153. At Bethany Beach, Delaware, the beach profile changes from season to season. In the summer, the beach tends to build out as gentle waves deposit material (A), but, during severe storms such as hurri-canes and in the winter, the beach erodes and a wave-cut scarp is created. A hurricane off the coast in August 1963 destroyed the beach (B). Photographs by the author, July 10, 1963 and August 12, 1963 (see p. 40).

A

B

Plate 154. Well-formed beach cusps were observed at Dana Point, California, on a March day in 1976 (A). Although the sea was relatively calm at the time, storm waves a day or two earlier had moved against the upper beach. Coarse material was moved to the horns, but the finer sand occupies the bay or floor in the depression between the horns. These are large beach cusps, indicating waves of considerable height and length. Beach cusps with very sharp divisions of material are found on a beach north of Kaikoura Peninsula, South Island, New Zealand (B). Photographs by the author, March 17, 1976 and September 21, 1975 (see p. 40).

Plate 155. Indurated beach rock occurs near Tangalla on the south coast of Ceylon. This beach rock consists of coarse-grained, fairly uniform quartz sand. At high tide this outcrop of rock is completely covered. Photograph by the author, January 15, 1972 (see p. 40).

Plate 156. The inner side of beach rock, where it disappears under the beach, is the youngest and most friable part of the rock; the oldest, most indurated bands are farthest seaward. The poorly indurated inner part of a beach rock outcrop is seen here on the beach at Boca Vieja on the north coast of Puerto Rico. Photograph by the author, June 17, 1971 (see p. 41).

Plate 157. The coast of Guadeloupe, especially the eastern portion of the island, is a classic beach rock area. Thick layers of beach rock with steeply dipping beds are found there. This photograph shows the beach rock clos-ing off a small lagoon at Pointe des Chateaux, Guade-loupe. Photograph by the author, June 22, 1971 (see p. 41).

Plate 158. Some beach rock outcrops are covered with green algae. At one time algae was thought to be respon-sible for cementation, but many areas with beach rock do not show any signs of organic cementation. This expo-sure of beach rock is on the inner side of a small bay north of Manati at Punta Marchiquita, on the north coast of Puerto Rico. Photograph by the author, December 29, 1965 (see p. 41).

Plate 159. A variety of cemented swamp and alluvial deposits can be classified under lagoon rock, which is similar in many ways to beach rock but is composed of muds and clays and usually found in tidal marshes rather than on the beach. An indurated lagoon rock outcrop was found north of Kino Bay at Santa Rosa point, on the Gulf of California coast of Mexico. Photograph by the author, May 24, 1972 (see p. 41).

Plate 160. Coquina and some beach rock look very similar although their origin may be entirely different. At Bahia de los Meurtos, near the southern tip of Baja California, Mexico, there is an extensive, nearly flat platform of cemented rock with a shell matrix. Because of the environment of this rock outcrop, it was thought to be of marine origin. But probably later, when it was uplifted and exposed to water percolating through its porous limestone, it was cemented. Photograph by the author, December 29, 1970 (see p. 41).

Plate 161. The internal structure of a megaripple on an intertidal sand flat at Plum Island, Massachusetts is shown here. The ebb current flowed from right to left. Scale is 0.3048 meter (one foot). Caption and photograph by Miles O. Hayes, 1971 (see p. 41).

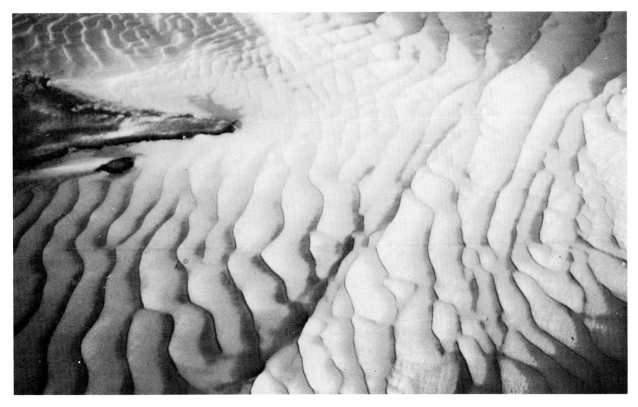

Plate 162. Megaripples and sand waves are large, gentle ripplelike features usually composed of sand that occur in nearshore marine situations formed by tidal currents. This photograph shows flood-oriented sand waves in the Parker River Estuary, Massachusetts. Flood current is moving from right to left. Scale is 1.52 meters (5 feet) and the wave length of sand waves averages between 12 and 24 meters (40 and 80 feet). Caption and photograph by Miles O. Hayes, 1971 (see p. 41).

Plate 163. Where tidal ranges are large, as is the case around the beach at Sigar Bay, South Island, New Zealand, megaripples and sand waves become exposed at low water. The smaller forms on the tidal flats (center right) are megaripples, the larger features (more to the left) are sand waves. Photograph by the author, August 10, 1975 (see p. 41).

Plate 164. Oscillatory wave ripples with symmetrical slopes, sharp crests, and rounded troughs are seen here on a tidal flat to the west of Puerto Peñasco at Cholla Bay, Mexico. These wave ripples result from the to-and-fro movement of the sea bottom produced by the passage and movement of waves. Tidal range in this area is as much as 6.10 meters (20 feet). Photograph by the author, November 24, 1972 (see p. 41).

Plate 165. Current ripples generally are asymmetrical and their crests are more rounded than wave-formed ripples. These cross-current ripples were found at low tide on a tidal flat at the north tip of Ocean City, New Jersey. The gentle slope face is the direction from which the current is moving. The steep slope is the angle of rest of the sand. Photograph by the author, December 26, 1974 (see p. 41).

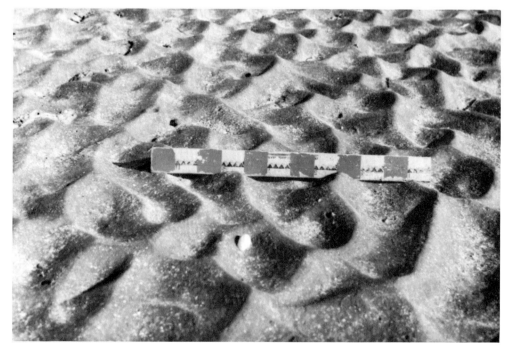

Plate 166. Current ripple marks form a symmetrical, irregular pattern when the velocity in the third stage begins to decrease. These irregular crests move down-stream with the current. These antidunes were found at Cholla Bay, Mexico, north of Puerto Peñasco. Photograph by the author, November 24, 1972 (see p. 42).

Plate 167. This photograph shows ripples on a tidal mudflat on the shore of Manukau Harbor, a few kilometers south of Auckland, New Zealand, The features form with runoff of water across the low 0.8-to-1.6-kilometer (0.5-to-1-mile) wide mudflat. The ripples are aligned transverse to the flow of water. A boulder interfering with the ripples can be seen clearly here. Caption and photograph by R. V. Fisher (see p. 42).

Plate 168. Oscillation and current ripples occur as compound forms on a wide sandy beach at the northern tip of Ocean City, New Jersey. Complex sand ripples are more common than simple forms. Photograph by the author, December 26, 1974 (see p. 42).

Plate 169. Lunate-linguoid ripples, even more complex than the ripples in Plate 168, were found on a tidal flat in the Parker River Estuary, Massachusetts. These ripples were formed by ebb currents. The wave length of these ripples is approximately 15.2 centimeters (6 inches). Photograph by Miles O. Hayes, 1971 (see p. 42).

Plate 170. Miniature river systems, called rill marks, occur on a beach at the nothern tip of Ocean City, New Jersey. As water flows down the beach to the sea, it often forms patterns that resemble branching plant stems. Photograph by the author, April 26, 1979 (see p. 42).

Plate 171. Rills and ripples often are closely associated, as is shown in this photograph. This view is of a beach at Puerto Peñasco, Mexico, at the head of the Gulf of California. Photograph by the author, November 30, 1974 (see p. 42).

Plate 172. These erosional rills were created by groundwater discharge from the beach-face area during ebb tide at Hampton Beach, New Hampshire. Small ditches, concave toward the lower part of the beach, form in the sand. Caption and photograph by Miles O. Hayes, 1971 (see p. 42).

Plate 173. This photograph shows swash marks on a beach face at Plum Island, Massachusetts. These very small coastal features do not attract very much attention, and only when they push coarser material ahead of them can they be easily detected. Caption and photograph by Miles O. Hayes, 1971 (see p. 42).

Plate 174. Crossbedding of a beach ridge on Crane Beach, Massachusetts, is shown here. This photograph was taken at low tide. The coarse ground layers consist of small pebbles, and the fine-grained layers are sand. Caption and photograph by Miles O. Hayes, 1971 (see p. 42).

Plate 175. This view is a cross-section of bimodal crossbedding at Nauset Beach, near Chatham, Cape Cod, Massachusetts. The wave-caused dark mineral accumulation was deposited during storms, and the whiter, finer quartz sand layers were deposited during quieter beach conditions. Photograph by J.V.A. Trumbull and John C. Hathaway, 1968 (see p. 42).

Plate 176. This photograph shows an isolated imbricated pebble (with current crescent) on Nauset Beach, Massachusetts. Current moved from right to left. Note the lineation of the sand grains in the lower right. Caption and photograph by Miles O. Hayes, 1971 (see p. 42).

Plate 177. Wind blowing across a beach can form wind shadows and sand ripples as can be seen on this photograph taken at Brigantine Beach, New Jersey. Photograph by the author, December 24, 1973 (see p. 42).

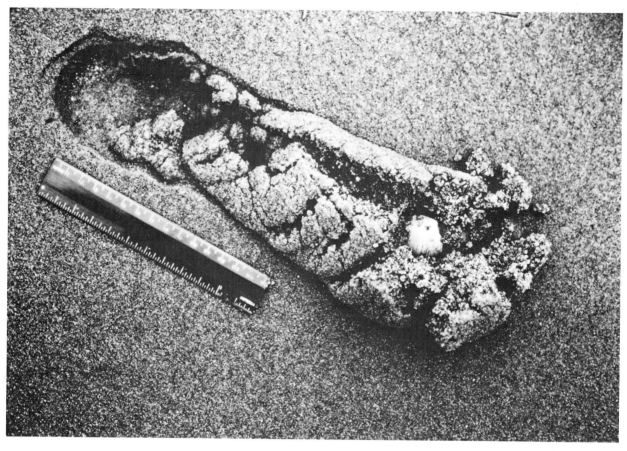

Plate 178. This photograph shows a gastropod burrowing in beach sand at Plum Island, Massachusetts. Scale is 0.30 meter (1 foot). Caption and photograph by Miles O. Hayes, 1971 (see p. 42).

Plate 179. Ice wedges in the sand on a day in March 1968 on Fire Island, Long Island, New York can be seen here. Many different shapes and forms of snow and ice can be created on a beach in the winter. Photograph by the author, March 10, 1968 (see p. 42).

Plate 180. This photograph is a closeup of live reef-top corals on Three Isles Key, off the northeast coast of Australia. This is a typical view of the miles and miles of shallow water reefs along the Great Barrier Reef. Photograph by David Hopley (*see* p. 43).

Plate 181. The island of Holbourne, which is off the north Queensland coast, 30 kilometers (19 miles) east of Bowen, has a large fringing reef. This photograph shows the exposed, inner, dead coral reef platform covered with algae, most of which is now also dead due to the destructive nature of tropical cyclones or to a sudden drop in water level caused by the breaking of the shingle barrier rim. The hills in the background are granitic bedrock, part of the continental rocks appearing as islands off the northeast coast of Australia. Photograph by David Hopley (*see* p. 43).

Plate 182. Many excellent examples of fringing reefs can be found. This photograph depicts spectacular fringing reefs along the north shore of Oahu, Hawaii, near Kahana Bay. There is a freshwater break in the reef where a small stream enters the sea. Photograph by Everett A. Wingert, December 12, 1952 (see p. 43).

Plate 183. One of the most picturesque fringing reefs occurs at Hanauma Bay on the island of Oahu, Hawaii. The reef is growing inside Koko Head Crater, an old volcano that has been breached on one side of its rim by the sea. Photograph by the author, July 1965 (see p. 43).

Plate 184. An almost ovoid-reef platform surrounds an atoll in the Maldives. This island appears as a dot in the Indian Ocean, southwest of India. Photograph by Kenneth Boston, June 1978 (see p. 43).

Plate 185. This photograph shows small patch reefs, which can be found associated with the main Great Barrier Reef off the northeast coast of Australia. This photograph was taken over Fairfax reef. These patch reefs can be seen as dark bands or circles around sand and shingle cays. In time they will grow and form one continuous reef system. Photograph by David Hopley (see p. 43).

A

B

Plate 186. These two photographs show linear coral reef platforms in two distant locations. Several atolls of the Maldive islands can be seen here (A). Mahé Island is in the foreground with Hulule Island in the distance. The curving arc of the Florida Keys can be seen on the NASA space photograph (B). The oolitic limestone platform to the southwest, of which Key West is a part, is quite different from the coral keys that extend northeast to the Florida mainland. Photographs by Kenneth Boston and courtesy of NASA (see p. 44).

Plate 187. Midway Island is representative of mid-Pacific type atolls, which rise in deep ocean basins from isolated volcanic cones (seamounts or guyots) with up to 2,000 meters (6,562 feet) of accumulated reef growth that may date back to the Cretaceous period. Photograph by the author, 1958 (see p. 44).

Plate 188. This is a typical fringing reef found around high continental islands off the northeast coast of Queensland, Australia. The smaller island in the foreground is Fly Island, and behind it is Hasannah Island. These islands are made up of remnants or outliers of the more resistant granitic rock found on the mainland. The fringing reefs grow best on the seaward side of these islands where they receive more food brought by waves and currents. Photograph by David Hopley (see p. 44).

Plate 189. This is an aerial view of a single sand cay, largely nonvegetated, near Lizard Island, off the north- east coast of Australia. The island is about 4.8 kilometers (3 miles) long. Photograph by David Hopley (see p. 44).

Plate 190. White coral breccia or coral conglomerate cemented into an eolitic limestone at Cayo Icacos, an island off the northeast coast of Puerto Rico, is shown here. The very white, layered rock is similar in many ways to the white limestone rock of the Bahamas. Photograph by the author, January 14, 1974 (see p. 44).

Plate 191. Sand cays with cemented ramparts consist- ing of eolianite or oolitic limestone generally have more vegetation than the cays made up purely of sand. La Cordillera Islands, off the northeast coast of Puerto Rico, represent an example of this type of cay. Note the lagoon fringed by mangrove trees that occurs in the interior (see Plate 201). Photograph by the author, January 13, 1974 (see p. 44).

Plate 192. An emergent coral-reef platform from the Pleistocene occurs at White Bay, east of Falmouth, on the north coast of Jamaica. This extensive dead coral reef is partially covered at high tide but not enough water is present then for the coral to grow. This appears to be an uplifted platform. Photograph by the author, January 8, 1975 (see p. 44).

Plate 193. Algae-covered beach rock at Bahia de Palma, near the city of Palma on the island of Mallorca in the western Mediterranean is shown here. This green algae can become very slippery when saturated with water. Photograph by the author, June 6, 1973 (see p. 45).

Plate 194. This photograph shows small erosional terraces rimmed by algae at Punta Marchiquita, Puerto Rico. These carollinelike algae can tolerate strong wave action if the waves are not too effectively armed with abrasive material. Photograph by the author, June 17, 1971 (see p. 45).

Plate 195. This photograph shows algae-covered bedrock at Devil's Punchbowl State Park along the northwest coast of Oregon. This small area of organisms has been set aside as a "seagarden." It is an excellent location to observe marine life of the Pacific Northwest Coast. Photograph by the author, July 16, 1979 (see p. 45).

Plate 196. A serpulid reef, built by the cementing of worm tubes in the rocks, is shown here on the south coast of Kauai, Hawaii. This reef occurs in patches for nearly 16 kilometers (10 miles) along the coast. Many marine organisms are associated with the worms in this very active tidal zone. Photograph by the author, July 1965 (see p. 45).

Plate 197. An exposed oyster reef, possibly of Pleisto-cene age, occurs on the shore of Bahia de los Muertos, near the southern tip of Baja California, Mexico. Uplift of this reef is on the order of 4.57 to 7.62 meters (15 to 25 feet). This is an active tectonic region with occasional earthquakes occurring south of La Paz. Photograph by the author, December 29, 1970 (see p. 45).

Plate 198. This photograph shows kelp and seaweed washed up on a pocket beach at Monterey, California. Photograph by the author, August 1965 (see p. 45).

Plate 199. The New Zealand coast has a great deal of kelp and seaweed lining the shore. This photograph shows kelp growing in a tidal pool on Kaikoura Penin- sula, South Island, New Zealand. Photograph by the author, September 21, 1975 (see p. 45).

Plate 200. A band of mangrove forests along the coast of southwest Florida is shown here. The tallest trees reach heights of 23 meters (75 feet) with trunks 1.22 meters (4 feet) in diameter. Most of the trees are *Rhi-zophora*, which have large prop roots. Some of the largest mangrove forests are found in Everglades National Park. Photograph courtesy of NASA, March 22, 1973 (see p. 46).

Plate 201. A *Rhizophora* mangrove swamp growing in a protected tidal lagoon on the island of Yap in the U.S. Pacific Island Trust Territory can be seen here. At low tide most of the roots are exposed and at high water the depth in the lagoon is about 0.91 meters (3 feet). Photograph by Warren Hamilton (see p. 46).

Plate 202. Mangrove swamps often extend inland up to 64 kilometers (40 miles) along many tidal rivers. Near Topolobampo, on the west coast of Mexico, narrow ribbons of mangrove swamp follow small rivers inland even in semiarid to arid environments. Two species of mangroves can be distinguished by two different shades of gray. The darker *Rhizophora* mangroves grow in deeper water and are found closer to the river. The lighter *Avicennia* mangroves extend farther out but are still in the tidal zone. Photograph by the author, December 24, 1970 (see p. 46).

Plate 203. The prop roots of *Rhizophora* mangroves form a dense tangled mass that is difficult to penetrate. Few large animals venture into this tangle of air-breathing roots. At White Bay, on the north coast of Jamaica, the prop roots spread out several meters from the trunks of the trees. Photograph by the author, January 8, 1975 (see p. 46).

Plate 204. The red mangrove, *Rhizophora,* has prop roots that branch out from its trunk like the legs of a tarantula. These large mangrove trees and nipa palms were found on the mudflats in the delta of the Ganges River in Bangladesh. Photograph by the author, October 1958 (see p. 46).

Plate 205. *Avicennia* mangroves have spikelike pneumataphores that project from several centimeters to a meter or two above the mud floor. At the north tip of La Paz Bay, on Baja California, these air-breathing roots are a considerable distance from the trees. Photograph by the author, December 31, 1970 (see p. 46).

Plate 206. Different species of mangroves have different root systems. This large buttress system is *Pelliciera rhizophorae*. The photograph was taken along the Pacific coast of Colombia, north of the San Juan River Delta. Caption and photograph by Robert C. West (see p. 46).

Plate 207. Mangroves are often hit by destructive hurricanes and typhoons. In this photograph, mangroves in Everglades National Park, Florida, have been killed by destructive winds breaking down the larger trees. Apparently when too many trees die and decay, a tannic acid forms in the water that kills other mangroves. Thus, after a particularly destructive storm, a whole region of mangroves will die. Photograph by the author, March 24, 1968 (see p. 46).

Plate 208. Mangrove trees in this photograph are being eroded on the north shore of Miāni Lagoon, 80 kilometers (50 miles) west of Karāchi, Pakistan. A close look at the root system reveals oysters, clams, and barnacles still clinging to their surfaces. In the foreground is the outrigger of a local fishing boat. Photograph by the author, January 24, 1961 (see p. 46).

Plate 209. Sand migrating across barrier spits and bars often advances onto mangrove thickets. Here, sand is moving against a mangrove thicket on a large spit to the west of Karāchi, Pakistan, near the fishing village of Son-miāni. Trees in this area do not grow large because of a harsh, arid climate and occasional frosts. Photograph by the author, September 23, 1945 (see p. 47).

Plate 210. Along desert coasts, such as those of Pakistan, Iran, and Saudi Arabia, small mangrove shrubs offer year-round lush vegetation for browse animals such as camels. Here, camels are walking along the edges of tidal mudflats trying to reach the leaves of the trees without getting stuck. Many animals die when their large feet get bogged down in the oozy muds; others lay on their sides and kick themselves out. This photograph was taken on the Iran-Pakistan border in the Dasht River Delta. Photograph by the author, October 23, 1968 (see p. 47).

Plate 211. Fossilized mangrove roots between 1,000 and 2,000 years old have been found on the northeast shore of Key Biscayne, Florida. This is one of the first reported occurrences of the fossilization of mangroves, because these plants usually decay very rapidly in the warmth of the muds and clays. This photograph shows the edge of a reef with a lattice structure made by horizontal and vertical rods of the old root system. Photograph by J. E. Hoffmeister and H. G. Multer, 1964 (see p. 47).

Plate 212. Other lower plants such as brackish-water ferns, low, woody shrubs, and nipa palms are often associated with mangroves in tidal environments. In south and southeast Asia, nipa palms *(Nipa fruticans)* form dense masses of fronds, which spring directly from a low stump. The fronds are a common thatching material in south Asia, and the sap is used to make gur or toddy. The leaf stalks give buouancy to sundri logs and are used for fishing floats. This photograph was taken in the Sundarbans of Bangladesh, south of the town of Khulna. Photograph by the author, January 1957 (see p. 47).

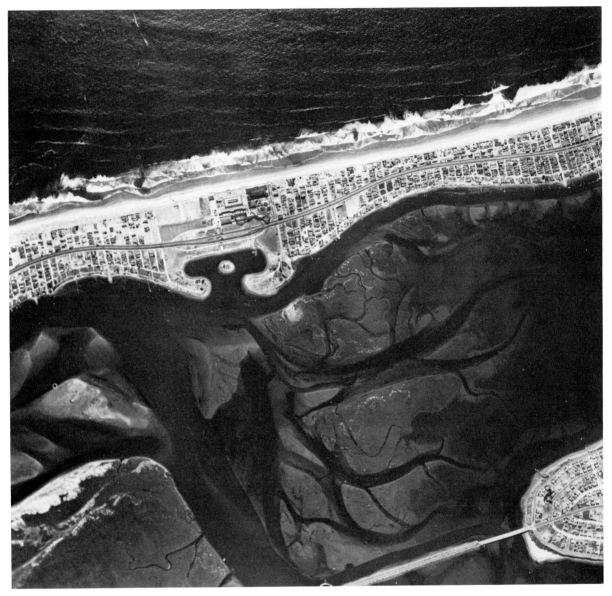

Plate 213. Tidal channels take on a particular pattern of sharp bends and 90° turns as a stream winds through a marsh area. This pattern develops because of the in-and-out flow of water. This photograph shows large tidal channels along the coast in Sussex County, to the west of Plum Island, Massachusetts. Photograph courtesy of U.S. Geological Survey, November 1, 1938 (see p. 47).

Plate 214. The marsh grass *Spartina* has its largest concentration along the Atlantic Ocean with an almost continuous growth from eastern Canada to Brazil. Here, a winter scene of marsh grass can be seen near the Great Egg Harbor Inlet of southern New Jersey. Photograph by the author, January 5, 1975 (see p. 47).

Plate 215. This photograph depicts tidal creek meanders in a salt marsh of the Hampton Estuary, New Hampshire. The abandoned meander loop has filled with fine-grained mud. Photograph by Miles O. Hayes, 1971 (see p. 47).

Plate 216. A large salt marsh occurs behind Plum Island, Massachusetts. Protected by the sand barrier, the tidal zone fills with fine-grained muds and clays and provides an excellent environment for salt grass to grow. Photograph by Miles O. Hayes, 1971 (see p. 47).

Plate 217. On the south coast of Jamaica tidal marshes extend into many bays. This view is near the town of Gut River along the coast of Long Bay. Photograph by the author, January 12, 1975 (see p. 47).

Plate 218. Along the north coast of Australia, to the west of Darwin, a vast marsh area has developed on the open, shallow water around Joseph Bonaparte Gulf. Few barrier bars and spits have developed along this coastal stretch. Scientists have only recently begun to study this isolated, hostile region. Photograph courtesy of the Department of Lands and Surveys, Government of Australia (see p. 47).

Plate 219. The salt marshes near Barnegat in southern New Jersey have a number of circular, residual, enclosed depressions and ponds that often become dry salt pans when the tide is out and fill with water at high tide. With high evaporation many become hypersaline. The origin of many of these ponds is still unknown. Photograph by the author, (see p. 47).

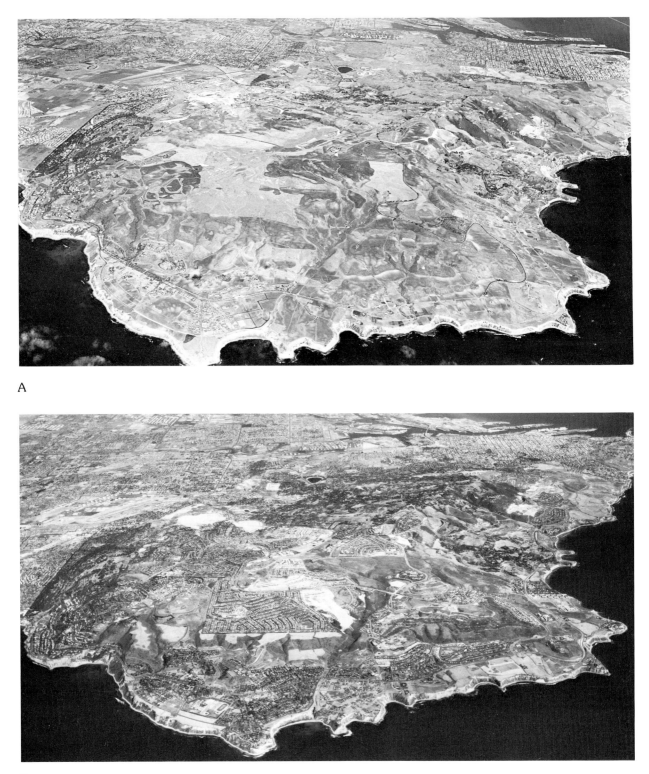

A

B

Plate 220. The coast of California has seen phenomenal development in the last sixteen years. These two photographs show very rapid growth at Palos Verdes Hills, California. In (A) large sections of nearly empty land can be seen across the coastal terraces. Development extends from both ends along the coast road. By 1969, development had not only filled in most of the lower terraces but was rapidly extending up the slopes to the higher terraces farther inland (B). Photographs by Francis P. Shepard, September 27, 1953 and October 7, 1969 (see p. 50).

Plate 221. The east coast of the United States can be considered a vanishing shoreline, because of the erosion of the beaches and the filling in of coastal marshes and lagoons for commercial and residential development. A typical example is in southern New Jersey, near Stone Harbor, where large sections of tidal marshland have been dredged for marinas and the fill used to raise the level of the land for housing developments. Before control of mosquitos through spraying took place, such residential development was impossible, but in the last twenty years great changes have been made. Recent restrictions on tidal-marsh use by the state legislators may curb this rapid destruction of the shore zone; the state of New Jersey, for example is at last putting controls on the use of tidelands. Photograph by the author, October 10, 1964 (see p. 50).

A

B

Plate 222. These two photographs illustrate how quickly settlement can move onto a fragile natural environment. Up until 1924 (A), the sand dunes at Palisades del Rey, California, were largely undisturbed except for one road that lead to a lighthouse and the Southern Pacific Railroad that followed the shoreline. But by 1928 (B), California was changing very rapidly and the development of Palisades del Rey was very quickly moving across the dunes with new roads and structures. View is looking south. Photographs by Francis P. Shepard, about 1924 and August 28, 1928 (see p. 50).

Plate 223. People in their efforts to get a view of the ocean have built houses on top of dunes near Crescent Beach, Florida. The low dunes have been leveled off, but erosion of the sand presents a problem. Stakes, vegetation stumps, and debris are placed around the structures to help hold the sand in place. To the left natural grasses on the dunes are much more successful. Photograph by the author, August 1969 (see p. 50).

Plate 224. Collection of sea water into ponds where the water evaporates and the salt remains is an ancient practice. Along the coast of Lebanon, the ancient Phoenicians used windmills to draw water into the ponds. This practice is still carried on by the descendants of these past traders. Photograph by the author, December 20, 1968 (see p. 50).

Plate 225. A serious oil spill from a tanker occurred at the entrance to San Francisco Harbor. This very clear photograph shows the dark circular bands of the thick pollutant. The date of this photograph is unknown. Photograph by John Estes (see p. 51).

Plate 226. This photograph shows an oil discharge from a ship at the San Diego Naval Base. Color photography can be used to reveal very thin oil slicks on overcast days. Blue filtered photography on black and white film is very useful for oil slick detection. Note the *Rhodamine WT* dye released from the end of the pier at the center of the photograph. Caption and photograph by R. T. Welch (see p. 51).

Plate 227. Because of seepage from offshore drilling and oil leakage from ships, large areas of the California coast have patches of oil and tar on the beaches and rock outcrops that are covered at high tide. This oil and tar residue was particularly bad at Goleta State Beach, west of Santa Barbara, in 1974. Photograph by the author, August 8, 1974 (see p. 51).

Plate 228. Large industrial complexes, such as the iron and steel plant at Sparrow's Point, Baltimore, Maryland, have contributed to the pollution of the Patapsco River and Chesapeake Bay. This photograph, taken in 1966, shows waste products being dumped off the end of the pier. Photograph courtesy of the Department of Geography, Clark University, Worcester, Massachusetts, 1966 (see p. 51).

Plate 229. The techniques of remote sensing, using color and black and white film, reveal how much people have polluted coastal regions. This photograph reveals the extent of pollution on marsh environments in the tidal salt marsh near Barnegat, New Jersey. The different shades of gray measure the health of the vegetation. Dark tones indicate healthy vegetation, and light gray and white areas, along canals and around bays, indicate vegetation that is suffering from pollution or too much salt. This photograph was taken from a helicopter that was spraying insecticide to kill mosquitos. Fortunately, DDT is no longer used as an insecticide along the east coast of the United States. Photograph by the author, August 7, 1971 (see p. 51).

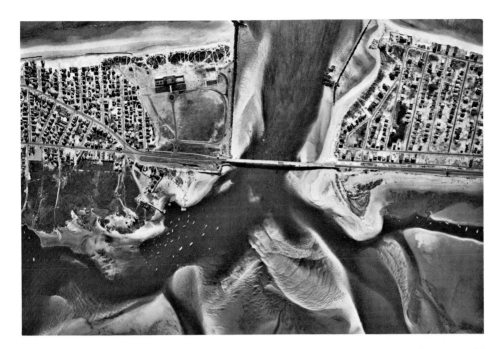

Plate 230. Jetties are long, rock or concrete structures built to protect the entrance to harbors, estuaries, lakes, or lagoons. Here, rock jetties have been built along Hampton Harbor Inlet to keep this estuary open to the Hampton River and tidal lagoons, which are used as small boat harbors. Small boats can be seen to the upper right of the bridge. These jetties have not been very successful as can be seen by the deposition in the inlet. Photograph courtesy of U.S. Geological Survey, August 19, 1958 (see p. 52).

Plate 231. Two long jetties have been built north of Cape May, New Jersey, to keep the entrance to the Cape May Canal open. This canal is a short cut between the Atlantic Ocean and Delaware Bay for small craft. The jetties were started about twenty years ago. The U.S. Army Corps of Engineers failed to realize that such a barrier would stop normal longshore drift of sand to the south. As a result, a wide sandy beach extends to the resorts of Wildwood Crest and Wildwood, but Cape May Point is being starved of sand, and severe erosion of the beaches and town is taking place. Photograph by the author, 1966 (see p. 52).

A

B

Plate 232. A very old breakwater, which has been re-built in recent years, occurs at the historic town of Byblos, Lebonon (A). The harbor was used by small Phoenician sailing ships for hundreds of years. This is one of the oldest, continuously used ports in the world. Modern breakwaters have been constructed at Tel Aviv, Israel, to encourage sand to form tombolos, which, in turn, create new beaches (B). Photographs by the author, February 27, 1972 and June 13, 1973 (see p. 52).

Plate 233. Seawalls are built along the shore to prevent erosion from wave action. This photograph shows a large, concrete seawall at Lynn, Massachusetts, built to prevent waves from undermining and eroding the town and coast road. Photograph by the author, August 11, 1972 (see p. 53).

Plate 234. This photograph shows a sloping seawall being repaired at Lynn, Massachusetts. Life of the old seawall was about twenty years. The new seawall is constructed as a series of steps to avoid undercutting and to provide a convenient way to the beach. Photograph by the author, June 1966 (see p. 53).

Plate 235. Bulkheads and revertments are built along the coast to protect shore structures or roads from wave action or currents. This photograph depicts a series of pilings used as a bulkhead to prevent waves from reaching new houses that have been built on stilts at Avalon, New Jersey. Photograph by the author, August 1967 (see p. 53).

Plate 236. These groins along the coast of Ocean City, New Jersey, were built to trap some of the sand that moves along the shore by littoral drift. They have not been very successful. Sand still has to be pumped onto the beach each spring to provide beaches for the tourist season. Photograph by the author, August 25, 1973 (see p. 53).

Plate 237. A groin field occurs along the east coast of Staten Island, New York, where the coast has been eroding severely as tides and currents circulate in Lower Bay, at the entrance to New York Harbor. This groin field has been successful in trapping sand at Midland and South beaches, but in other coastal areas these engineering structures have not been so successful. Photograph by the author, April 1967 (see p. 53).

Plate 238. There are a variety of methods used to stop coastal erosion, one of which is to dump rubble over a cliff to help absorb wave energy. This method was used at Sunset Cliffs in San Diego, California. Photograph by the author, July 1, 1972 (see p. 54).

Plate 239. At Rehobeth Beach, Delaware, the U.S. Army Corps of Engineers has been pumping find sand from the lagoon areas onto the resort beach. This process has been going on for a number of years and will probably need to be continued for a number of years to come. Photograph by the author, August 10, 1963 (see p. 54).

Plate 240. Dunes are being built by the placement of 1.22-meter (4-foot) snow fences along Cape Hatteras National Seashore, North Carolina, by the U.S. Army Corps of Engineers. The fences have been successful, as can be seen here. Photograph by the author, July 1963 (see p. 54).

Plate 241. Several different types of fences have been put up to trap sand and form dunes along the east coast of the United States. On Fire Island, Long Island, snow fences were put up to form dunes but trapped snow on a winter day instead. Photograph by the author, March 1968 (see p. 54).

A

B

Plate 242. These two views show very little change in the coast at Sunset Cliffs, near Point Loma, San Diego, California, between March 1968 (A) and March 1978 (B). Note that even the gravel at the base of the cliffs has changed very little in ten years. Photograph by Francis P. Shepard, March 1968, and the author, March 1978 (see p. 56).

A

B

Plate 243. These two pictures illustrate the filled state of a small beach at Scripps Oceanographic Institution, La Jolla, California, in August 1938 (A) and the cut state in March 1938 (B). Note that the rocks are almost entirely covered in (A). Photographs by Francis P. Shepard (see p. 56).

Plate 244. The March 1962 "northeaster" did a great deal of damage to the southern New Jersey coast. At Avalon the waves at high tide not only damaged the structures in the foreground but carried sand from the beach across the barrier island and deposited it around structures and even in the tidal lagoon in the background. In just three days this section of the coast had been significantly altered. Photograph by the author, March 24, 1962 (see p. 57).

Plate 245. This photograph shows what is left of a small hotel in La Pesca, Mexico, after the eye of Hurricane Anita passed over the fishing village on September 2, 1977. The 249 kilometers-per-hour (155 miles-per-hour) winds damaged most structures severely, even those built of concrete and stucco. Photograph by the author, January 8, 1978 (see p. 57).

Plate 246. Humans have been changing the coastlines of the world for thousands of years, but only recently have the changes been on such a grandiose scale. Today, entire lagoon and marsh areas are converted into enormous marinas, such as the large enterprise at the Municipal Yacht Harbor in San Diego, California. Photograph courtesy of Department of Geography, University of California, Los Angeles (see p. 57).

Plate 247. A significant change in the biotic environment of the Colorado River Delta has been caused by the use of so much river water for irrigation that salinity has greatly increased in the lower river region. This view shows the extensive salt flats that have formed recently at the mouth of the river. Photograph courtesy of department of Geography, University of California, Riverside (see p. 57).

References

Agassiz, A., 1903, On the Formation of Barriers and of the Different Types of Atolls, *Royal Soc. (London) Proc.* **71**:412-414.

Albertson, N. L., Y. B. Dai, R. A. Fensen, and H. Rouse, 1950, Diffusion of Submerged Jets, *Am. Soc. Civil Engineers Trans., Jour. Waterways and Harbors Div.* **115**:639-697.

Bascom, W. H., 1964, Waves and Beaches: The Dynamics of the Ocean Surface, Anchor Books, Doubleday & Co., Garden City, N. Y., 267 p.

Bates, C. C., 1953, Rational Theory of Delta Formation, *Am. Assoc. Petroleum Geologists Bull.* **37**:2119-2162.

Baulig, H., 1956, *Vocabulaire Franco-Anglo-Allemand de Geomorphologie,* Publ. Fac. Lettres No. 130, University of Strasbourg, Paris, 230 p.

Billings, M. P., 1954, *Structural Geology,* 2nd ed., Prentice-Hall, Englewood Cliffs, N. J., 514 p.

Bird, E. C. F., 1968, *Coasts,* MIT Press, Cambridge, Mass., 246 p.

Bloch, M. R., 1965, A Hypothesis for the Change of Ocean Levels Depending on the Albedo of the Polar Ice Caps, *Palaeogeography, Palaeoclimatology, Palaeoecology* **1**:127-142.

Bloom, A. L., 1978, *Geomorphology: A Systematic Analysis of Late Cenozoic Landforms,* Prentice-Hall, Englewood Cliffs, N.J., 510 p.

Bourcart, J., 1938, La Marge continentale, *Soc. Géol. France Bull.* **8**(5):393-474.

Burton, I., R. W. Kates, and R. E. Snead, 1969, The Human Ecology of Coastal Flood Hazard in Megalopolis, *Department of Geography Research Paper 115,* University of Chicago, Chicago, 196 p.

Carey, A. E., 1903, The Sanding-up of Tidal Harbours, *Inst. Civil Engineers Proc.* **156**:215-302.

Chapman, V. J., 1960, *Salt Marshes and Salt Deserts of the World,* Wiley Interscience, New York, 392 p.

Cotton, C. A., 1952, Criteria for the Classification of Coasts, *17th Internat. Geog. Congress Proc.,* Washington, D.C., pp. 315-345.

Curray, J. R., 1960, Sediments and History of Holocene Transgression, Continental Shelf, Northwest Gulf of Mexico, in *Recent Sediments, Northwest Gulf of Mexico,* F. P. Shepard et al., eds., American Association of Petroleum Geologists, Tulsa, Okla., pp. 221-266.

Curray, J. R., 1961, Late Quaternary Sea Level: A Discussion, *Geol. Soc. America Bull.* **72**:1701-1712.

Curray, J. R., F. P. Shepard, and H. H. Veeh, 1970, Late Quaternary Sea-Level Studies in Micronesia: CARMARSEL Expedition, *Geol. Soc. America Bull.* **81**:1865-1880.

Daly, R. A., 1915, The Glacial-Control Theory of Coral Reefs, *Am. Acad. Arts and Sci. Proc.* **51**(4):155-251.

Dana, J. D., 1849, in United States Exploring Expedition, During the Years 1838, 1839, 1840, 1842 and 1843, Under the Command of Charles Wilkes, vol. 10, Philadelphia, pp. 380-390.

Darwin, C., 1896, The Structure and Distribution of Coral Reefs, 3rd ed., Appleton, New York, 344 p.

Davies, J. L., 1973, *Geographical Variation in Coastal Development,* Hafner Publishing Co., New York, 204 p.

Davis, W. M., 1896, The Outline of Cape Cod, *Am. Acad. Arts and Sci. Proc.* **31**:303-332.

Davis, W. M., 1915, Shaler Memorial Study of Coral Reefs, *Am. Jour. Sci.* **40**:223-271.

Embleton, C., and C. A. M. King, 1968, *Glacial and Periglacial Geomorphology,* St. Martin's Press, New York, 608 p.

Evans, O. F., 1942, The Origin of Spits, Bars, and Related Structures, *Jour. Geology* **50**:846-863.

Fairbridge, R. W., 1950a, Recent and Pleistocene Coral Reefs of Australia, *Jour. Geology* **58**:330-401.

Fairbridge, R. W., 1950b, Landslide Patterns on Oceanic Volcanoes and Atolls, *Geog. Jour.* **115**:84-88.

Fairbridge, R. W., 1961, Eustatic Changes in Sea Level, in *Physics and Chemistry of the Earth,* vol. 4, L. H. Ahrens et al., eds., Pergamon Press, London, pp. 99-185.

Fairbridge, R. W., 1966, *The Encyclopedia of Oceanography,* Dowden, Hutchinson & Ross, Stroudsburg, Pa., 1021 p.

Fairbridge, R. W., 1968, *The Encyclopedia of Geomorphology,* Rinehold Book Corporation, New York, 1295 p.

Fairbridge, R. W., 1980, The Estuary: Its Definition and Geodynamic Cycle, in *Chemistry and Biogeochemistry of Estuaries,* E. Olausson and I. Cato, eds., Wiley-Interscience,

New York, pp. 1-35.

Flint, R. F., 1971, *Glacial and Quaternary Geology*, John Wiley and Sons, New York, 892 p.

Fujii, S., and N. Fuji, 1967, Postglacial Sea Level in the Japanese Island, *Jour. Geoscience* **10**:43-51.

Gabler, R. E., R. Sager, S. Brazier, and J. Pourciau, 1975, *Introduction to Physical Geography*, Rinehart Press, Holt, Rinehart & Winston, New York, 801 p.

Gilbert, G. K., 1885, Topographic Features of Lake Shores, *5th Annual Report*, U.S. Geological Survey, pp. 69-123.

Gresswell, R. K., 1957, *The Physical Geography of Beaches and Coastlines*, Hulton Educational Publications, London, 128 p.

Gross, M. G., 1972, *Oceanography: A View of the Earth*, Prentice-Hall, Englewood Cliffs, N.J., 581 p.

Guilcher, A., 1954, *Morphologie Littorale et Sous-Marine*, Presses Univ. France, Paris, 216 p.

Guilcher, A., 1958, *Coastal and Submarine Morphology*, B. W. Sparks and R. H. W. Kneese, trans., Methuen & Co., London, 274 p.

Gulliver, F. P., 1889, Shoreline Topography, *Am. Acad. Arts and Sci. Proc.* **34**:151-258.

Inman, D. L., and R. A. Bagnold, 1963, Beach and Nearshore Processes, Part II: Littoral Processes, in *The Sea*, M. N. Hill, ed., Wiley Interscience, New York, pp. 529-553.

Inman, D. L., and B. M. Brush, 1973, The Coastal Challenge, *Science* **181**:20-32.

Jelgersma, S., 1961, Holocene Sea Level Changes in the Netherlands, Meded. Geol. Stinchting Ser. C-VI-7, 100 p.

Jessen, O., 1943, Die Randschwellen der Kontinente, *Peter manns Geog. Mitt.* **241**:1-205.

Johnson, D. W., 1919, *Shore Processes and Shoreline Development*, John Wiley and Sons, New York, 584 p.

Johnson, D. W., 1925, *The New England-Acadian Shoreline*, John Wiley and Sons, New York, 608 p.

Johnson, D. W., 1957, The Littoral Drift Problem at Shoreline Harbours, *Am. Soc. Civil Engineers Proc., Jour. Waterways and Harbors Div.* **83**:1-37.

Kaye, C. A., 1959, Shoreline Features and Quaternary Shoreline Changes, Puerto Rico, *U.S. Geol. Survey Prof. Paper 317-B*, pp. 49-140.

King, C. A. M., 1959, *Beaches and Coasts*, Edward Arnold, London, 403 p.

Komar, P. D., 1976, *Beach Processes and Sedimentation*, Prentice-Hall, Englewood Cliffs, N.J., 429 p.

Krauss, R. W., 1960, The Role of Algae in the Formation of Beach Rocks in Certain Islands of the Caribbean, *Coastal Studies Institute Technical Report No. 11*, Part E, Louisiana State University, Baton Rouge, 49 p.

Kuenen, Ph. H., 1948, The Formation of Beach Cusps, *Jour. Geology* **56**:34-40.

Kuenen, Ph. H., 1950, *Marine Geology*, John Wiley and Sons, New York, 568 p.

Lewis, W. V., 1931, The Effect of Wave Incidence on the Configuration of a Shingle Beach, *Geog. Jour.* **78**:129-148.

McCormick, M E., 1973, *Ocean Engineering Wave Mechanics*, John Wiley and Sons, New York, 179 p.

MacNeil, F. S., 1954, The Shape of Atolls: An Inheritance from Subaerial Erosion Forms, *Am. Jour. Sci.* **252**:402-427.

Martonne, E. de, 1909, Traite de géographie physique, A. Colin, Paris, 910 p.

Mason, C. C., and R. L. Folk, 1958, Differentation of Beach, Dune, and Aeolian Flat Environments by Size Analysis, Mustang Island, Texas, *Jour. Sed. Petrology* **28**:211-226.

Milliman, J. D., and K. O. Emery, 1968, Sea Levels During the Past 35,000 Years, *Science* **162**:1121-1123.

Morgan, J. P., J. M. Coleman, and S. M. Gagliano, 1968, Mudlumps: Diapiric Structures in Mississippi Delta Sediments, in *Diapirism and Diapirs*, American Association of Petroleum Geologists Memoir No. 8, American Association of Petroleum Geologists, Tulsa, Okla., pp. 145-161.

Nash, E., 1962, Beach and Sand Dune Erosion Control at Cape Hatteras National Seashore: A Five Year Review (1956-1961), U.S. Department of the Interior, National Service, Manteo, N.C.

Nesteroff, W., 1956, Le Substratum Orgainque dans les Depots Calcaires, sa Signification, *Soc. Géol. France Bull.* **6**:381-389.

Off, T., 1963, Rhythmic Linear Sand Bodies Caused by Tidal Currents, *Am. Assoc. Petroleum Geologists Bull.* **47**:324-341.

Ota, V., 1975, Late Quaternary Vertical Movement in Japan Estimated from Deformed Shorelines, *Royal Soc. New Zealand Bull.* **13**:231-239.

Palmer, H. D., 1971, Observations on the Erosion of Submarine Outcrops, La Jolla Submarine Canyon, California, *Geol. Soc. America Abs. with Programs* **3**(7):666.

Palmer, H. D., D. W. Scholl, and J. Green, 1965, A Peculiar Pedestalate Terrace, San Nicolas Island, California, *Jour. Sed. Petrology* 45:507-511.

Price, W. A., 1951, Barrier Island, Not Offshore Bar, *Science* **113**:487-488.

Price, W. A., 1953, The Classification of Shorelines and Coasts, and Its Application to the Gulf of Mexico, mimeographed, Preliminary Report, *Contribution 15*, Texas A & M University, Department of Oceanography. 111 p.

Price, W. A., 1963, Patterns of Flow and Channeling in Tidal Inlets, *Jour. Sed. Petrology* **33**:279-290.

Redfield, A. C., 1967, Postglacial Change in Sea Level in the Western North Atlantic Ocean, *Science* **157**:687-692.

Ricthofen, F. von, 1886, Führer für Forschungsreisende, Gebrüder Janecke, Hanover, 734 p.

Ritchie, W., and K. Walton, 1972, The Evolution of the Sands of Forire and the Ythan Estuary, in *North East Scotland Geographical Essays*, C. M. Clapperton, ed., Department of Geography, University of Aberdeen, Scotland, pp. 12-15

Russell, R. J., 1957, Aspects of Alluvial Morphology, *Kon. Ned. Aardrijkskd. Genootsch.* **74**:377-388.

Russell, R. J., 1964, Techniques of Eustasy Studies, *Zeitschr. Geomorphologie* **8**:25-42.

Russell, R. J., 1967, *River Plains and Sea Coasts*, University of California Press, Los Angeles and Berkeley, 173 p.

Savage, R. P., 1959, Notes on the Formation of Beach Ridges, *U. S. Army Corps of Engineers Beach Erosion Board Bull.* **13**:31-35.

Schmidt, W., 1923, Die Scherms an der Rotmeekuste von el-Hedschas, *Petermanns Geog. Mitt.* **69**:118-121.

Schofield, J. C., 1961, Sea Level Fluctuations During the Last

4000 Years as Recorded by Chenier Plain, Firth of Thames, New Zealand, *New Zealand Jour. Geol. Geophys.* **3**:461-485.

Scholl, D. W., and M. Stuiver, 1967, Recent Submergence of Southern Florida: A Comparison with Adjacent Coasts and Other Eustatic Data, *Geol Soc. America Bull.* **78**:437-454.

Shepard, F. P., 1937, Revised Classification of Marine Shorelines, *Jour. Geology* **45**:602-624.

Shepard, F. P., 1938, Beach Cusps and Tides: A Discussion, *Am. Jour. Sci.* **35**:309-310.

Shepard, F. P., 1948, *Submarine Geology*, Harper and Brothers, New York, 348 p.

Shepard, F. P., 1952, Revised Nomenclature for Depositional Coastal Features, *Amer. Assoc. Petroleum Geologists Bull.* **36**:1902-1912.

Shepard, F. P., 1963, Thirty-five Thousand Years of Sea Level, in *Essays in Marine Geology in Honor of K. O. Emery*, Thomas S. Clements, ed., University of Southern California Press, Los Angeles, pp. 1-10.

Shepard, F. P., 1972, Submarine Canyons, *Earth-Sci. Rev.* **8**:1-12.

Shepard, F. P., and J. R. Curray, 1967, Carbon-14 Determination of Sea Level Changes in Stable Areas, in *Progress in Oceanography: The Quaternary History of the Ocean Basins*, M. Sears, ed., vol. 4, Pergamon Press, London, pp. 283-291.

Shepard, F. P., and R. F. Dill, 1966, *Submarine Canyons and Other Valleys of the Ocean Floor*, Rand McNally, New York, 381 p.

Shepard, F. P., and H. R. Wanless, 1971, *Our Changing Coastlines*, McGraw-Hill Book Co., New York, 579 p.

Shepard, F. P., K. O. Emery, and E. C. La Fond, 1941, Rip Currents: A Process of Geological Importance, *Jour. Geology* **49**:337-339.

Smith, H. T. U., 1954, Coastal Dunes, *Coastal Geog. Conf. Proc.*, U.S. Office of Naval Research, and the National Research Committee on Geography.

Snead, R. E., 1964, Active Mud Volcanoes of Buluchistan, West Pakistan, *Geog. Rev.* **54**(4):546-560.

Snead, R. E., 1966, Physical Geography Reconnaissance: Las Bela Coastal Plain, West Pakistan, *Louisiana State University Research Pub. No. 13*, Louisiana State University, Baton Rouge, 118 p.

Snead, R. E., 1967, Recent Morphological Changes Along the Coast of West Pakistan, *Assoc. Am. Geographers Annals* **57**(3):550-565.

Snead, R. E., 1969, Physical Geography Reconnaissance: West Pakistan Coastal Zone, *University of New Mexico Publications in Geography 1*, University of New Mexico Press, Albuquerque, 55 p.

Snead, R. E., 1970, *Physical Geography of the Makran Coastal Plain of Iran*, National Technical Information Service, U.S. Department of Commerce, Springfield, Va., 715 p.

Snead, R. E., 1978, *Satellite Imagery: World Physical Features and Landforms*, Harper & Row, New York, 60 p.; 100 35mm slides.

Stamp, L. D., 1961, *A Glossary of Geographical Terms*, John Wiley and Sons, New York, 539 p.

Steers, J. A., 1964, *The Coastline of England and Wales*, 2nd ed., Cambridge University Press, Cambridge, England, 750 p.

Stewart, J. Q., 1962, The Great Atlantic Coast Tides of 5-8 March 1962, *Weatherwise* **15**:117-120.

Strahler, A. N., 1969, *Physical Geography*, 3rd ed., John Wiley and Sons, New York, 733 p.

Strahler, A. N., 1971, *The Earth Sciences*, 2nd ed., Harper & Row, New York, 824 p.

Suess, E., 1885-1909, *Das Antlitz der Erde*, Tempsky, Vienna; English translation, 1906, *The Face of the Earth*, H. B. C. Sollas and W. J. Sollas, trans., Clarendon Press, Oxford, 5 vols.

Tanner, W. F., 1960, Florida Coastal Classification, *Gulf Coast Assoc. Geol. Socs. Trans.* **10**:259-266.

Te Punga, M. T., 1957, Live Anticlines in Western Wellington, *New Zealand Jour. Sci. and Technology*, sec. B, **38**:443-446.

Thornbury, W. D., 1962, *Principles of Geomorphology*, John Wiley and Sons, New York, 618 p.

Thornbury, W. D., 1969, *Principles of Geomorphology*, 2nd ed., John Wiley and Sons, New York, 594 p.

Thrush, P. W., 1968, *Dictionary of Mining, Mineral and Related Terms*, U.S. Bureau of Mines, Washington, D.C., 1269 p.

U.S. Army Corps of Engineers, 1964, Land Against the Sea, *U.S. Army Corps of Engineers Coastal Eng. Research Center Misc. Paper 4-64*, U.S. Army Corps of Engineers, Coastal Engineering Center, Washington, D.C., 43 p.

U.S. Army Corps of Engineers, 1971a, *Shore Management Guidelines, National Shoreline Study*, U.S. Government Printing Office, Washington, D.C., 56 p.

U.S. Army Corps of Engineers, 1971b, *Shore Protection Guidelines, National Shoreline Study*, U.S. Government Printing Office, Washington, D.C., 59 p.

Valentin, H., 1952, Die Kusten der Erde, *Petermanns Geog. Mitt. Erganzungsheft 246*, EB Hermann Haack, Gotha, 118 p.

Van Andel, Tj. H., and J. Laborel, 1964, Recent High Relative Sea Level Strand Near Recife, Brazil, *Science* **145**(3632):580-581.

Watson, J. G., 1928, Mangrove Forests of the Malay Peninsula, *Malayan Forest Records* **6**:274.

West, R. C., 1956, Mangrove Swamps of the Pacific Coast of Colombia, *Assoc. Am. Geographers Annals* **46**(1):98-121.

Wiegel, R. L., 1953, *Waves, Tides, Currents and Beaches: Glossary of Terms and List of Standard Symbols*, Council on Wave Research, Engineering Foundation, University of California, Berkeley, 71 p.

Wiegel, R. L., 1959, Sand Bypassing at Santa Barbara, California, *Am. Soc. Civil Engineer Proc., Jour. Waterways and Harbors Div.* **85**:1-30.

Wiegel, R. L., 1964, *Oceanographical Engineering*, Prentice-Hall, Englewood Cliffs, N.J., 532 p.

Wooldridge, S. W., and R. S. Morgan, 1937, *The Physical Basis of Geography*, Longmans, Green and Co., London, 445 p.

Zenkovitch, V. P., 1967, *Processes of Coastal Development*, D. G. Fry, Trans., J. A. Steers, ed., Oliver and Boyd, Edinburgh, 738 p.

Glossary

abrasion A wearing away. Geologists use the term specifically for wearing of rock as a result of impact such as occurs when sand or gravel propelled by currents of air or water strike rock with sufficient force to polish or erode its surface mechanically.

aeolian Original (English) spelling of eolian, q.v.

aggradation Building of a surface as a result of continuous or intermittent deposition; in general, the process of increasing the volume of a deposit as a result of contributions of material transported by currents of water or wind. The surfaces of the deposits are relatively flat. See **accretion.**

aggradation plain A plain formed by deposition of terrigenous deposits, mainly alluvium.

aggrade To flatten; specifically, to increase in volume by deposition of sediment, as on a flood plain, along a channel, or in a waterbody.

aggregate A mixture of substances, separable by mechanical means.

alga(e) Simple plants (thallophyte) containing chlorophyll that normally grow in water. Practically all seaweeds are included.

algae flat Surface resulting from the accumulation of algae deposits on rocks of various kinds, such as bed rock or eolianite. In detail, the flat consists of steps of rimmed basins that typically remain filled by sea water, with flow from one to another after the most elevated receive replenishment by waves.

algae ridge Slight elevation deposited by lime-secreting algae along the crest of a coral reef. Algae ridges are conspicuous parts of reefs in the Pacific and Indian oceans, but not in the Gulf of Mexico, Caribbean Sea, or Atlantic Ocean.

algae rock Rock of biogenic origin consisting wholly or mainly of algae deposits.

alluvial cone An incomplete cone with apex ordinarily located where an alluviating stream crosses a valley wall and enters a flood plain or heading some distance upvalley. Composed of deposits left by the stream. Alluvial cones vary in radius from a few meters to hundreds of kilometers. On a larger scale, the flood plain of a large river. In arid regions the cones attain greatest steepness, up to 20° but more ordinarily about 6°, but radial gradients in humid regions may be only a few centimeters or meters per kilometer. In the United States they are commonly called alluvial fans because, as viewed from the air or on maps, radial streams, which are ephemeral in position, resemble the ribs of a fan. The cones are built as natural levees along the radiating distributaries. New channels develop between older natural levees, so lower parts of the surface are alluviated. With frequent shifts in channel position the cone surfaces become fairly smooth, being interrupted by channels most recently active. In areas subject to occasional intensive floods the alluvium may contain huge boulders; in most humid regions, silt or sand.

alluvial fan (or cone) Where a stream emerges from a narrow valley or canyon, it deposits a large part of its sediment load over the plain in a fan shape. If the slope of this deposit is quite steep, it is called an **alluvial cone.** Alluvial fan is a term popular among Americans for alluvial cone. Europeans have usually regarded the geometric shape of the deposit as more significant than its changing surface characteristics.

alluviation The process of accumulating deposits of gravel, sand, silt, or clay at places in rivers, lakes, or estuaries where flow is checked.

alluvium As used in the United States, deposits by rivers of silt, sand, or other debris derived from rocks. Recency of deposition is implied; older deposits have been called diluvium, and deposits that have become masses of rock such as sandstone, although recognized as alluvial, are excluded. Engineers are inclined to regard it as soil, a usage condemned by soil scientists. Many people include lake deposits or other than river-transported sediments. In legal context the French equivalent, **alluvion,** is used.

alongshore   Parallel to and near the shoreline; same as **longshore.**

alongshore current   Same as **longshore current.**

amphidromic   Descriptive of an area in an ocean where effect of tidal waves is cancelled and little or no change in the elevation of water occurs. Tidal waves radiate from these nodal points.

amplitude   Magnitude; distance between extremes; as applied to wave, loosely, wave height, but more strictly, displacement from mean value or one-half the mean vertical separation of crests from troughs, or from still-water level to wave-crest elevations.

amplitude, tide   See **tide amplitude.**

amplitude, wave   See **wave amplitude.**

anastomose (adj., **anastomotic)**   To branch. Applied to stream channels that branch and rejoin at comparatively frequent intervals. This stream pattern implies the presence of readily entrained load, so is characteristic of places where the channel crosses coarse silt or sand, and appears in many cases where stream gradients are locally steepened, as well as downstream from heavily loaded tributaries. Also known as braiding.

anastomosing channel system   A system of interlaced channels formed by consequent runoff passing around pre-existing obstructions of alluvium or bedrock.

annelid   Certain segmented worms with distinct heads, most of which live in the marine environment, including types that build tubes that form rock masses (worm rock) or destroy stratification in unconsolidated bottom sediments.

antidunes   Transient ripples, ordinarily small but in some cases several feet high, in stream beds floored with readily erodible material, mainly sand, that occur only under conditions of rapid (torrential) flow. Their distinctive characteristics are (1) movement upstream because downstream faces are eroded rapidly, with most of the sediment coming to rest on the next antidune downstream, causing crests to advance against the current; and (2) cyclic appearance and complete removal, which occurs in very few minutes. They imply extreme movement of bed sediment downcurrent, both when formed and throughout the cycle.

aquifer   A geologic formation that is water-bearing and that transmits water from one point to another. A permeable layer through which ground water flows freely, in contrast to aquiclude, a layer that is relatively impermeable. Aquifers supply water in wells, springs, etc. Flow is down hydraulic gradients, ordinarily along

directions of valleys or trends of alluvial deposits or strata in rock.

aragonite   Mineral with calcium carbonate in orthorhombic crystal form. Characteristic of certain organic marine oozes in shallow water, also one of the main constituents of common shells and coral. Aragonite rapidly changes to calcite, a more compact and enduring form with identical chemical composition.

arch, sea   See **sea arch.**

archipelago   A group of islands; a sea studded with many islands.

arête   Sharp, serrate ridge in glaciated mountains, usually between two cirques.

argillaceous   Rich in clay, as applied to sediment or rocks.

arid   Deficient in precipitation. Commonly thought of as a climate in which irrigation is practiced; more precisely defined in terms of precipitation-temperature ratios. Extremely arid climate (vegetation, etc), desert, has less than 25 centimeters, (10 inches) of annual precipitation in moderately hot areas, such as midlatitudes, half again as much in lower latitudes, where evaporation is more intense. Summer maxima in precipitation increase the amount needed to escape desert condition because the rainfall arrives when evaporation is fastest. Between deserts and humid climates with adequate precipitation, such as is needed to support forest growth, is the semiarid steppe climate, where the vegetation is somewhat more closely spaced than in deserts and consists largely of grass. All climatic divisions are gradational, and boundary positions shift from year to year. The term is extended to include description of vegetation, soil, and other characteristics of moisture-deficient regions.

arkose   Clastic sediment or consolidated rock consisting predominantly of quartz and feldspar and derived from disintegration of granite or closely associated crystalline rocks. Arkosic deposits survive for great lengths of time in arid climates, where the decomposition of feldspars takes place more slowly than it does in areas where precipitation is commonplace. In contrast is graywacke.

artificial nourishment   The process of replenishing a beach with material (usually sand) obtained from another location. Replenishing a beach material by artificial means, for example, by the deposition of dredged materials.

atoll   A more or less ring-shaped island composed wholly of organic material (algae, coral, etc.) that has accumulated *in situ,* ordinarily containing a central body of water (lagoon) that is connected with the surrounding sea (chiefly on lee coasts). Mainly found in the Pacific and Indian oceans, but some develop in the Gulf of Mexico and Caribbean Sea. Commonly the highest elevations occur on sand dunes and rarely amount to more than 6 meters, (20 feet). It should be noted that the term "coral island" for most of these tropical islands is incorrect, as calcareous algae (Lithothamnion) often forms much more than 50 percent of them. Some of the cays of the Florida Banks, the northwest Cuban coast, and parts of the Australian banks contain many atoll-like islands, which are composed of noncoral detritus.

atoll reef   A ring-shaped coral reef, often topped by a low sand island, enclosing a body of water.

attenuation   (1) A lessening of the amplitude of a wave with distance from the origin. (2) The decrease of water-particle motion with increasing depth. Particle motion resulting from surface oscillatory waves attenuates rapidly with depth, and practically disappears at a depth equal to a surface wavelength.

attrition   Abrasion; frictional wear. Characterizes places worn away by loss of surface material. Term applied to wear of rock particles in transit.

authigenic   Formed in place, as in the case of minerals crystalized in igneous rock and many substances of chemical or biological origin in sediments.

avant cote   Offshore zone in front of the beach.

Avicennia   A common type of mangrove, varying in habit from low shrubs to stately trees, characterized by being surrounded by pneumatophores (air roots) that project from the ground like spears of asparagus. The genus includes the common black mangrove, which grows as a pioneer on offshore bars and on many mudflats. It also includes some white mangroves.

avulsion   Ordinarily, a legal term indicating sudden loss of land by one person with resulting gain by another under natural processes. Commonly emphasis is placed on the loss, as during storms when waves attack coasts or during floods when land is removed along river banks. The act performed by a stream when it suddenly breaks through its banks in an unexpected manner and forms another channel or cuts off a large quantity of land from one owner and adds it to the land of another.

awash   Situated so that the top is intermittently washed by waves or tidal action. Condition of being exposed or just bare at any stage of the tide between high water and chart datum. Condition of an object that is nearly flush with the water level. (Nautical definition.)

awash rocks   Rocks exposed at any stage of the tide between mean high water and the sounding datum, or exactly awash at these levels.

backbeach   The backshore of a beach. See also **backshore.**

backrush   The seaward return of the water following the uprush of the waves. For any given tide stage, the point of farthest return seaward of the backrush is known as the limit of backrush or limit of backwash. See **backwash.**

backshore   That zone of the shore or beach lying between the foreshore and the coastline and acted upon by waves only during severe storms, especially when combined with exceptionally high water. It comprises the berm or berms. Upper part of beach, which remains dry except under unusual conditions and free of cover by uprush associated with ordinary wave arrivals. See also **backbeach.**

backslope   Inclination of the surface of a natural levee between the levee crest and adjacent backswamp basin. Ordinarily steepest near the crest.

backswamp   Basin between natural levees in an alluvial valley, with particular reference to its lower parts. If forested, such basins are true swamps; but if covered by grass, they are marshes. In many cases they have agricultural use, particularly if drained Lush vegetation accounts for the presence of highly organic deposits in humid climates. Many backswamps contain lakes and wet areas due to ineffective drainage systems.

backwash   Water flowing down the slope of a beach. Opposite of uprush. The seaward return of water from a wave after it has just reached it greatest runup on the shore, generally at right angles to the shoreline. Water or waves thrown back by an obstruction such as a ship, breakwater, or cliff. See **backrush.**

ball   Low ridge approximately parallel to a shoreline between runnels or troughs, exposed at less than high tide; longshore bar; a feature on the lower (commonly submerged) beach. Also called ridge, and with many other meanings. See **longshore bar.**

bar   An offshore ridge or mound of sand, gravel, or other unconsolidated material that is submerged (at least at high tide), especially at the mouth of a river or estuary, or lying parallel to, and a short distance from, the beach. A slightly submerged sand or gravel ridge, often found at the mouth of a bay. A deposit of alluvium either in a channel or along its side, commonly composed of coarser sediment than that underlying it; also, a shoal area nearshore or out in a lake, bay, etc. Bars generally form at river mouths and along convex banks of alluviating streams. In meteorology, atmospheric pressure of 29.5306 inches of mercury at 0°C (32°F), presumably the world's average. A submerged or emerged embankment of sand, gravel, or other unconsolidated material built on the sea floor in shallow water by waves and currents. See **baymouth bar, cuspate bar, sand bar, offshore bar, midbay, bay head.**

bar, longshore   See **longshore bar.**

bar, offshore   See **barrier beach.**

barchan   Dune with crescentic ground plan, with horns at the ends of its concave leeward front and sharp contrast between steep front downwind and more gentle stoss back. A common form of sand dune in areas where there is considerable lag gravel present on the surface, covering the loose sediments from which the sand is derived and across which it travels. Found isolated, in families etc., with new dunes originating at horns of mother dunes. These are ordinarily whalebacks that become barchans after growing in size.

barking sand   Sand emitting a noise similar to the bark of a dog when walked on. It occurs typically on flat surfaces and emits the sound when dry. Most generally known as occurring on black beaches in the Hawaiian Islands but also is present in many other places.

barrier   A sand beach, island, or spit extending roughly parallel to the coast and separated from the mainland by a lagoon. Present along large parts of the Atlantic and Gulf coasts, and along much of the Arctic coast of Alastka.

barrier beach   a straight or gently curved beach separated from the mainland by a lagoon. A bar essentially parallel to the shore, the crest of which is above normal high-water level or exposed during high water. Also called offshore barrier, barrier island, and sand reef.

barrier chain   A series of barrier islands, barrier spits, and barrier beaches that extend along a considerable length of coast.

barrier flat   A marshy flat on the lagoon side of a barrier spit or barrier island, largely formed by sand or silt carried across the barrier through sluiceways during major storms.

barrier island   A detached portion of a barrier beach between two inlets. Elongate island formed as a result of wave processes. Examples typically parallel the coast and are commonly separated from the nearby mainland by a lagoon or bay. Surplus sand may accumulate in dunes to the rear of an outer beach. In places these dunes may be breached by wave overwash, which transports sand toward the lagoon to accumulate as a barrier flat.

barrier lagoon   A bay roughly parallel to the coast and separated from the open ocean by barrier islands. Also the body of water encircled by coral islands and reefs, in which case it may be called an atoll lagoon.

barrier reef   Coral reef converging with capes, etc., and most widely removed from a shore in enclaves, embayments, etc. Likely to be separated from beaches along the shore by a more or less linear lagoon that is open to the sea at various passes, which are located as a rule above valleys cut to a lower sea level. Generally, barrier reefs follow the coasts for long distances and are cut through at irregular intervals by channels or passes. Often separated from the coast by a lagoon that is too deep for coral growth. The Great Barrier Reef of Australia is a complex of reefs forming an interrupted chain that includes some high islands.

barrier spit   A barrier connected with the mainland at one end, extending part way across a bay or estuary. Similar to a barrier island, only connected to the mainland.

bars, reticulated   See **reticulated bars.**

bars, transverse   See **transverse bars.**

base level   Presumed lowest level to which fluvial processes accomplish erosion. Temporary base levels occur at higher elevation—a lake, river, or some body of rock, etc.—preventing erosion below limits set by such features. From a theoretical standpoint the ultimate base level, also called level base, is an imaginary surface rising gently from sea level, according to some mathematical rule. The location of the base level is commonly in dispute, but it is the ultimate surface toward which rivers may erode.

basin, boat   See **boat basin.**

bay   A recess or inlet in the shore of a sea or lake between two capes or headlands, not as large as a gulf but larger than a cove. It originated by popular usage and may refer to a large estuary or even to a rarely flooded marsh. Hudson Bay is essentially a small epicontinental sea. The Bay of Biscay is part of the Atlantic Ocean between widely separated capes, and more than half of its area is over 100 fathoms deep. See also **bight, embayment.**

bay barrier   A sandy barrier that separates or nearly separates a bay from an ocean.

baymouth bar   Bar extending between headlands or other topographic limits of a bay or estuary.

bayou   Any water body that is locally called a bayou. Many are relatively stagnant, but in some the flow is vigorous, even down waterfalls. Some are cutoff lakes, others are tidal channels, estuaries, or active or abandoned river distributaries. The term in no sense is scientific or precise. It is most commonly used in Gulf coast states. A minor sluggish waterway or estuarial creek, tributary to, or connecting, other streams or bodies of water. Its course is usually through lowlands or swamps. Sometimes called slough.

beach   A deposit along a shore extending between inner and outer limits of active wave transport, hence including upper (exposed to air when water level is lowest) and lower (submerged at all times) parts, both of which tend to exhibit upward concavities in profile that are commonly separated by the step, where upward convexity exists, where gradient is steeper, and where sediment constituents are larger. Also, the area so defined, extending out to a depth where wave-produced entrainment ceases, except at times of extraordinary sea state. Most popular definitions, such as area exposed at low tide, have little value, and many more or less scientific definitions of a beach, and especially its parts, are not particularly useful. The zone of unconsolidated material or physiographic form, or to the line of permanent vegetation (usually the effective limit of storm waves). The seaward limit of a beach, unless otherwise specified, is the low water line. A beach includes foreshore and backshore.

beach berm A nearly horizontal part of the beach or backshore formed by the deposit of material by wave action. Some beaches have no berms, others have one or several.

beach cusps Ephemeral ridges on the upper beach terminating in horns toward the shoreline and separated by small bays. Their spacing is ordinarily quite uniform and is related to wave energy at the time of their origin, being wider at higher levels if more than one series is present. Their composition normally is of coarser material than the parts of the beach they overlie. This suggests depositional origin resulting from accumulation of material carried in from the step zone by waves. Cusps typically form when waves approach the shoreline at approximately right angles and are eroded when waves come from other angles. See **cusp.**

beach drift The material moved in a zigzag path along the foreshore by the action of the uprush and backwash of waves breaking at an angle with the shore.

beach drifting The transfer of sand or gravel along the shore by littoral currents.

beach erosion The carrying away of beach materials by wave action, tidal currents, littoral currents, or wind.

beach face The section of the beach normally exposed to the action of the wave uprush. The foreshore of a beach. (Not synonymous with shoreface.)

beach profile (1) The intersection of the ground surface with a vertical plane; may extend from the top of the dune line to the seaward limit of sand movement. (2) A sectional elevation through the beach and surf perpendicular to the shoreline.

beach ridge Ordinarily, permanent linear accumulations of coarse sand or shingle on a prograding upper beach. Fine sand tends to form sheets rather than ridges. Beach ridges may occur singly or in series, the youngest being most shoreward; their heights vary up to 6 meters (20 feet) or so and the ridges commonly survive as a result of vegetational cover or of cementation if the sand is calcareous and the climate warm. There are conflicting theories as to origin, but high

states of the sea, uprush beyond ordinary limits, and creation of higher-level berms are involved. They should not be confused with cheniers because beach ridges are fronted by beach, rather than marsh deposits, and originate as a result of contrasts in effectiveness of sand transport by uprush toward their locations. An essentially continuous mound of beach material that has been heaped up by wave or other action. In England they are called fulls. During storms, coast sediment, sand, gravel, or shells may pile up just landward of the beach. Very similar ridges may form behind the beach, composed of sand blown from the beach (see **dune ridge**).

beach rock Cemented beach material formed in situ at or close to the level of the water table, hence at about sea level if the tidal range is small or at about the level of high neap tide if the range is large. A variety of water-table rock. Without interruption the cemented layer commonly extends inland if unconsolidated rock is present, to be exposed along stream banks or encountered in excavations or borings. Traditionally the reference is to material cemented by calcium carbonate (especially in the form of calcite), something possible only if groundwater temperature remains about 20°C (68°F) for at least several months of the year (lime dissolves more rapidly if water is colder), hence is restricted to tropical or semitropical climates. In colder climates a similar cementation involves iron compounds, as a rule. When first exposed the incipient beach rock is readily crushed by hand, but later may become as hard and durable as concrete. Bands (pavements) are present where coastal recession has been intermittent. On tropical beaches where there is much shell or coral detritus, the loose beach sediment may be cemented into a firm rock, often within a few years of deposition. In the United States, beachrock if found in the Florida Keys and along many Hawaiian beaches.

beach scarp An almost perpendicular slope along the beach foreshore, an erosional feature due to wave action. It may vary in height from a few centimeters to several meters, depending on wave action and the nature and composition of the beach.

beach width The horizontal dimension of the beach measured normal to the shoreline or from the water's edge inland.

bench A flat, especially of small area, that stands somewhat above another level. Flats formed on resistant layers of rock are typical. The term is not appropriate for the surface of an alluvial terrace. If a considerable area is involved, the feature is commonly regarded as a platform or plateau. A level, or gently sloping erosion plane inclined seaward. A nearly horizontal area at about the level of maximum high water on the sea side of a dike protecting marsh land.

berm   A flat of depositional origin, specifically on a beach, dating from a time when that portion of the beach aggraded to a higher level than the one present at the time of observation. Berms are washed away when sea state is high and commonly are replaced as wave energy subsides. Also, a comparatively narrow bench in other locations, as along a channel bank; a batture. A low, nearly horizontal portion of the upper part of the beach formed by the deposit of material by wave action. Some beaches have no berms, others have one or several. See **beach berm.**

berm crest   The seaward limit of a berm. Outer edge of a berm. Also called berm edge.

berm edge   See **berm crest.**

bight   Shoreline indentation concave toward the sea. Bights vary in size from a fraction of a kilometer to nearly 1,126 kilometers (southern Australia). As the term is in popular use rather than scientific use, there is little advantage in formulating a more exact definition. A bend in a coastline forming an open bay. A bay formed by such a bend. A slight indentation in a coast forming an open bay, usually crescent-shaped.

bill   A small, narrow cape; for example, Portland Bill on south coast of England.

billow   Usually a great wave or surge of water; any wave.

biosphere   The part of the earth's atmosphere, hydrosphere, and lithosphere capable of supporting life.

blowout   Depression in dune fields and in parts of individual sand dunes excavated as a result of sand removal by wind.

blowout dune   A break in the plant cover of coastal dunes allows landward transfer of the dune sand, developing a depressed passage (blowout) across the dune ridge and generally building a higher U-shaped dune inland from the coastal dune ridge.

bluff   A high, steep bank or cliff.

boat basin   A naturally or artificially enclosed or nearly enclosed Harbor area for small craft.

bold coast   A prominent land mass that rises steeply from the sea.

bomb   A mass of semifluid lava forcibly ejected from a vent and shaped to a spindlelike form while hardening during air transport.

boom   A floating structure, usually of timber logs, used to protect the face of a dam or other structure built in or on water from damage by wave action, from floating material being dashed against it by the waves, or used to deflect floating material away from such a structure.

bore   The steep front of a wave of translation in which there is forward movement of water and a distinct rise of level with passage of the wave. Ordinarily associated with rising tide as a discrete change in water level, but also appears along coasts when tsunami or other widespread increases in water level occur; most evident in estuaries and river mouths, but under conditions of extreme calm may be noted elsewhere. Term does not include fronts of advancing waves that become translatory on approaching a shore, because change in level is temporary and alternates between rises and falls. In the Amazon Estuary the bore amounts to several feet and is used to move boats upstream in surfboard fashion. A very rapid rise of the tide in which the advancing water presents an abrupt front of considerable height. In shallow estuaries, where the range of tide is large, the high water is propagated inward faster than the low water because of the greater depth at high water. If the high water overtakes the low water, an abrupt front is presented with the high water crest finally falling forward as the tide continues to advance. Also called eager.

brackish water   Somewhat saline water, generally with at least 500 parts per million or more of salt. With 1,000 ppm the taste is strongly saline and above 5,000 ppm the water is considered unfit for human use, although in some places people use it and livestock tolerate 10,000 ppm. Salinity may be caused by admixed sea water, contact with salt beds, or other contaminants. Occurs either in surface waterbodies or in groundwater.

braided channel   Anastomotic (see **anastomose**); channel frequently branching and rejoining after separation by visible bars or islands with lenticular shapes.

breaker   A wave, typically of at least fair amplitude, losing its form and in part being in process of changing from a mass of water into water with considerable air content (foam), normally as a result of friction against a shoaling bottom. As the wave feels the bottom it begins to deform, until there is considerable contrast in velocity of water movement, the water toward the surface being faster, resulting in piling up of water that may topple over its support, forming a breaker. A wave breaking on a shore, over a reef, etc. Breakers may be classified into four types: (1) spilling. Bubbles and turbulent water spill down front face of wave. The upper 25 percent of the front face may become vertical before breaking. Breaking generally across over quite a distance. (2) plunging. Crest curls over air pocket; breaking is usually with a crash. Smooth splash-up usually follows. (3) collapsing. Breaking occurs over lower half of wave. Minimal air pocket and usually no splash-up. Bubbles and foam present. (4) surging. Wave peaks up, but bottom rushes forward from under wave, and wave slides up beach face with little or no bubble production. Water surface remains almost plane except where ripples may be produced on the beachface during runback.

breaker depth   The still water depth at the point where a wave breaks. Also breaking depth.

breakwater   An artificial structure designed to protect some portion of the coast from wave erosion or to create a comparatively quiet area of water behind it, as in a harbor, anchorage, or basin.

bruguiera   A genus of mangrove developing pneumatophores (see **Avicennia**) but occurring inland of and at somewhat higher elevations than the common black mangrove, forming dense forests in some places.

bulkhead   A structure or partition to retain or prevent sliding of the land. A secondary purpose is to protect the upland against damage from wave action. See also **seawall.**

calcarenite   Calcareous sand or rock, commonly containing at least one-half organic lime, such as pieces or fragments of calcareous algae, shells, or coral; limestone or dolomite (calcium plus magnesium carbonate). The term is applied to eolianite (dune rock) with calcium carbonate cement.

calcareous   Containing appreciable calcium carbonate (lime).

calcite   Mineral composed of calcium carbonate in crystalline grains (hexagonal rhombohedrons). With similar composition but slightly differing crystal form it is known as aragonite. Calcite has three perfect cleavages that cause it to break into rhombs. It is a compact and lasting form of calcium carbonate.

caldera   Deep, more or less circular volcanic crater formed either explosively or by subsidence, or by a combination of the two. The depth ordinarily is more than twice the basin's diameter. In some cases, where bottomed below sea level, calderas form harbors.

calving   Breaking off, detaching, etc., as calf from a cow; detachment of blocks of considerable size from an ice front, especially in water, where they may float and become icebergs. The term is used by some for the detachment of blocks associated with retreat of a cliff or bank of a river.

cape   A popular term meaning a feature along the shore where the land protrudes or a significant change in shoreline direction occurs. Application of the term is by no means uniform. While generally the feature is likely to be conspicuous, in many cases it is not. Point is used in a similar sense, and other words, such as head, or simply a geographical place name are used in many cases. A relatively extensive land area jutting seaward from a continent or large island that prominently marks a change in, or interrupts notably, the coastal trend; a prominent feature.

case hardening   Precipitation of mineral matter in a toughened outer layer of a rock being weathered.

cave, (sea)   See **sea cave.**

cavern (solutional)   Underground openings of appreciable extent developed by solution of percolating groundwater.

cavernous weathering   Development of pits and depressions in a rock surface during weathering.

cay   British spelling of key, a low, flat island or mound ordinarily composed of sand or organic materials, for example, coral, algae, etc. By extension, an artificial structure (properly, quay) such as a protected embankment or a landing place. Both British and Americans pronounce the word "kee." The spelling "kay" is sometimes used in the West Indies.

cementation   A form of induration; specifically, binding together mineral or rock material, ordinarily by the introduction of silica, carbonate, or iron compounds as cement.

channel   (1) A natural or artificial waterway of perceptible extent which either periodically or continuously contains moving water, or which forms a connecting link between two bodies of water. (2) The part of a body of water deep enough to be used for navigation through an area otherwise too shallow for navigation. (3) A large strait, such as the English Channel. (4) The deepest part of a stream, bay, or strait through which the main volume or current of water flows.

chenier   A beach ridge generally including much shell detritus piled up on a flat coastal plain during a hurricane or major storm. The name comes from Louisiana where oak trees (chene, in French) grow along the ridges. An abandoned beach located some distance from the shore as a result of deposition of fine sediment on its seaward side. Should not be regarded as synonymous with beach ridge. The origin of cheniers depends on variable sediment supply. When nearby rivers furnish little, a beach forms, but when the supply is large, a marsh builds in front of the beach.

chenier plain   A low, marshy coastal plain that includes cheniers.

chop   The short-crested waves that may spring up quickly in a moderate breeze and break easily at the crest. Also called wind chop.

choppy sea   Short, rough waves tumbling with short and quick motion. Also called choppong sea and clocking sea.

cinder cone   A more or less steep-sided subcircular of symmetrical conical hill formed by clastic volcanic material (tephra) around an explosive vent or small crater in the center, piled up during an explosive volcanic eruption. The angle of the slope is the angle of rest of the loose material composing the cone. Some cinder cones have formed islands that have been rapidly eroded away.

clay dune   In the Laguna Madre of southern Texas, salts such as gypsum (hydrated calcium sulphate) are precipitated during the summer dry season. This salt then binds together masses of clay, forming grains of sand size; and these may be piled up into dunes by the wind.

cliff   A high, steep face of rock; a precipice. An escarpment eroded by wave action. See also **sea cliff.**

coast   Region extending inland from the sea, ordinarily as far as the first topographic change in the land surface; also, popularly, a stretch of the shore, together with land nearby; in general, an area where maritime influences prevail. The land zone immediately adjacent to a body of standing water.

coastal   Pertaining to a coast.

coastal area   The land and sea area bordering the shoreline.

coastal current   Drift of water about parallel to the shore and outside the surf zone, whatever the cause. (1) Those currents that flow roughly parallel to the shore and constitute a relatively uniform drift in the deeper water adjacent to the surf zone. These currents may be tidal, transient, wind-driven, or currents associated with the distribution of mass in local water. (2) For navigational purposes, the term is used to designate a current in coastwise shipping lanes where the tidal current is frequently rotary.

coastal plain   The plain composed of horizontal or gently sloping strata of clastic materials fronting the coast, and generally representing a strip of sea bottom that has emerged from the sea in recent geologic time. Relatively flat land extending back from the sea, ordinarily to some prominent topographic rise. The term is used both in restricted and in broader context, an example of the latter being the large coastal plain along the Atlantic and Gulf states, which is bounded by the Fall Line (in many places an abrupt rise along the boundary between younger, less consolidated, and older, more resistant, rock).

coastline   (1) Technically, the line that forms the boundary between the coast and the shore. (2) Commonly, the line that forms the boundary between the land and the water. (3) Approximate position of the shoreline, ordinarily as displayed on a map, chart, or other means of showing position on a comparatively small scale; or the feature itself. Less restricted in definition than shoreline.

cobble (cobblestone)   Small boulders or rounded rocks ranging in diameter from approximately 64 to 256 millimeters (2 to 10 inches; (-6 phi to -8 phi).

compound shoreline   A term describing a coast having relatively straight barrier features seaward from lagoons, etc., behind which an irregular, commonly more or less estuarine, shoreline is present as a result of drowning during the last major rise of sea level.

concretion   Nodular or irregular concentration of a mineral substance introduced into sedimentary or other rocks in solution, such as masses of silica in limestone, iron compounds in sandstone, etc., which result from the fact that similar molecules carried in solution, ordinarily in ground water, attract each other and grow as aggregates, commonly around some nucleus, which may be organic, such as a fossil or speck of carbon. Interesting objects may be found by breaking concretions—fossil leaves, insects, bones, etc. Concretions grade into extensive, more or less tabular, layers along permeable beds or the upper surface of groundwater, etc. Original bedding of rock commonly passes through a concretion undisturbed, but not in all cases.

cone   Anything shaped more or less like a mathematical cone (formed by swinging a line around a central vortex); specifically, talus or alluvial cone, q.v., even though the surface may be nearly horizontal; the form assumed by lava or tephra issuing from one or several closely associated vents; of depressions, surface of the water table resulting from abnormal loss of ground water by pumping, etc.

conglomerate   A clastic sedimentary rock made up of more or less rounded fragments in which an appreciable volume is of sizes of granules or larger. Some degree of consolidation differentiates it from gravel (in a general sense). Puddingstone.

continental shelf   Ordinarily, a comparatively flat bottom surrounding continents or islands, extending from low-water level outward to a comparatively abrupt steepening of slope, the continental slope. The shelf is widest, as a rule, seaward from broad coastal plains (typical of many shores of the Atlantic, rarer around the Pacific). The depth of the outer edge is commonly about 50 fathoms but may be less than or several times that depth.

continental slope   Area of increased gradient leading from the edge of a continental shelf into greater depth, commonly the ocean floor.

contraposed coast   Coast with outlines formed at an earlier time, later covered by deposits, and still later exhumed, after the covering layers have been removed.

coquina   A coarse-grained, porous, friable variety of limestone, chiefly made up of fragments of shells of species of mollusks and of coral, cemented together as rock. A kind of beachrock common on the Atlantic coast of Florida.

coral   (1) biology: Marine coelenterates (Madreporaria), solitary or colonial, which form a hard external covering of calcium compounds, on other materials. The corals that form large reefs are limited to warm, shallow waters, and those forming solitary, minute growths may be found in colder waters to great depths. (2) geology: The concentration of coral polyps, composed almost wholly of calcium carbonate, forming reefs, and treelike and globular masses. May also include calcareous algae and other organisms producing calcareous secretions, such as bryozoans and hydrozoans. In warmer seas the coralline growths are commonly massive and may contribute appreciably to the formation of reefs; in cold seas corals grow as individuals or in very small colonies. Corals are common as fossils in rocks, and (assisted by algae and other kinds of organisms) living corals produce important masses of biogenic rock.

coral limestone   A limestone composed of coral fragments.

coralline limestone   A limestone composed of or containing many corals or coral-like remains.

coral reef   In warmer seas a large accumulation of coral and remains of other organisms, commonly a short distance offshore where the bottom is firm and the water is clear, with appreciable penetration of daylight. Under similar conditions isolated accumulations may grow (patch reef, etc.). A true reef should preserve the relative growth positions of its constituent organisms when alive. Accumulations of fragments of reefal origin occur in reef flats, etc. A limestone shoal water area built in subtropical or tropical seas by corals, marine algae, and other calcium carbonate-secreting organisms. See **reef**.

countercurrent   A current, commonly near shore, moving in a direction opposite to that of the predominant oceanic current. For example, the southwestward-flowing littoral currents along the southeastern United States, shoreward from northeastward-flowing Gulf Stream.

country rock   Type of rock characteristic of a particular area. Commonly used to refer to rock invaded by dikes or other intrusive bodies of igneous rock or by mineral veins; rock surrounding an igneous outcrop if widespread in comparison to the intrusion; rock encountered by erosion through a superficial layer of recent origin, as below alluvial or glacial deposits.

cove   An indented recess on a coast, particularly one providing shelter to small craft, such as a small bay or stream mouth; a type of beach with conspicuous concavity in outline and limited length. Often inside a larger embayment.

crenulate   Characterized by numerous lobes or scallops, as a crenulate coast.

crossbedding   A system of minor stratification or bedding oblique to the attitude of stratification that predominates locally. These minor structures are common in sediments deposited by currents, as in accumulations of sand or deposits along stream channels, and in many cases are caused by variations in intensity or directions of flow. In some cases torrential flow is involved.

cross sea   Confused, irregular state of the sea due to different groups of waves from different directions raised by local winds.

current   (1) A horizontal movement of gas or liquid, specifically in air or water in most cases. May be intermittent and of small size, as in the case of a rip current, or steady and huge in dimensions, as in the case of major ocean currents. Also, applied to the flow of streams in confined channels. Many related and other usages. The direction of a current is the one toward which it moves (opposite to the terminology used for waves or wind). (2) The flowing of water, or other liquid or gas. (3) That portion of a stream of water that is moving with a velocity much greater than the average or in which the progress of the water is principally concentrated. (4) Ocean currents can be classified in a number of different ways. Some important types are: (a) Periodic currents, due to the effect of tides; such currents may be rotating rather than having a simple back-and-forth motion. The currents accompanying tides are known as tidal currents. (b) Temporary currents, due to seasonal winds; (c) Permanent currents, also called Ocean Currents, constitute a part of the general oceanic circulation (Gulf Stream, Japan Current, applied to a slow broad movement of the Gulf Stream and the Japan Current, as distinguished from the narrower and swifter movements called stream currents. (d) Nearshore currents, caused principally by waves breaking along a shore. (5) See also coastal currents; offshore current, rip current, tidal current.

current, coastal   See **coastal current**.

current, drift   See **drift current**.

current, ebb   See **ebb current**.

current, littoral   See **littoral current**.

current, longshore   See **longshore current**.

current, rip   See **rip current**.

current, tidal   See **tidal current**.

cusp   (1) One of a series of low mounds of beach material separated by crescent-shaped troughs spaced at more or less regular intervals along the beach face. (2) Short ridges transverse to the beach, extending out to cuspate points. Between these cusps are hollows. The cusps are spaced at somewhat uniform distances along beaches. They represent a combination of constructive and destructive processes. (3) Projection of land, sand, etc., with an apex pointed seaward and embayments or depressions on both sides. See also **beach cusps**.

cuspate   Having a cusp shape, as of a spit, foreland, or stretch of coast.

cuspate bar A crescent-shaped bar uniting with the shore at each end. It may be formed by a single spit growing from shore and then turning back to again meet the shore, or by two spits growing from the shore and uniting to form a bar of sharply cuspate form. A series of loops in a longshore bar, as at Horn Island, Mississippi.

cuspate foreland A projecting point in a barrier coast, such as the Carolina capes and Cape Krusenstern and Point Barrow in northern Alaska.

cuspate sand key A cuspate sand deposit formed by an outflowing tide outside a tidal inlet. If the sand key is angular it is called cuspate, but, if it is rounded, it may be called lunate.

cuspate spit Cuspate projections of a beach into a lagoon.

dalmatian Type of coast characterized by parallel trends of its shorelines following those of rock structures.

debris line A line near the limit of storm-wave uprush marking the landward limit of debris deposits.

dead cliff A former sea cliff, ordinarily elevated and no longer subject to alteration by marine processes.

decay of waves The change waves undergo after they leave a generating area (fetch) and pass through a calm, or region of lighter winds. In the process of decay, the significant wave height decreases and the significant wavelength increases.

deep (1) Restricted area, ordinarily a trough not far from the coast of a continent, where the depth is greater than that of adjoining sea floor. Deeps, like peaks of a mountain range, are given names. Many are also called trenches. Also, many other usages. (2) An area of the ocean considerably deeper than the surrounding waters. (3) Secondary and smaller bounded areas within the great ocean basins with depths exceeding 5,000 to 6,000 meters (roughly 16,000 to 20,000 feet).

deep water (1) Water so deep that surface waves are little affected by the ocean bottom. Generally, water deeper than one-half the surface wavelength is considered deep water. (2) Water which extends far downward. It is a relative term.

deepwater wave A surface wave of length less than twice the depth of water. It moves with a velocity independent of water depth. Also, a wave in water the depth of which is greater than one-half the wavelength.

deflation The removal of loose material from a beach or other land surface by wind action.

degradation (1) A bringing to flatness, particularly at a lower elevation, as the wearing away of hills and mountains and other relief features. Denudation, q.v., is an associated process. (2) The geologic process by means of which various parts of the surface of the earth are worn away and their general level lowered, by the action of wind and water.

delta (1) The area of land created by deposition where streams enter bodies of water such as lakes, estuaries, or the sea. Geologists regard the deposit itself as constituting the delta, but where originally described, in Egypt, the added land area was indicated. Coarser sediments ordinarily are deposited along distributary streams and finer, in basins between, with fine, prodelta clay offshore. A distinct fluvatile deposit made at a river's débouchér.

delta-flank depression Low and commonly embayed areas on either or both sides of large deltas, originating because the weight of the delta deposit has lowered land in the vicinity. In some examples, important rivers belonging to and contributing sediments to a large delta are diverted into a delta-flank depression, and their deposits may accumulate to neutralize topographic effects of subsidence.

deltaic Pertaining to a delta. Specifically used to describe coastal plains formed by successive or adjacent deltas. Descriptive of channel patterns originating under water as these fronts advance, as during the filling of an estuary; these are characterized by branching submarine natural levees, lenticular islands between channels that later come together, and complicated systems of deposits that persist after the area has become land. Mobile Bay, Alabama, is an excellent example, and much of the Atchafalaya Basin, Louisiana, exemplifies the process. Submarine origin is responsible for patterns and forms differing from those of typical flood plains.

denudation To denude is to uncover. Denudation refers to lowering of relief by stripping away rocks and exposing those below, whereas degradation refers to general surface flattening that develops as a result of the process. Popularly, but rather unscientifically, these and other processes are likely to be lumped under the term "erosion."

depth Vertical distance from water surface to sea or other waterbody floor; on charts, from a surface associated with a specific tidal position. Also applied to other features, such as distance to a particular layer in the water such as the limit of penetration of light of some wavelength; in navigation, the controlling depth of a channel is the minimum depth present to be cleared by the craft in question. Also many other usages.

depth of breaking See **breaker depth.**

design wave In the design of harbors, harbor works, etc., the type or types of wave selected as having the characteristics against which protection is desired. Various criteria for their selection exist.

differential erosion Selective removal of rock material in accordance with erosive susceptibility and agency.

diffracted wave   Wave with front changed in direction by an obstacle, as distinguished from changes caused by reflection or refraction. Waves are bent on encountering a rock, barrier such as a groin, etc., in the shadow of which waves are propagated with other than initial frontal directions.

diffraction   The phenomenon occurring when water waves are propagated into a sheltered region formed by a breakwater or similar barrier that interrupts a portion of the otherwise regular train of waves, resulting in a change in the characteristics of the waves.

dike (dyke)   (1) Artificial levee, a more or less linear embankment constructed for the purpose of confining water in the vicinity of a stream channel or near the shore of a large waterbody; geologically, a more or less tabular mass of mineral or rock cutting across country rock and standing vertically or nearly so, whether exposed to the atmosphere or not. As a verb, to construct a dike. See **sill**. (2) A wall or mound built around a low-lying area to prevent flooding (as a levee).

direction of current   Direction toward which current is flowing.

direction of waves   Direction from which waves are coming.

direction of wind   Direction from which wind is blowing.

discharge (stream)   Quantity of water moving along a channel, commonly measured in terms of cubic meters (feet, etc.) per second (cusecs) passing some specific cross-section of the channel; in some cases, the volume moved during some time interval of much greater length (day, month, year, etc.). As a verb, to move into. Many other usages.

disintegration   As used by geologists, the reduction of a rock or mineral mechanically; a process of fragmentation, resulting in detritus or clastic particles.

dispersion   Act of dispersing; state of being dispersed; the separation of complex light into its contained wave lengths, as by a prism, or to create effects visible in a rainbow; also, in analogous phenomena, such as dispersing electric waves or a complex gravity wave in water, the separation of the disturbance into its component parts.

dissected   With reference to land surface, cut into valleys, ridges, etc., by removal of materials, by flow of water or ice as a rule; roughened topography. Sometimes used to describe submerged surfaces.

distributary   (1) Channel branching from another in the direction of water flow, particularly if it does not rejoin farther downstream. Channels down the slope of an alluvial cone or that individually lead to a body of water across a delta are typical. In some cases a distri-butary eventually diverts the flow of its parent stream. (2) In the lower part of its course, a river may break up into several channels which enter the sea or other bodies of water at different places. Distributary channels are found in most deltas.

diurnal   (1) Daily; specifically, as applied to ocean tides, one high and one low level per day. Also applied to other actions having a 24-hour cycle or rhythm. (2) Having a period or cycle of approximately one tidal day.

diurnal tide   A tide with one high water and one low water in a tidal day.

divergence   (1) In refraction phenomena, the increasing of distance between orthogonals in the direction of wave travel. Denotes an area of decreasing wave heights and energy concentration. (2) In wind-setup phenomena, the decrease in setup observed under that which would occur in an equivalent rectangular basin of uniform depth, caused by changes in platform or depth. Also the increase in basin width or depth causing such decrease in setup. (3) Separation in directions of flow along a line, plane, or zone. Ordinarily applied to circulation in air or water.

double ebb (tidal)   An ebb current having two maxima of velocity separated by a smaller ebb velocity.

downdrift   The direction of predominant movement of littoral materials.

drift current   A broad, shallow, slow-moving ocean or lake current. Opposite of stream current. See **current**.

drowning   Flooding by rise of water or subsidence of land. Extended to mean covering of flooded areas by alluvial deposits. Estuaries are a common example of drowning, ordinarily as a result of rising sea level. After sufficient time the deposits accumulating in estuaries drown the topography present when the estuary was formed. Most coasts were drowned during the recent rise of sea level, in which hills were detached from the mainland and islands were created where their summits were highest. In coastal regions an important effect of drowning is the associated rise of the water table.

drumlin   Elongate oval hill formed of debris accumulated beneath a slowly advancing glacier. The long axis of the hill and steeper frontal slope mark the direction of movement of the subsequently vanished glaciers. An unstratified hill of glacial drift. A whaleback-shaped hill deposited by an ice sheet, usually in groups.

dune   A topographic form characterized by a steeper face on the side toward which it advances and a more gentle slope upwind or upcurrent, whether exposed to the atmosphere, as in the case of a sand dune in an arid region or near a beach, or covered by water, as in the case of small ripple marks or larger sand waves. Commonly, dunes are composed of sand, but in some cases of finer sediment such as clay. The upwind or upcurrent (stoss) side of a dune is eroded and the other (lee) side is built forward. Dunes that have ceased moving are regarded as fixed and may be covered by vegetation and exhibit soil development. The migration of a dune is an example of collection bed transport. In torrential currents of water, the direction of movement of a dune crest (summit) may be upcurrent, in which case it is called an antidune; extremely rapid downcurrent transport occurs at the time antidunes are present. Bed forms are smaller than bars but larger than ripples that are out of phase with any water-surface gravity waves associated with them.

dune field   Extensive deposits on sand in an area where the supply is abundant. As a characteristic, individual dunes somewhat resemble barchans but are highly irregular in shape and crowded; erg areas of the Sahara are an example.

dune ridge   A ridge of sand blown a short distance inland from the beach. Where the shore is being extended into the sea (prograded), there may be a series of subparallel dune ridges, as at Cape Henry, Virginia.

dune rock   See **eolianite**.

duration   In wave forecasting, the length of time the wind blows in nearly the same direction over the fetch (generating area).

duricrust   Ground surface mineral incrustation formed by water solutioning and precipitation, usually in deserts.

ebb   To move outward and downward, as a falling tide, as opposed to flood; decrease in intensity, etc.; description of condition of a tide between high and succeeding low water.

ebb current   The tidal current away from shore or down a tidal stream. Usually associated with the decrease in the height of the tide.

ebb tide   (1) A nontechnical term used for falling tide or ebb current. In technical language, ebb refers to current. (2) Falling tide between high and low tidal stages. At such times, currents flow out of bays into the ocean.

eddy   (1) Rotating mass of water around an axis that is vertical or nearly so; a vortex; a whirlpool if the rotation is rapid. Rotation is caused by shear, either created by some obstruction or by proximity of currents flowing with differing speeds or directions. Water moves toward the central part of an eddy, downward flow occurs in the axial area. Term is also applied to similar structures in wind currents; for example, small "dust devils," or on a grand scale to cyclones. On a microscopic scale eddies are associated with turbulent flow. Some eddies are fixed in position, while others move more or less downcurrent. Secondary, spinoff,

eddies are commonly generated. (2) A circular movement of water formed on the side of a main current. Eddies may be created at points where the main stream passes projecting obstructions or where two adjacent currents flow counter to each other. In extreme cases a whirlpool forms.

edge wave   Ocean wave of limited width that moves along a coast with its axis at about right angles to the coast. Called a king wave in some countries. These waves result from wave currents arriving within about 20° of the trend of the shore, forming an envelope that may build to heights of several tens of meters; ordinarily accompanied by a characteristic road that increases with closeness that is caused by the violence with which cobbles and other solids are displaced and moved by the edge wave current. The crest, normal to the shore, lowers rapidly in the seaward direction.

embayment   (1) An indentation in a shoreline forming an open bay. (2) The formation of a bay. (3) Depression reentrant in the margin of a land with a tendency to be submerged and/or subside.

emergence   Rise of land relative to sea level; uplift to a position above its surroundings; act of becoming increasingly accepted as a theory or an idea.

end moraine   Debris deposited at the terminus of a glacier and forming a ridge remaining to mark a particular glacial stage after the glacier has melted back or vanished.

en echelon   In steps. Used by geologists to describe repetitive features arranged in parallel but offset rows, such as ridges having similar strikes and close association but that are separated.

energy coefficient   The ratio of the energy in a wave per unit crest length transmitted forward with the wave at a point in shallow water to the energy in a wave per unit crest length transmitted forward with the wave in deep water. Distance between a pair of orthogonals at a selected point to the distance between the same pair of orthogonals in deep water.

eolian   Associated with wind, which most commonly acts as a transport agent; for example, eolian sand (characterized as a rule by rounded, sometimes pitted, grains) and eolianite.

eolian deposits   Wind-deposited sediments, such as sand dunes.

eolianite (aeolianite)   Dune rock, sandstone that originated as a result of transport of sand in wind and that owes its induration to calcareous cement, present because the sand has high lime content. Crossbedding and other characteristics of wind deposits are typically evident. Often composed of minute shells or shell fragments.

eolian sands (blown sands)   Sediments of sand size or smaller that have been transported by winds. They may be recognized in marine deposits off desert coasts by the greater angularity of the grains compared with waterborne particles.

ephemeral   Transient; lasting for only a short time, as part of a day. Applied to streams that flow directly as a result of runoff from a local rain, etc., but whose beds are normally dry. Intermittent streams ordinarily flow for longer periods of time; for example, seasonally.

epicontinental   Upon a continent. Specifically, a sea above a continental shelf, or any epeiric sea, such as Hudson Bay, the Gulf of Mexico, and Mediterranean Sea.

equatorial tides   Tides occurring semimonthly as the result of the moon being over the equator. At these times the tendency of the moon to produce a diurnal inequality in the tide is at a minimum.

erg   Extensive area covered by sand, as in some deserts. If somewhat smaller areas are involved, they commonly are called dune fields, q.v. A sand sea.

erosion   (Root word, as in rodent, means to gnaw). Wearing away; specifically, entrainment; detachment of particles, of whatever size or by whatever means, as illustrated by effects of currents, water, wind, ice, etc., in contact with surfaces of land, wetted perimeters of channels, etc. Commonly applied to the entire process of wearing away of landmasses, an unfortunate usage because erosion is but one of many processes involved. Erosion is immediately succeeded by transport.

escarpment   (1) A more or less continuous line of cliffs or steep slopes facing in one general direction that are cuased by erosion or faulting. (2) A cliffed terminus of an elevated area, such as a fault scarp, as on the northeast coast of San Clemente Island off California, or on an erosional escarpment, such as the cliffed north shore of Molokai Island, Hawaii. An escarpment may be entirely below sea level, as the Gorda Escarpment in the Pacific Ocean off California on the south side of the San Andreas Fault. Also called scarp.

estuarine   Associated with the presence of an estuary.

estuary   (1) Drowned river mouth in most cases, especially where the shoreline penetrates considerable distance inland. Ordinarily implying some intrusion of brackish or saline water. Originally, tidal influences were regarded as essential, but the tendency has been to broaden the meaning of the term to include examples in which tidal influences are negligible, or even absent. Unfortunately, the term is sometimes extended to mean bodies of water separated from the sea by islands of any origin. Bays with arms extending along drowned stream valleys are included, as well as valleys deepened by ice scour, as in the case of fiords of Norway, etc. (2) Drowned valley of a river including its tributaries, generally elongate at an angle to the

shoreline. Some other authors include in the definitions lagoons elongate parallel to the shoreline. (3) The part of a river that is affected by tides. (4) The region of a river mouth in which the fresh water of the river mixes with the salt water of the sea. A firth, a frith.

eustatic   Refers to a worldwide rise or fall in sea level resulting, for example, from the return to the ocean of meltwater at the end of a glacial episode. This is independent of local elevation or depression of coastal lands.

eye   In meteorology, usually the "eye of the storm" (hurricane); the roughly circular area of comparatively light winds and fair weather found at the center of a severe tropical cyclone.

fan, alluvial   See **alluvial fan.**

fault   A fracture along which there has been differential movement of the blocks on opposite sides. The movement may be principally vertical, so that one block is elevated, or lateral, in which case there is a different direction of movement of the blocks on either side, as in the San Andreas Fault of California. Movement may involve both vertical and lateral components.

fault block   The elevated mass of rock on the upthrow side of a fault surface.

feeder beach   Source of sand for nourishment of downcurrent beaches (mainly for recreational or protective purposes). In most cases the sand is obtained by dredging and replenished as needed.

fen   Relatively flat area typically covered by marsh vegetation. The fens in England have become much drier in recent centuries as a result both of improved drainage and of isostatic uplift.

fetch   (1) As used in describing the formation of wind waves, the fetch is the horizontal length of the generating area in the direction of the wind; that is, the distance between the rear and the front boundaries of the generating area. In general, the fetch boundaries are determined by coastlines or by one of the following: (a) fanning out of the isobars; (b) curvature of the isobars; or (c) meteorological fronts. (2) Occasionally, the area, rather than length. (3) In some literature the term signifies the distance from the weather shore to where the formation of waves commences. (4) Sometimes used synonymously with fetch length.

firth   (1) As used in Scotland, a deep estuary, not a fiord. (2) A narrow arm of the sea; also the opening of a river into the sea. An estuary.

fissure   An opening extending downward in rock or ice, originating as a cleft or parting; an open joint; a deep furrow.

fixed channel   A stream whose course is determined by its incision into bedrock or other materials that effectively resist erosion. This is the normal condition of eroding channels in regions of hills, mountains, or flat territory where sides and beds of channels consist of solid rock. In alluvial regions channels are fixed in tenacious clay or where they have cut down locally into bedrock below the alluvium. Channel positions are also fixed along faults and other geologic structures.

fixed dune   Stabilized dune, protected by vegetation, cementation, etc., from modification by wind action. Fixation in some cases has persisted long enough for soil profile development to begin.

fjard (fiard)   Irregular embayment, fjordlike but with subdued relief surrounding it. The irregular coast of Sweden exhibits many examples

fjord (fiord)   An estuary or arm of one extending along a valley deepened by ice and drowned either, and commonly both, by admission of the sea as a result of rise of level or by wasting away of the glacial ice. In most cases the valleys were occupied by rivers prior to ice advance that somewhat reshaped them by scour. Anchorage for ships typically occurs only in limited areas where the bedrock is covered by recently accumulated sediments. Charts suggest far more value as harbors than actually exists. Bottom depths are highly variable, which is also true of glaciated surfaces of bedrock in mountains, etc.

floating marsh   Flotant; quaking marsh, etc.; vegetation-covered areas held together by intertwined roots and plant debris above water or soft ooze. In some cases the accumulation is too thin to support a human's weight, but typically it may be crossed and eventually becomes firm land. Shaking one's body normally results in perceptible vibration of the surrounding area. Developed over fresh or slightly brackish water. Marsh close to a shore is ordinarily firm in comparison.

floe berg   Large masses of sea ice broken off from ancient floes of great thickness when they are forced upon the shore and presenting the appearance of small icebergs.

floe ice   Floe ice consists of drift ice frozen into small fields, a floe carrying the meaning of a small field. An area of ice other than fast ice whose limits are between 0.3 to 0.6 meter (1 and 2 feet) in thickness. Floes thicker than this are known as heavy floes. Floe ice prevents navigation.

flood   Higher stages of river regime; incoming or rising tide; also many other meanings.

flood current   The movement of a tidal current toward the shore or up a tidal stream. In the semidiurnal type of reversing current, the terms "greater flood" and "lesser flood" are applied respectively to the flood currents of greater and lesser velocity each day. The terms "maximum flood" and "minimum flood" are applied to the maximum and minimum velocities of a flood current the velocity of which alternately increases and decreases without coming to a slack or reversing. Maximum flood is also applicable to any flood current at the time of greatest velocity.

flood plain   The surface of sediment deposited by a stream after it becomes land (adjective, floodplain). Flood plains are the result of alluviation. In typical cases they are subject to overflow during floods; ordinarily the flooding is restricted to lower areas, which accumulate alluvium as consequence. Higher parts (natural levees) result from more active alluviation along the sides of active channels, and backswamps occur in basins between them. If stream channels deepen enough to terminate flooding, flood plains stand elevated and are called alluvial or stream terraces. Alluvial cones are flood plains if they are relatively flat and extend into broad alluvial valleys, but after diversion of the master stream forming them they are subject to dissection and are regarded as standing above the flood plain.

flood tide   (1) Rising ocean surface preceding high tide stage; often produces a current that flows into a bay. (2) The period of tide between low water and the succeeding high water; a rising tide.

flucculation   Aggregation of colloids or clay particles into visible particles, flocs, ordinarily are electrolytic agencies occurring when fresh water reaches a slightly saline environment. Produced in various ways in the laboratory. Flocs (flo-cules) are commonly heavier than water, so precipitate to the bottom. In estuaries and tidal channels the precipitate forms ooze that eventually becomes clay. Traditionally, aggregations in soils or sediments.

fluvial   Pertaining to channels of water—streams, creeks, rivers, etc.; potamic.

fog   Minute water droplets suspended in the atmosphere close to the ground; cloud surrounding a person. In navigation, etc., the droplets must reduce visibility to 1 kilometer (0.62 mile) or less.

fore dune (foredune)   A dune immediately behind a shoreline. Such dunes commonly are small and form rows.

forerunner   (1) Low, long-period ocean swell that commonly precedes the main swell from a distant storm, especially a tropical cyclone. (2) Low-amplitude, long-period swell not detectable by eye, and arriving before the main body of waves from a storm.

foreshore   The part of the shore lying between the crest of the seaward berm (or upper limit of wave wash at high tide) and the ordinary low-water mark, that is ordinarily traversed by the uprush and backrush of the waves as the tides rise and fall. The same as the beach face where unconsolidated material is present. The portion of the shore between ordinary high and low water marks, as on a beach.

fracture   Act of breaking or state of being broken; rupture; condition exhibited by an elastic solid when stressed sufficiently. Characteristic of rigidity and not ductility, in which the yield results from flow. Incipient fracture is called cleavage, and true fracture results in joints, faults, or fissures. Minerals and amorphous substances, if sufficiently rigid, fracture irregularly, in many cases leaving rounded surfaces that are regarded as conchoidal (shell-like) but fracture may be uneven, fibrous, or hackly, etc.

fringing reef   (1) Reef building by marine organisms, commonly corals and algae, in shallow water along the shore, as on several Hawaiian Islands. In the Cedar Keys area of the Florida Gulf coast, many fringing reefs are made of oyster shells. (2) A coral reef attached directly to an insular or continental shore. (3) An organic reef ranging from slightly offshore to essentially on the strand.

front of the fetch   In wave forecasting, the end of the generating area toward which the wind is blowing.

fulls   See **beach ridge.**

fumarole   A vent or hole through which a column of superheated steam with associated gases rise, usually in recent lava flows or ash flows, as in the Valley of Ten Thousand Smokes, near Mt. Katmai, Alaska.

gale   A wind between a strong breeze and a storm (in the Beaufort Scale). A continuous wind blowing in degrees of a moderate, fresh, strong, or whole gale and varying in velocity from 28 to 35 nautical miles per hour.

generating area   In wave forecasting, the continuous area of water surface over which the wind blows in nearly a constant direction. Sometimes used synonymously with fetch length. Also **fetch.**

generation of waves   (1) The creation of waves by natural or mechanical means. (2) The creation and growth of waves caused by a wind blowing over a water surface for a certain period of time. The area involved is called the generating area or fetch.

geology   The science that treats the origin, history, and structure of the earth, as recorded in the rocks; together with the forces and processes now operating to modify rocks.

geomorphology   (1) Earth science concerned with forms on the earth's surface and changes taking place as landforms develop, drawing on conclusions of geographic, geologic, pedologic, climatologic, hydraulic, and other disciplines. Formerly called physiography when its emphasis was mainly on processes of degradation of the surface. (2) That branch of physical geography that deals with the form of the earth, the general configuration of its surface, the distribution of the land, water, etc. (3) The investigation of the history of geologic changes through the interpretation of topographic forms.

geosyncline   An elongate large area downwarped structurally in which sedimentary rocks accumulate in great thickness, whether actively forming or preserved in older rocks. Most mountain ranges having diastrophic origin formed in areas where geosyncline existed.

glacial deposits (drift)   Sediments and rock fragments deposited after transport by ice.

glacial drift   Sediment accumulated as a result of glaciation, under a glacier, at its margins or beyond, as glaciofluvial and glacial marine deposits.

glacial marine   Deposits formed in seawater at or near the margins of an ice sheet or glacier, as in Alaskan fiords, or the Ross Ice Shelf adjoining Antarctica. Also included are sediments dropped from icebergs.

glacial till   A boulder clay, and unsorted and unstratified sediment deposited directly by a glacier in moraines or drumlins and not reworked by meltwater.

glaciation   The alteration of any part of the earth's surface in consequence of the movement of land ice.

glacier   Flowing ice on land. Modern terminology inclines toward recognition of glaciers and ice caps as continental ice, island ice, valley ice, etc.

glaciofluvial   A term applied to sediments introduced into an area by glaciers but transported beyond the ice front by meltwater streams. Includes outwash and valley train deposits.

grau   Term used in southern France for a narrow coastal opening into a lagoon or similar waterbody.

gravity wave   (1) A wave whose velocity is controlled primarily by gravity. If a breeze of less than 2 knots blows across water, small ripples (wavelets) form almost instantly, and if wind velocity diminishes, these disappear about as rapidly; but when the wind velocity exceeds 2 knots, more stable gravity waves are formed and progress with the wind. (2) A wave whose velocity of propagation is controlled primarily by gravity. Water waves more than 5 centimeters (2 inches) long are considered gravity waves. Waves longer than 2.5 centimeters (1 inch) and shorter than 5 centimeters (2 inches) are in an indeterminate zone between capillary and gravity waves. See **ripple.**

groin   A shore-protection and improvement structure (built usually to trap littoral drift or retard erosion of the shore). It is narrow in width (measured parallel to the shoreline); and its length may vary from less than one hundred to several hundred meters (extending from a point landward of the shoreline out into the water). Groins may be classified as permeable (with openings through them) or impermeable (a solid or nearly solid structure). Also spelled groyne.

groove   In the terminology applied to coral reefs, a small trough leading down the reef face, alternating with buttresses. Together, these, as well as surge channels, dampen the energy of advancing waves most effectively. More commonly, a shallow, linear depression created by abrasion, as on a firm surface crossed by moving ice containing rocks.

ground swell   A long, high ocean swell, rising to prominent height as the water shallows. When the increase in amplitude reaches almost the breaking point, individual swells are called blind rollers. These may mark local areas of shoaling.

gulf   A relatively large portion of sea, partly enclosed by land.

habitat   The place where an organism lives. The term is usually used more specifically than environment. It is used with descriptive words to emphasize distinct features, such as swamp habitat, barren habitat, rock habitat, stream habitat, lakeshore habitat.

half-tide level   A plane midway between mean high water and mean low water. Also called mean tide level.

harbor   Shelter; place of security and comfort; portion of a water body where ships are protected, because the area is either in part landlocked or artificially sheltered. Good anchorage is a favorable but not necessary qualification, something also true of wharves or other structures.

headland   (1) Cape or comparatively bold promontory jutting seaward. (2) A high, steep-faced promontory extending into the sea.

head of rip   The part of a rip current that has widened out seaward of the breakers. See also **rip current.**

head sea   Sea coming from the front. A ship moving in the direction from which the waves are coming is said to be in a head sea.

heave   (1) The vertical rise or fall of the waves or sea. (2) The translational movement of a craft parallel to its vertical axis. (3) The net transport of a floating body resulting from wave action.

heavy sea   A sea in which the waves run high.

higher high water   The higher of the two high waters of any tidal day. The single high water occurring daily during periods when the tide is diurnal is considered to be a higher high water.

higher low water   The higher of the two low waters of any tidal day.

high tide (high water)   The maximum elevation reached by each rising tide. See **tide.** The height may be solely due to the periodic tidal forces or it may have superimposed on it the effects of prevailing meteorological conditions.

high water line   In strictness, the intersection of the plane of mean high water with the shore. The shoreline delineated on the nautical charts of the U.S. Coast and Geodetic Survey is an approximation of the high water line. For specific occurrences, the highest elevation on the shore reached during a storm or rising tide, including meteorological effects.

high water mark   A reference mark on a structure or natural object, indicating the maximum stage of tide or flood.

hinge line   During the Pleistocene ice age, heavily glaciated areas were depressed under the weight of the ice, and marginal areas were elevated. When the glaciers melted, these movements were reversed. The hinge line is the junction between elevated and depressed areas. Also applies to line between upraised and downdropped areas due to faulting.

Holocene   Latest part of geologic time, variously defined. A term originating and most widely used in Europe but gaining popularity elsewhere. A common definition regards it as dating from the time the ice crossed the Baltic during its last major retreat; others consider the start as indicated by changes in pollen spectra that suggest warmer temperatures. In general, the start is regarded as a few thousand years ago. The term is reminiscent of the importance attached by Americans to the time that ice retreated across Niagara River, initiating the cutting of the gorge below the falls and hence starting the Recent, something that recent investigators regard as inconsequential or even as an erroneous concept. More fundamental are times such as when the ice initiated its last major retreat or dating of the various complications involved in the retreat.

hook   A curve at the end of a spit formed by tidal currents entering a bay. Present in most tidal inlets. Sandy Hook, outside New York Harbor, is a well-known example.

hurricane   (1) A large, cyclonic mass of air commonly originating on the western side of the Atlantic or Pacific oceans a few degrees north or south of the equator, moving with a generally poleward component and somewhat westward to a latitude of $25°$ or higher, after which it recurves and moves eastward. Maximum velocities toward the central eye are less than in tornadoes, but range upward from 128.7 to 241.3 kilometers per hour (80 to 150 miles per hour). As most of the energy comes from condensation of water vapor, the energy of the storm diminishes rapidly over land. (2) An intense tropical cyclone in which winds tend to spiral inward toward a core of low pressure, with maximum surface wind velocities that equal or exceed 120.6 kilometers per hour (75 miles per hour; 65 knots) for several minutes or longer at some points. "Tropical storm" is the term applied if maximum winds are less than 120.6 kilometers per hour (75 miles per hour).

hurricane surge (wave)   A sudden rise in sea level caused by a violent cyclonic wind system of considerable size. The surge builds to greater heights if it approaches across a wide and comparatively shallow continental shelf, to lesser heights around islands surrounded by deep water. Lower barometric pressure associated with the eye of the storm plus wind drive account for the disturbance that, like tsunami or surges of explosive origin, increases in amplitude on reaching shallow water.

hydrography   (1) The description and study of seas, lakes, rivers, and other waters. (2) The science of locating aids and dangers to navigation. (3) The description of physical properties of the waters of a region.

hydrosphere   Water layer of the earth, with gaseous atmosphere above and lithosphere of rock below. Ordinarily refers to water in ocean basins, rather than on continents.

hypersaline   Euhaline; descriptive of water with more than usual salinity, ordinarily more than in local sea water, as in a lagoon affected by evaporation in excess of inflow from the sea.

ice age   Older term for Pleistocene, the earlier part of the Quaternary division of geologic time. Characterized by extreme variations in cover by continental ice and corresponding effects on sea level (highest with least continental ice). Realistically, the Ice Age hasn't ended because there is at least one-third as much continental ice today as during any Pleistocene glacial stage; this ice includes more than 80 percent of the world's fresh water.

iceberg   A large floating mass of ice detached from a glacier at sea level.

ice cap   (1) Extensive mass of ice covering land, as is present on Antarctica. Generally regarded as continental ice if the area is large, island or mountain ice if less extensive. Typically the surface does not reflect underlying topography, but crevasses or other forms indicate abrupt changes in slope. (2) In Alaska, as well as in Greenland and Antarctica, large upland areas are largely buried beneath glacial ice. Glacial flow generally takes place radially from the highest parts of such an ice field. The Pleistocene continental glaciers of such an ice field. The Pleistocene continental glaciers of North America and Europe were large ice fields. (3) A sheet of sea ice extending over a considerable area. It is of such extent that its termination cannot be seen from the crow's nest of a ship.

impermeable groin   A groin through which sand cannot pass. See **groin.**

indurate   To increase hardness, firmness, durability, strength, etc., of sediments, changing them to bodies of rock in the popular sense. These commonly result from cementation but may arise from other causes,

such as baking, development of oxides, or other alterations of minerals.

inlet   (1) A narrow strip of water running into the land or between islands, such as the entrance through a barrier reef into a lagoon (pass), or a small bay or creek; a tidal inlet.

inshore   Being near, moving, or directed toward the shore; the zone of variable width between the shoreline and the breaker zone (applied either to the water or the beach). Same as shoreface.

inshore current   (1) Horizontal movement of water inside the surf zone (includes longshore and rip currents). (2) Any current in or landward of the breaker zone. (3) Any current inside the surf zone. (4) In beach terminology, the zone of variable width extending from the low-water line through the breaker zone.

insular   (1) Of or pertaining to an island or islands. (2) Detached; standing alone.

interglacial stage   During the Pleistocene period, four major glacial episodes are recognized in North America and Europe. In the three intervening stages, glaciers of the earth melted back even farther than they have today. During parts of interglacials, sea levels were higher than now, and marine beaches and terraces were formed at many places higher than those along the present shores.

internal wave   A wave in the interface between two density layers of water or other fluid.

intertidal   Between high and low water marks, indicating the tidal range along a coast.

island   (1) A body of land extending above, and completely surrounded by water at the mean high water stage. (2) An area of dry land entirely surrounded by water or a swamp. (3) An area of swamp entirely surrounded by open water. (4) Landmass surrounded by water, having dimensions less than those of a continent and greater than those of rock, sea stack, etc. Islet may be used.

island arc   A group of islands elongate in arrangement and ordinarily, with axial concavity in the direction of not-far-distant mainland; for example, Aleutians, Japanese, Indonesian. Arcuate disposition of andesite volcanoes, usually along an ocean trench.

island ice   Ice cap covering a significant part of an island (other than being localized in valleys). Used in distinction to terms such as continental ice or valley ice.

islet   A very small and minor island.

isostatic adjustment   When an additional weight, such as a glacier or deposits of a large delta, are placed on a portion of the earth's crust, it subsides under the load. If this weight is removed, as by melting of the glacier or erosion of the delta sediments, the area will rise.

jet flow   Flow concentrated into a distinct current whose velocity is higher than that existing in the surrounding media (air or water, as a rule). Where occurring out from the mouth of a stream entering a lake or the sea, the jet widens, decreases in energy, and eventually dies out.

jetty   (1) (U.S. usage). On open seacoasts, a structure extending into a body of water, and designed to prevent shoaling of a channel by littoral materials, and to direct and confine the stream or tidal flow. Jetties are built at the mouth of a river or tidal inlet to help deepen and stabilize a channel. (2) (British usage). Jetty is synonymous with warf or pier. See **training wall.**

joint   A fracture in rock that may be open or closed between blocks that have not been offset by shear with the same orientation (fault). Many joints are essentially planar and commonly are arranged in parallel sets, of which two or more may be present. Coasts developed as a result of jointing. Curving examples result in more or less domal topographic forms that are present on many crystalline-rock coasts.

kame   Glaciofluvial deposit, commonly conate in shape and often associated with moraines and kettles.

karst   A feature or an area characterized by having been formed by processes associated with solubility of limestone. Named after a region in Yugoslavia where it is well developed, with conspicuous lapiés, sinkholes, underground drainage, caves, etc. Karst features are most spectacular in rugged regions but are not confined to them. The many circular lakes, ponds, or depressions in the Florida peninsula and those on the High Plains of Texas may be regarded as flat karst. Contrasts in karstic modification related to degrees of solubility of limestone occur in the Mammoth Cave area, Kentucky, and elsewhere. Along limestone coasts landforms such as ridges, islands, sea stacks, etc., occur in less soluble limestone.

karst topography   In soluble rocks, such as limestone, dolomite, and gypsum, a complex of solution cavities (like caves and sink holes) allow surface streams to disappear, flowing into the underlying caves. In western peninsular Florida, a karst area developed during the Pleistocene time of lowered sea levels is now partly drowned by postglacial rise in sea level, leaving numerous lakes.

kelp   A member of an order of brown algae with large, leaflike structures and bulbous stems, commonly with a holdfast that may grip large boulders. Kelp grows in colder sea water (coast of California, southern Chile, South Africa, New Zealand, etc.) and in places forms wide beds that dampen waves most effectively. During intense storms great masses of kelp may be detached and thrown onto upper beaches, together with rocks attached by holdfasts. Kelp has many uses (source of iodine, ash used in making glass, useful fertilizer, etc.) and provides areas of good fishing. See also **seaweed.**

kettlehole   Near the margin of a receeding glacier, outwash deposits of sand and gravel may bury masses of ice. As these buried blocks later melt, the sediments above collapse, forming a depression. Commonly, small lakes form in kettleholes.

key   See **cay.**

knoll   (1) Loosely speaking, a submerged elevation of rounded shape rising from the ocean floor, but less prominent than a seamount. (2) Underwater mounds, in a line parallel to shore; similar to an intermittent bar. (3) On land, a little round hill; a mound.

lagoon   Shallow body of water at least intermittently connected with the sea or other larger body of water across a beach or other barrier. Typically, lagoonal water is brackish or saline, although broad lower parts of rivers behind sand bars are not excluded because their water may be fresh, particularly at times of maximum river inflow. Many lagoons are elongate parallel to the coast. The basin within an atoll, commonly connected with the sea at one or more places, is also included.

landslide   Downslope movement of a comparatively large mass of rock debris, usually rather suddenly.

landslide surge   Large water displacement by a landslide entering standing water.

lateral moraine   The deposit formed along the sides of a valley glacier, composed of debris carried to the glacier by avalanches from bordering cliffs. This type of moraine may survive after the glacier mas melted, leaving a terrace on the side of a valley.

lava   Molten or solidified rock that issued from a fracture in country rock or volcanic vent. The most abundant variety is basalt in oceanic basins on continents, but may be andesite (a somewhat more siliceous and lighter—both in color and weight—lava) near continental margins around the Pacific Ocean. Many other types (rhyolite, dacite, etc.) are also relatively abundant on continents.

lava cone   A cone-shaped mountain built by successive lava flows. It has gentler slopes than a cinder cone. Good examples are in the Hawaiian Islands and the Aleutians.

lava fan   Arcuate coastal bulges due to lavas entering the sea, for example, in Maui, Hawaii.

lee   Sheltered side; downcurrent side; shelter, generally from effects of wind, waves, drifting snow, etc. Side toward which wind blows is called windward (in navigation) and the opposite side, lee. Opposite of stoss.

length of wave The horizontal distance between similar points on two successive waves measured perpendicularly to the crest.

lenticular Lens-shaped, converging toward ends of a longer axis, as in islands, sedimentary deposits, bars of sediment, or some feature present in rock.

levee (1) A landing place, pier, or quay. (2) A dike or embankment to prevent inundation. (3) Artificial or natural dike, including examples with very gentle lateral slopes.

limestone Rock composed predominantly (80 percent or more in some definitions) of calcium carbonate (lime), in many cases associated with magnesium carbonate.

limit of backwash The seaward limit of the backwash at any given tide stage.

limit of uprush The landward limit of the uprush at any given tide stage.

lithification Result of processes associated with increased induration of rock, for example, conversion of sand (unindurated, unconsolidated rock) into sandstone, or clay into claystone, etc.

littoral Near shore. By some definitions limited to the tidal zone; by others, to depths of 100 fathoms. A littoral current, caused by wave action, running more or less parallel to the shore (longshore current). Littoral deposits accumulate in nearshore, ordinarily shallow, water.

littoral current A current moving parallel to the shore, usually developed by wave fronts that have an angular approach to the shore. The current causes shifting of beach sand along the shore.

littoral deposits Deposits of littoral drift.

littoral drift The sedimentary material moved in the littoral zone under the influence of waves and currents.

littoral transport The movement of littoral drift in the littoral zone under the influence of waves and currents. Includes movement parallel (longshore transport) and perpendicular (on-offshore transport) to the shore.

littoral zone In beach terminology, an indefinite zone extending seaward from the shoreline to just beyond the breaker zone.

lobe Subdelta; a division of a delta associated with deposition along an individual stream system that is a major channel or distributary of the river responsible for the entire alluvial deposit. Individual part extending forward, as of a glacier, lava flow, etc.

loess Wind-blown dust, mainly silt-size clasts.

longcrested waves A wave, the crest length of which is long compared to the wave length.

longitudinal dune Dune with elongate axis in the direction of the wind. A seif dune in most regards but should have a sharply curved advancing front, giving the dune a fishhook shape with a long shank pointing toward the prevailing wind direction.

longshore Parallel to and near the shoreline.

longshore bar A slightly submerged sand ridge generally parallel to the shore a short distance from the beach. At some places there are series of parallel longshore bars at increasing distances from the beach.

longshore current (longshore drift) A current located in the surf zone, moving generally parallel to the shoreline, generated by waves breaking at an angle with the shoreline. Current that runs along and roughly parallel to the shore. Commonly, it is a result of wave arrivals in shoaling water at angles less than normal to the shoreline and submarine contours, and acts as the feeder of rip currents. Also called an alongshore current. See **littoral current** and **beach drifting.**

longshore trough Elongate depression between longshore bars.

long wave This refers to the term tidal wave as used by Sir Horace Lamb in his book *Hydrodynamics*. It refers to the gravitational oscillations in bodies of water possessing the characteristic feature of the oceanic tides produced by the action of the sun and moon; that is, waves in which the motion of the fluid is mainly horizontal and therefore sensibly the same for all particles in a vertical line. Also called shallow water wave or very shallow water wave.

lower beach Portion of the beach submerged at all times, extending out as far as ordinary high waves entrain and transport sediment from and along the bottom, commonly extending inland as far as the step (if present) dividing it from the upper beach.

lower high water The lower of the two high waters of any tidal day.

lower low water The lower of the two low waters of any tidal day. The single low water occurring daily during periods when the tide is diurnal is considered to be a lower low water.

low island A term used mainly in the Pacific and Indian oceans for islands (many of which are atolls) formed by accumulations of coral, algae, etc., and their debris, and rising only a few meters above sea level. Although subject to overwash during severe storms, great numbers of low islands are inhabited. Their vegetational variety is narrowly restricted. The only useful trees ordinarily are coconut palms and pandanus.

low tide (low water) The minimum elevation reached by each falling tide. See **tide.**

lunate bar A crescent-shaped, submerged sand bar commonly developed directly outside the entrance to a harbor or estuary.

lunette dune   An arcuate dune form commonly developed just downwind from a blowout or pan.

mammillated surface   A series of rounded, breast-like hills, usually of glacial origin.

mangrove   One of several genera of trees or shrubs characteristic of many tropical or subtropical coasts, that are ordinarily very tolerant of saline water with which they come in contact. In most examples mangroves grow in close formation, forming swamps that are difficult to cross. Some are used for tannin, for their wood, and to some extent animals for food by browsing. Many are only a few meters high, but in favorable environments mangroves form tall, stately trees. Their decomposition results in accumulations of peat that may become tens of meters thick. Mangrove peat may have greater total volume than that formed by other plants (moss, sedges, grass, etc.). There are many varieties, lumped roughly under terms black, red, and white. There are two important varieties. Red mangrove, *Rhizophora,* can establish itself and grow in normal seawater; it forms the seaward margin of mangrove coasts. Black mangrove, *Avicenna,* cannot colonize in open marine water but inhabits areas behind the red mangrove stand; it is covered only at very high tides.

marsh   (1) Strictly, a low, relatively flat area that is wet for appreciable periods and commonly contains considerable water surface, supporting widespread vegetational cover of grasses and other plants smaller than trees or large bushes (which may grow in patches on higher and drier areas locally). Distinguished from a swamp, which is similar but is typically covered by shrubs or trees; but both terms, with somewhat different meanings, are used loosely. (2) An area of soft, wet, or periodically inundated land, generally treeless and usually characterized by grasses and other low growth.

mass movement   Downslope transport of surface material (soil, rock debris, etc.) as a result of gravity, commonly assisted by water (as a lubricant or from the force of its expansion on becoming ice). Includes slow creep, results of solifluction, slump, slide, debris avalanche, etc.

mass transport   In regard to surface gravity waves (progressive) the nonperiodic movement of water in the direction of wave travel.

mass transport, shoreward   The movement of water due to wave motion, which carries water through the breaker zone in the direction of wave propagation. Part of the nearshore current system.

mean depth   The average depth of the water area between the still water level and the shoreface profile from the waterline to any chosen distance seaward.

meander   (Verb). To develop systematic sinuosity (as a stream with an alluvial bed) as a result of processes of deposition, sediment entrainment, bank caving, etc. (Noun). A more or less S-shaped bend developed as a result of meandering. Excluded are sinuosities caused by agencies or controls other than those directly involved hydraulic processes that cause transfer of alluvium along the channel. As used by surveyors, the determination of the approximate course of a river by straight lines between points along the bank—in distinction to contouring, which implies detailed control and more accurate delineation.

mean higher high water   The average height of the higher high water over a 19-year period. For shorter periods of observation, corrections are applied to eliminate known variations and reduce the result to the equivalent of a mean 19-year value.

mean high water   The average height of the high water over a 19-year period. For shorter periods of observation, corrections are applied to eliminate known variations and reduce the result to the equivalent of a mean 19-year value. All high-water heights are included in the average where the type of tide is either semidiurnal or mixed. Only the higher high water heights are included in the average where the type of tide is diurnal. So determined, mean high water in the latter case is the same as mean higher high water.

mean lower low water   The average height of the lower low waters over a 19-year period. For shorter periods of observations, corrections are applied to eliminate known variations and reduce the results to the equivalent of a mean 19-year value. Frequently abbreviated to lower low water.

mean low water   The average height of the low water over a 19-year period. For shorter periods of observations, corrections are applied to eliminate known variations and reduce the results to the equivalent of a mean 19-year value. All low-water heights are included in the average where the type of tide is either semidiurnal or mixed. Only lower low water heights are included in the average where the type of tide is diurnal. So determined, mean low water in the latter case in the same as mean lower low water.

mean range of tide   The difference in height between mean high water and mean low water.

mean rise of tide   The height of mean high water above the plane of reference or datum of chart.

mean sea level   The average height of the surface of the sea for all stages of the tide over a 19-year period, usually determined from hourly height readings. Not necessarily equal to mean tide level. See **sea level.**

mean tide level   A plane midway between mean high

water and mean low water. Not necessarily equal to mean sea level. Also called half-tide level.

mean water level   The mean surface level as determined by averaging the heights of the water at equal intervals of time, usually at hourly intervals.

medial moraine   Where the lateral moraines of two glaciers have joined and extended below the junction as a dark band of debris in the combined glacier.

megaripple   A more or less dunelike form associated with collective bed movement, generally of sand but in some cases of coarser materials, associated with comparatively high current velocities, as offshore from river mouths or estuaries, forming and moving most rapidly during a sharp drop in water level when tide ebbs or when rivers attain high discharge and velocity levels. Outlines are irregular as a rule; heights range up to a few meters; spacing is likely to be variable, from a few meters to several hundred. Ripple marks are smaller, sand waves larger. See **sand wave.**

meltwater   Water derived from ice, specifically from glacial ice, which from large volumes of continental ice causes a rise in sea level.

minimum fetch   The least distance in which steady state wave conditions will develop for a wind of a given speed blowing at a given duration of time.

mixed tide   Type of tide in which the presence of a diurnal wave is conspicuous by a large inequality in either the high or low water heights with two high waters and two low waters usually occurring each tidal day. In a strict sense, all tides are mixed, but the name is usually applied without definite limits to the tides intermediate to those predominantly semidiurnal and those predominantly diurnal.

monsoonal   Seasonal. Ordinarily descriptive of contrasts in precipitation, wind direction, etc. A monsoon wind occurs typically at the same season each year. The underlying cause is development of pressure gradients, such as result from continentality in climates. Also used to describe vegetation characteristic of areas subject to monsoonal conditions; for example, forests that grow vigorously at some season but are more or less defoliated and open during the opposite season.

moraine   Rock debris on or deposited by a glacier, or the topographic form resulting. However, if the deposit has little relief and is spread as a sheet, it is considered drift. Moraines are described in regard to position on a glacier. A deposit left by a glacier at its terminus (end moraine), along the side of a valley glacier (lateral moraine), down the glacier from the junction of tributaries (medial moraine), and as a thin glacial deposit over most of the glaciated area (ground moraine). Moraines are generally ridges, but a ground moraine may form a level plain. But after deposition, conspicuous moraines are ordinarily terminal. Residual deposits left by melted ice bear many different names.

mouth   The exit or point of discharge of a stream into another stream or a lake or sea.

muck   A dark earth capable of absorbing much water. Because of moisture content it has a consistency like that of moist or wet loam or humus. It is marked by the presence of organic matter in an advanced state of decomposition, in proportions of less than 50 percent but greater than 18 or 20 percent. It is fertile, rich in nitrogen, and relatively low in mineral content.

mud   General and popular rather than scientific term for sticky sediment when wet. Consists mainly of clay- or silt-sized particles admixed, but may have considerable organic or sand content. If the organic content is high, called muck. A fluid-to-plastic mixture of finely divided particles of solid material and water.

mud flat (mudflat)   (1) Deposit of ooze, clay, silt, etc., to water level along a shore. If tidal range is appreciable, the flat is ordinarily submerged at high tide. Also, similar deposits elsewhere, as along stream banks or in lower parts of basins. (2) A muddy, low-lying strip of ground by the shore, or an island, usually submerged more or less completely by the rise of the tide.

mudflow   A deposit formed by the rapid flow of water-saturated clay or shale. Flow of a more or less saturated and mixed mass of rock, sediment, soil, etc., down a slope. Larger rocks may be incorporated or carried along on the surface.

mudflow fan   Splay resulting from a mudflow, or in particular its lower part if spread across flat territory.

mudlumps (mud lumps)   Elevations or structures caused by the rise of clayey material through covering silt or sand. Known only in the Mississippi River Delta but suspected elsewhere. The rising sediment accumulated offshore as prodelta clay and when later buried under increasing load of delta deposits it behaves as a plastic and flows upward as a diapiric (crossing layers) intrusion, emerging as mounds, most of which are nearshore islands up to several acres in extent and 3 meters (10 feet) or so in height. Gas (mainly marsh gas derived from decomposition of plants) and water commonly rise and escape in association with the rise of the mud. Most mudlumps are elongate in the direction of some fracture and display highly varied and complex structures, in the main anticline.

mud volcano   Cone-shaped mound rising either on land or through water, in some cases several tens of meters or more but ordinarily much lower. Formed as a result of clayey mud rising and reaching the surface at some vent of restricted size. Commonly there is continuing flow of water or escape of gas. Large examples occur near the coast of West Pakistan, smaller examples are common in marshy areas receiving considerable loads of new sediment.

nautical mile   The length of a minute of arc 1/21,600 of an average great circle of the earth. Generally one minute of latitude is considered equal to one nautical mile. The accepted U.S. value as of 1 July 1959 is 1,852 meters or 6,076.115 feet, approximately 1.15 times as long as the statute mile of 1,609 meters (5,280 feet). Also known as the geographical mile.

neap rise   The height of neap high water above the plane of reference or datum of chart.

neap tidal current   Tidal current of decreased velocity occurring semimonthly as the result of the moon being in quadrature.

neap tide   (1) A tide occurring near the time of quadrature of the moon with the sun. The neap tidal range is usually 10 to 30 percent less than the mean tidal range. (2) Tide of low range experienced about every two weeks, when the directions to the sun and moon are about at right angles (between new and full moon, when spring tide occurs). The level of high neap tide is commonly that at which escape of ground water may be observed along springlines on beaches. (3) Tide of decreased range occurring semimonthly as the result of the moon being in quadrature. The neap range of tide is the average semidiurnal range occurring at the time of neap tides and is most conveniently computed from the harmonic constants. It is smaller than the mean range where the type of tide is either semidiurnal or mixed and is of no practical significance where the type of tide is diurnal. The average height of the high waters of the neap tide is called neap high water or high water neaps, and the average height of the corresponding low water is called neap low water or low water neaps.

nearshore   (1) In proximity to the shore. Used with several meanings: inshore, q.v., in the most restricted sense; in a broader sense, includes parts of the sea bottom with characteristics of islands or continents rather than ocean bottoms; from the environmental standpoint, water out to depth of 30 fathoms. Hence, when this term is encountered it is necessary to determine by context which meaning is meant. (2) In beach terminology an indefinite zone extending seaward from the shoreline somewhat beyond the breaker zone. (3) The part or zone of the sea approach lying between the 3-fathom line and the shoreline at mean low water springs.

nearshore (zone)   In beach terminology an indefinite zone extending seaward from the shoreline well beyond the breaker zone. It defines the area of nearshore currents.

nip   Somewhat horizontal cut, particularly on a sea cliff, in the zone where wave impact or solution is most intense, that is, at and just above sea level. Also, similar notches or areas of erosional attack elsewhere.

nodal point   (1) This term has been taken from usage in harmonic vibration of strings to denote a point on the shore where the predominant direction of littoral drift changes from upcoast to downcoast or vice versa. Also called neutral point. (2) Area where little rise and fall of tide occurs in comparison to areas adjacent. See **amphidromic.**

nodal zone   An area in which the predominant direction of the longshore transport changes.

node   That part of a standing wave where the vertical motion is least and the horizontal velocities are greatest. Nodes are associated with clapotis and with seiche action resulting from wave reflections.

notch   A more or less cavelike indentation at about high-tide level at the base of a sea cliff. Most commonly notches result from solution of limestone. They are capped by visors. Many other usages for indentations of other origins.

nourishment   The process of replenishing a beach. It may be brought about naturally, by longshore transport, or artificially by the deposition of dredged materials.

nuées ardentes   Glowing clouds of super heated tephra and gases.

nunatak   An isolated hill or peak that projects above the surface of a glacier.

ocean   The great body of salt water that occupies two-thirds of the surface of the earth, or one of its major subdivisions. The sea.

oceanography   Science involving study of the oceans—physical and chemical characteristics, marine biology, ocean bottoms and boundaries, etc. Some physical scientists prefer the term "oceanology," limiting oceanography to the study of the marine environment. (1) That science treating of the oceans, their forms, physical features and phenomena. (2) The study of the sea, embracing and indicating all knowledge pertaining to the sea's physical boundaries, the chemistry and physics of sea water, and marine biology.

offshore   (1) A comparatively flat zone that extends in from the edge of the continental shelf and variously defined as to inland extent, ordinarily as far as the slope of the beach, more generally, away from the shoreline toward the body of water it faces, whether sea or land. Also, away from a coast. (2) In beach terminology, the comparatively flat zone of variable width, extending from the breaker zone to the seaward edge of the continental shelf. It is continually submerged (3) A direction seaward from the shore.

offshore bar   Accumulation, ordinarily sand or shingle, more or less parallel to the shoreline, that remains submerged at least most of the time.

offshore barrier   See **barrier beach.**

offshore current   (1) Any current in the offshore zone. (2) Any current flowing away from shore. (3) Nontidal current setting about parallel to the shore outside the surf zone.

offshore wind   A wind blowing seaward from the land in the coastal area.

onshore   A direction landward from the sea.

onshore current   Any current flowing toward the shore.

onshore wind   A wind blowing landward from the sea in the coastal area.

oolitic limestone   A limestone formed largely of cemented round calcareous grains.

ooze   Soft mud or slime consisting largely of noncrystalline (amorphous) minerals, ordinarily with considerable organic content (commonly 30 percent or more of plant debris, animal hard parts, etc.). Clay minerals are likely to constitute an appreciable part of the deposit, which may accumulate in water of any salinity. The most widespread organic oozes occur on floors of oceans, but other kinds are found in bottoms of lakes, various channels, and within low basins.

orbit   In water waves, the path of a water particle affected by the wave motion. In deepwater waves the orbit is nearly circular and in shallow-water waves the orbit is nearly elliptical. In general, the orbits are slightly open in the direction of wave motion giving rise to mass transport.

orbital current   The flow of water accompanying the orbital movement of the water particles in a wave. Not to be confused with wave-generated littoral currents.

organic coast   A coast whose morphologic configurations are due to organic activity.

organic reef   A moundlike deposit based on a framework of wave-resistant, sediment-binding organisms.

orthogonal   (1) Line extending shoreward connecting points that are at right angles to the trend of advancing wave crests (directly toward the shoreline if waves parallel the shore; otherwise converging toward points of land or shoaling bottom). Also called rays, similar to rays of theoretical optics in which the advance of light (or other forms of electromagnetic energy) is considered in terms of wave motion. (2) A member of a family of curves everywhere perpendicular to the family of curves representing wave crests on a refraction diagram; analogous to rays in the theory of geometrical optics.

oscillatory wave   A wave in which each individual particle oscillates about a point with little or no permanent change in mean position. The term is commonly applied to progressive oscillatory waves in which only the form advances, the individual particles moving in closed or nearly closed orbits. Distinguished from a wave of translation. See also **orbit.**

outwash   Stratified glacial debris deposited by meltwater.

outwash plain   A plain built by meltwater from the front of a glacier, often composed of gravel near the ice front and sand at a greater distance. Modern outwash plains flank the piedmont glaciers of southern Alaska. A Pleistocene example is the southern part of Long Island, New York.

overfalls   Breaking waves caused by a conflict of currents or by the wind moving against the current.

oversplash   The water that splashes over the top of a breakwater, seawall, etc.

overtop   Pertaining to water, to move across a surface that ordinarily confines its current or extent, for example, over the crest of a natural levee; also, to move over other water, as lighter fresh over heavier saline water, or water near the surface that because of its greater velocity or superposition moves across or falls upon other water, as in the case of a wave of translation or breaker.

overtopping   Passing of water over the top of a structure as a result of wave runup or surge action.

overwash   That part of the uprush that runs over the crest of a berm or structure and does not flow directly back to the sea or lake.

overwash fan (deposit)   Sediment accumulated from overwash transport.

overwash plain   A plain built into the side of a coastal lagoon adjoining a barrier by overwashes (washovers) through sluiceways during hurricanes and other violent storms.

oyster reef   An organic reef composed of oyster and other molluscan shells.

pack ice   (1) A rough, solid mass of broken ice floes forming a heavy obstruction, preventing navigation. (2) A collection of large pieces of floating ice of indefinite extent. (3) A considerable area of floating ice in Polar Seas, more or less flat, broken into large pieces by the action of the wind and waves and driven together in an almost continuous and nearly coherent mass. (4) The principal difference between pack ice and floe ice is that the formation of the pack requires polar ice of many years' standing, while floe ice and ice fields can be formed from one-year ice.

parabolic dune   A dune having in plan the shape of a

parabola, with concave side toward the wind. Term loosely used for dunes that are more or less U- or V-shaped, with concave side toward the wind. A barchan dune has its concave front on its lee side. It may form at the downwind end of a blowout or by the merging of two longitudinal dunes.

parapet   A low wall built along the edge of a structure as on a seawall or quay.

parasitic cone   A small volcanic cone on the slope of a larger volcano. Frequently the product of a single eruption.

parent material   The disintegrated rock material, usually unconsolidated and unchanged or only slightly changed, that underlies and generally gives rise to the true soil by the natural process of soil development. Also called source material. Term also used to mean the initial state of the soil system or the state of the soil system at soil formation time zero. In an extended sense, substances that contribute to the forming and content of the form or feature observed.

pass   (1) A channel leading to a lake or the sea in a river delta, ordinarily useful to boats, even if only small skiffs. The term has many other meanings, generally implying usefulness in crossing from one place to another, as through a gap in a coral reef, valley between hills or mountains, or route across mountain summits. (2) A pass in a delta that does not lead inland to some useful stream channel is regarded as blind. (3) A navigable channel, especially at a river's mouth. (4) A narrow connecting channel between two bodies of an inlet (5) An opening through a barrier reef or sand bar.

patch reef   A localized and ordinarily small structure of organic origin, mainly of calcium carbonate, concentrated by growths of algae, corals, or other reefal organisms. Each patch reef is distinctly separated from others in its vicinity. In some cases patch reefs rise several tens of meters from the bottom to, or near the level of, low tide; some form dangerous shoals. They are commonly present in atoll lagoons, but are numerous in the Bahamas and many other places where there are no atolls.

pavement   Coarser rock fragments or mineral grains left as a residual cover on finer and ordinarily heterogeneous deposits, as a result of finer particles on the surface having been eroded and transported away (winnowed). A widespread condition in arid lands, where sand and smaller particles are blown away by wind, leaving a surface cover of gravel, which is typically thin. A similar deposit commonly forms during intervals between sediment accumulation on beds of streams, lakes, etc., also as a result of winnowing. The term also describes a single band of beach rock, especially if its inner and outer boundaries are rather sharply defined.

peat   Carbonaceous material resulting from partial decomposition of vegetation such as collects in shallow water or as a result of increase in volume, such as accumulations of moss that remain saturated with water in cool regions. Ordinarily brown at first, the color gradually darkens and original plant structures become less evident. Greatest volumes probably occur in the tropics (mangrove origin) but peat derived from sphagnum moss is also abundant, as well as peat derived from sedges and grasses, especially in marshes. After much consolidation peat becomes coal or lignite, which is a member of a series of substances leading to bituminous coal.

pebbles   Smooth, rounded stones ranging in diameter from approximately 2 to 64 millimeters (0.08 to 2.52 inches).

pedestal rock   A tall, slender erosion remnant; sea stack, butte, monument.

pen   One of a series of parallel jetties for berthing several destroyers, submarines, or small craft.

peneplain   Surface that is almost flat or in a condition of very low relief as a result of prolonged denudation; the final result of a cycle of erosion. W. M. Davis, who originated the term, rejected D. W. Johnson's attempt to change the spelling to "peneplane" because the resulting surface should retain undulations and not be geometrical. Until the end of the 1920s the concept of peneplanation was applied, usually uncritically, to various kinds of surfaces, many of which were of depositional origin, resulting in widespread rejection of the term. Davis lacked sufficient appreciation of isostatic compensation and the time necessary to develop peneplanation. Some regard extensive shield areas as the only approximate examples.

peninsula   An elongated portion of land nearly surrounded by water and connected to a larger body of land, usually by a neck or an isthmus.

periglacial   Descriptive of phenomena, processes, and forms resembling in some regards those associated with the presence of large masses of continental ice, in alpine areas or those subject to frequent alternations between freeze and thaw, either under existing climatic conditions or those of the Pleistocene when ice covers were not far away. Terracettes, undulating surfaces, cryoturbation, intensified erosion near margins of snow or ice, intensified solifluction, etc., are characteristic evidences.

period   Interval between times of wave approach, ordinarily from 5 to 16 seconds; also, intervals between expressions of other rhythmically or cyclically occurring phenomena.

periodic current   A current caused by the tide-producing forces of the moon and the sun, a part of the same general movement of the sea that is manifested in the vertical rise and fall of the tides. *See also* **flood current** and **ebb current.**

permafrost Layer of soil or bedrock that has remained frozen, ordinarily since the time of the last major continental glaciation. The temperature has remained below about −5°C (23°F) in locations not covered by ice for long periods (ice acts as insulation against loss of heat by radiation into the atmosphere), as over large parts of Alaska, northern Canada, and Siberia (where the base of permafrost lies as far as 457.2 meters (1,500 feet) below the surface). Above is the active area, subject to thawing out during the warm part of the year (from centimeters to a few meters thick). The older names, now largely replaced, were "frozen ground" or "permanently frozen subsoil."

piedmont fan A fanlike deposit built by ephemeral streams on a plain adjoining a mountain area.

piedmont glacier Alpine valley glaciers may extend beyond a mountain front where they spread out, forming a bulbous projection. Malaspina Glacier in southern Alaska is the largest North American piedmont glacier.

pier (1) A structure built out into the water for use as a landing place, pleasure resort, etc., usually with its greatest dimension at right angles to the shore. (2) A structure extending into navigable water for berthing of vessels. (3) Support for a bridge or other object; structure extending into navigable water for use as a landing place for ships or boats, but also for fishing or as promenade (in some cases above shallow water). (4) In the Great Lakes, a term sometimes improperly applied to jetties.

piling, sheet See **sheet piling.**

plain, coastal See **coastal plain**

plastic flow Movement of rock material in response to pressure; little or no rigidity exhibited. Examples include flowing in response to increase in overlying weight, as mud rising to form a mudlump or salt rising in a salt dome. A condition that is general at considerable depth below the earth's surface, where rock material moves by convection or down pressure gradients in other than liquid phase (hence flow of magma, etc., is excluded). Plastic deformation or flow may be induced by increased water content; for example, occurs readily below highway fills across clay containing large amounts of water. In some tropical areas the accumulation of mangrove debris (mainly roots) results in raising the level of the surface, reportedly as much as 9.1 meters (30 feet), within which a condition approaching water saturation exists, creating instability that at times is relieved by violent plastic flow (known to have covered villages and killed people during the advance). Similar "bursting of the bog" occurrences, particularly in sphagnum moss, have been reported in cooler climates.

plateau (1) (Geographical). An elevated plain, tableland, or flat-topped region of considerable extent. A land area (usually extensive) having a relatively level surface raised sharply above adjacent land on at least one side; table land. A similar undersea feature. (2) (Oceanographical). An elevation from the bottom of the ocean with a more or less flat top and steep sides. (3) Aside from well-known meanings (important or extensive level above something lower, etc.), in the Seychelles the term is used to mean uppermost berm, or storm beach, particularly when wide and supporting coconut groves (walks).

platform An area where denudation of bedrock has created relative flatness. Also, the mean elevation of continental surfaces and of ocean floors. In general, a surface elevated above another; for example, a stage above a floor; but the term is not appropriate for the surface of an alluvial deposit such as a terrace.

plate tectonics The array of theories and concepts pertaining to seafloor spreading, continental drift, and crustal subduction.

playa Spanish word for beach. Curiously, the term was applied in the American Southwest to enclosed lakes and basin floors, probably because when dry they commonly exhibit white surfaces, hence in that regard resemble beaches.

Pleistocene Older portion of the Quaternary, preceding the Recent. Commonly regarded as glacial period, but this concept is weakened by the presence of huge volumes of continental ice today, especially in Antarctica and Greenland, so that many authorities do not accept the idea that postglacial time has arrived. The Pleistocene began at least 2 million years ago, possibly much earlier (some suggest 4 million), whereas the Recent is probably not an interval greater than 50 to 80 thousand years. Many regard it as starting 18 thousand years ago; some, 10 thousand. If the basis of separating Pleistocene from Recent is the start of the last general rise of sea level, these smaller estimates are certainly incorrect because material in the Recent deposits on continental shelves is dated as old as 37 thousand years by radioactive assay methods. Faunas identified as Pleistocene by earlier paleontologists are now recognized as inseparable from Recent faunas.

plunge point (1) For a plunging wave, the point at which the wave curls over and breaks. (2) The final breaking point of the waves just before the water rushes up the beach.

pollution Introduction of foreign, and commonly undesirable, substances, especially into the atmosphere or bodies of water. Extended use includes cause of change.

port   A place where vessels may discharge or receive cargo; may be the entire harbor including its approaches and anchorages, or may be the commercial part of a harbor where the quays, wharves, facilities for transfer of cargo, docks, and repair shops are situated.

pothole (pot hole)   (1) A circular depression scoured in a stream bed by clasts carried in a rotating current. (2) A small hole in rock, commonly circular in plan, resulting from wear by boulders swirled around by violent currents. Potholes occur along rivers and many coasts and in numerous examples along streams of water flowing below glaciers. In the latter case, it is thought, the abrading agent may not be boulders but either finer sediment or even small masses of ice. In many cases some rounded boulders are present in the holes.

primary coast   A coast largely unmodified by shore processes. May be the product of rise or fall in sea level, delta growth, glacial action, volcanic eruptions, or earth movements.

profile, beach   See **beach profile.**

profile of equilibrium   Idealistic concept of the profile extending offshore or along a river channel indicating balanced conditions between processes tending either to steepen or aggrade. At best, verification is based on statistical averages, ordinarily over a time base of insufficient length; hence a doubtful first-order deductive estimate.

prograde, progradation   Where a coast is being extended seaward, as if by deposition of a succession of beach or dune ridges, it is said to be prograding.

progression (of a beach). This is the same as growth or advance of a beach.

progressive wave   (1) A wave that moves relative to a fixed coordinate system in a fluid. The direction in which it moves is termed the direction of wave propagation. (2) A wave that is manifested by the progressive movement of the wave form.

promontory   High point of land or rock jutting into the sea along a coast; headland. Also, such features in large lakes.

propagation of waves   The transmission of waves through water.

prop roots   Tree roots rising partially above the ground and spreading to provide support for the plant. Characteristic of some mangroves and all pandanus trees.

pumice   Excessively cellular lava resulting from explosive volcanic action, commonly light colored and because of high air content buoyant on water, permanently or until water displaces air in cells. In ground condition, an effective abrasive.

race   A strong or rapid current of water or the passage confining such flow; marine and many other applications, such as mill race that brings a flow of water to a water wheel.

rampart   Protecting wall, as on the outer side of a bench facing the sea. Although the term commonly refers to built structures it also covers, by extension, natural features.

range of tide   The difference in height between consecutive high and low waters. The mean range is the difference in height between mean high water and mean low water. The great diurnal range or diurnal range is the difference in height between mean higher high water and mean lower low water. Where the type of tide is diurnal, the mean range is the same as the diurnal range.

reach   (1) An arm of the sea extending into the land. (2) A straight section of restricted waterway of considerable extent; may be similar to a narrows, except much longer in extent. (3) An extended portion of water, as in a straight portion of a stream or river. (4) A level stretch, as between locks in a canal. (5) A promontory, tongue or extended portion of land. (6) Segment of a channel between bends, especially along meandering channels. In a broader sense the term is used to describe greater distances along stream courses that are more or less unified by some characteristic. Distance between river gages. Also many other usages and meanings.

rebound   Elevation of a land area after a large glacier, the weight of which had caused it to subside, has melted away. This is a form of isostatic adjustment.

Recent   Latest division of the Quaternary, following the Pleistocene. The boundary between the two divisions is in dispute because so commonly it has been based on strictly local evidence. Some geologists and the U.S. Geological Survey regard it as equivalent to Holocene; as used in Europe and by some in the United States considered as marking the retreat of continental ice across the Baltic; a possibly more fundamental definition, proposed in 1872, regards the interval as starting when sea level initiated its last major rise (considered by some as about 18,000 years ago, but more probably 50,000 to 80,000). This concept is in keeping with tradition among geologists of defining ages of rock units in stratigraphic terms, because with rise of sea level came a new group of deposits across older rocks on continental shelves and eventually into estuarine and valley positions.

recession (of a beach)   (1) A continuing landward movement of the shoreline. (2) A net landward movement of the shoreline over a specified time. Coastal recession is commonly regarded as the result of local changes brought about by wave action under existing conditions, rather than as effects of submergence, which is a more widespread and fundamental long-term consideration. Also retrogression. (3) The back melting of the frontal area of a glacier where melting is more rapid than the advance of the new glacial ice. It does not involve a reversal in the direction of glacial flow.

reef (1) A rocky or coral elevation in the sea dangerous to surface navigation; it may or may not be above the sounding datum in elevation. A coral reef is primarily a mixture of coral and calcareous algae (Lithothamnion). A large mass of coral, algae, and associated organisms is ordinarily called a coral reef, but in some cases the reference is more specific, for example, algal or bryozoan reef. Also many other usages. See **coral reef.** (2) There are also oyster reefs, serpuloid reefs, etc. (3) An offshore consolidated rock hazard to navigation with a least depth of 10 fathoms (about 20 meters) or less.

reef, atoll See **atoll reef.**

reef, barrier See **barrier reef.**

reef face (front) Outer surface of a coral reef facing the sea, extending from the crest downward into the water to limits of organic accumulation, rather commonly to a sandy bench or inclined sand accumulation. It is the environment in which coral, algae, and other organisms are best supplied with food or nutrients and hence grow most rapidly.

reef flat Surface of a deposit formed on the landward side of a coral reef, consisting in part of coral debris in various orientations together with living or remains of dead organisms. The flat may be submerged in places or as a whole, but rises only to about the low-tide level, except in isolated areas where accumulation of fragments has been particularly intense. The transition to reef or lithothamnion (algal) ridge is gradual. May be active or fossil (fossil-reef flats occur at various levels). As an adjective, commonly refers to deposits forming a reef flat.

reef, fringing See **fringing reef.**

reef, sand See **bar.**

reflected wave That part of an incident wave that is returned seaward when a wave impinges on a steep beach, barrier, or other reflecting surface.

refraction of water waves (1) The process by which the direction of a wave moving in shallow water at an angle to the contours is changed. The part of the wave advancing in shallower water moves more slowly than that part still advancing in deeper water, causing the wave crest to bend toward alignment with the underwater contours. (2) The bending of wave crests by currents.

reticulate bars (1) A criss-cross pattern of slightly submerged sand ridges. Formed by littoral currents that change direction from time to time. (2) Bars with a criss-cross pattern, with both sets diagonal to the shoreline.

revetment Retaining wall or facing created to prevent retreat of banks of a stream, canal, etc. It may be composed of masonry, blocks of concrete, fascine mats of trees, etc. To be effective it must extend down to and for a considerable distance across a stream bed; otherwise, it is undermined rapidly if the stream has considerable velocity and turbulence; but unless solidly built the protection rendered is temporary. Most permanent is a change of a channel into a flume by paving extending above its entire wetted perimeters.

Rhizophora The common red mangrove, which occurs along sides of rivers and estuaries as well as forming forests with trees 24.3 meters (80 feet) or so in height. Characterized by stilt or prop roots. Although present on some coral keys, it is not as capable of pioneering in a marine environment as the common black mangrove, and apparently is more dependent on freshwater supply.

ria A long, narrow inlet, with depth gradually diminishing inward.

ria coast A coast characterized by the presence of indentations, ordinarily having comparatively low relief. The term "ria" has aroused considerable discussion as to whether it should be general or specific as to origin (for example, only drowned valleys), with the tendency being toward acceptance in the more general sense. Where originally applied, rias were restricted to cases where the indentation agreed with rock structure directions.

ridge Typically, an elongate rise in elevation (in contrast to swale, valley, runnel, etc., that adjoins it); the crest of a mountain or crests between significant valleys leading down mountainsides. Also many other usages, for example, low deposit (ordinarily by calcareous algae) on the outer side of a reef, low accumulation of sand between troughs (runnels) exposed at low tide in readily entrained sediments (mainly sand).

ridge, beach See **beach ridge.**

ridge and swale topography More or less concentric bands of elevated land (ridges) alternating with depressions (swales), specifically the result of depositional processes associated with advancing point bars. The swales may be ponded, or they may serve as active channels during floods or as temporary or permanent chutes, a few of which succeed in diverting all or a considerable part of the stream flow, shortening river distance and being called chute cutoffs.

rift A valley depression along a large fault. Particularly applied to the Mid-Atlantic Ridge.

right lateral fault A fault in which the continuation of a stratum that terminates at the fault will be found to the right of the observer. The San Andreas is a right lateral fault.

rill marks   Tiny drainage channels in a beach caused by the flow seaward of water left in the sands of the upper part of the beach after the retreat of the tide or after the dying down of storm waves.

rip   A body of water made rough by waves meeting an opposing current, particularly a tidal current; often found where tidal currents are converging and sinking.

rip current   (1) Concentrated return flow of water piled up by incoming wind and waves along a shore, the flow in many cases attaining considerable velocity and comparatively narrow width. Feeder currents run parallel to the shore, concentrating water in an unstable position, with rising head, a condition that periodically is relieved by rip currents through the surf zone. After crossing the breakers the rip current widens and diminishes in velocity, commonly turning in the general direction of the offshore current or producing a mild swirl. A swimmer caught in a rip current does well to relax, knowing that after crossing the surf zone he will have little difficulty in regaining the shore. (2) A strong surface current flowing seaward from the shore. It usually appears as a visible band of agitated water and is the return movement of water piled up on the shore by incoming waves and wind. With the seaward movement concentrated in a limited band its velocity is somewhat accentuated. A rip consists of three parts: the feeder currents flowing parallel to the shore inside the breakers; the neck, where the feeder currents converge and flow through the breakers in a narrow band or rip; and the head, where the current widens and slackens outside the breaker line. A rip current is often miscalled a rip tide. Also rip surf.

ripple   (1) The light fretting or ruffling on the surface of the water caused by a breeze. (2) The smallest class of waves and one in which the force of restoration is, to a significant degree, both surface tension and gravity. (3) The ruffling of the surface of the water, hence a little curling wave or undulation. (4) A wave less than 5 centimeters (2 inches) long controlled to a significant degree by both surface tension and gravity. See **gravity wave.**

ripple mark   Ordinarily, a small ridge that alternates with nearly parallel depressions in unconsolidated bed materials, commonly sand, in bodies of water such as channels, lakes, outer beaches, sand dunes, etc. If of large size, ripple marks are known as megaripples, but they grade upward into sand waves, dunes, etc. Originate as a result of stress against the bed induced by currents. Many last only for a brief interval, as between tides, but others have become preserved as structures in rock, including some of the oldest ones. Heights may vary between a centimeter or so to several centimeters (megaripples, several meters) and spacing from 7.6 to 10.1 centimeters (3 or 4 inches) to a meter, commonly, but in larger varieties, several meters.

rips   Agitation of water caused by the meeting of currents or by a rapid current setting over an irregular bottom. A tide rip.

rip tide   Improper name for rip current.

rivermouth bars   Bars formed across mouths of rivers, in some cases preventing outflow, causing formation of a lagoon, which may be ephemeral, occurring during dry periods or when flow is so reduced that the discharge (if any) occurs as seepage through the bars. These bars (which may be wholly or partially submerged) occur across rivers with any amount of discharge, forming upchannel downslopes to some characteristic depth and creating shoals that restrict drafts of entering vessels; but are absent if channels are very deep, as at the mouths of many estuaries. Where sediment supply is large, some estuaries, as in coastal Louisiana, are blocked so that lakes form inland form bars, across which outlets are restricted in depths and widths.

rocks, awash   See **awash rocks**

rockweed   Any coarse seaweed growing attached to rocks.

runnel   (1) A corrugation trough of the foreshore, or the bottom just offshore, formed by wave and/or tidal action. Larger than the trough between ripple marks. (2) A small brook or channel. A trough, generally about parallel to the shore, separated by low ridges (ordinarily on a sandy bottom), exposed as a rule when the tide ebbs across a comparatively flat bottom, as a rule several orders of magnitude larger than ripple marks (which commonly are present on its surface).

runup   The rush of water up a structure or beach on the breaking of a wave. Also uprush. The amount of runup is the vertical height above stillwater level that the rush of water reaches. The covering of all or some part of the swash zone.

salina   Marsh or pond separated from the sea but flooded at times of high tide. Also called saltern and, in some of the West Indies, flash.

salinity   Weight ratio between dissolved salts and water containing them, commonly expressed in parts per thousand (o/oo) or per million (ppm). Applied specifically to sea and brackish water, as a rule, and also to groundwater. In sea water the ratio measured is ordinarily chlorinity, and it is regarded that salinity amounts to chlorinity multiplied by 1.80655. In other kinds of water, various proportions of salts exist, but ordinarily the water is considered saline if there is a considerable amount of sodium chloride present. The property of salinity is also recognized in muds and rocks.

saltation (1) That method of sand movement in a fluid in which individual particles leave the bed by bounding nearly vertically and, because the motion of the fluid is not strong or turbulent enough to retain them in suspension, return to the bed at some distance downstream. The travel path of the particles is a series of hops and bounds. (2) Intermittent transport in a current involving frequent contact with the bed alternating with transport in suspension. Sedimentary particles advance forward during jumps, coming to rest or rolling or sliding during intervals when lodged on the bed. The process is characteristic of movement of bed load. Movement of sediment particles by bouncing.

salt dome Deformed geologic structure caused by central rise of a core or plug of salt from considerable depth. These have various surface expressions; the core may underlie a mound or hill up to several hundred meters high, or for the reason that the upper part of the column is continuously dissolved by groundwater a depression of the surface may result, commonly containing a pond or lake in areas of sufficient precipitation or flow of groundwater. Residual minerals concentrated above the core form cap rock in which economic quantities of sulfur may accumulate. In strata deformed by rise of the plug, important accumulations of petroleum are trapped.

salt marsh A marsh periodically flooded by salt water. Comparatively flat coastal tracts commonly flooded at high tide and covered with grass, sedges, etc., and other plants that are able to tolerate the degree of salinity present.

sand (1) Mineral or rock particles from about 0.06 to about 2 millimeters in diameter (varying according to classification scheme used). Coarser than silt, finer than gravel. Along shores of continents quartz is commonly the most abundant mineral present, but the term refers to size, not to composition, and includes organic material, such as fragments of corals, algae, etc., and a great variety of rock or mineral particles. (In phi units the size range is from about $+4$ to -1). (2) An unconsolidated (geologically) mixture of inorganic soil (that may include disintegrated shells and disintegrated coral) consisting of small but easily distinguishable grains ranging in size from about 1/20 to 2.0 millimeters, depending on the size classification used.

sand bar (1) Partially visible or wholly submerged accumulation of sand extending across the mouth of a channel; sand accumulations along other parts of channels. A spit, as distinguished from a bar, is attached visibly to the land at one of its ends. (2) In a river, a ridge of sand built to or near the surface by river currents. See **bar.**

sand dome Small elevated sand surface on a beach, created by entrapment of air.

sand dune A dune formed of sand.

sand field Extensive sand cover in which many dune-line irregularities characteristically are present on the surface. Sand fields lie behind some extensive beaches and also occur inland. In deserts they are called ergs or, by some, sand seas.

sand sheet Thin layer of sand covering some other surface.

sand spit A narrow sand embankment, created by an excess of deposition at its seaward terminus, with its distal end (the end away from the point of origin) terminating in open water.

sandstone Sedimentary rock or particles between 1/16 and 2 millimeters (-1 phi and $+4$ phi).

sand wave (megaripple) (1) A large wavelike sediment feature composed of sand in very shallow water. Wavelength may reach 100 meters (328 feet); amplitude is about 0.5 meters (1.6 feet). (2) Advancing mass of sand in collective bed movement in channels and across bottoms in lakes or the sea. Many examples move upslope toward point bars or toward beaches, always in a direction of decreasing turbulence. Some advance seaward toward bars near river mouths. Dimensions exceed those of megaripples as a rule; amplitudes may be from several to more than 6 meters (20 feet) and spacing between crests from about 9 to 183 meters (10 to 200 yards).

sapped cliff Cliff with a relatively resistant rock ledge that has been undercut, often by spring flow or eolian blasting.

scarp, beach See **beach scarp.**

scour Mechanical wear on the bottom of a channel or bed of a body of water, ordinarily resulting from erosion associated with turbulence and frictional drag of currents. In alluvium, channels scour and fill alternately as they deepen or become more shoal-like.

sea (1) The ocean; more specifically, some large part of the ocean; also, very large bodies of water even if located inland and not connected with the ocean system; for example, Sea of Galilee. Mediterraneans are located within continents but are connected with the ocean, ordinarily through narrow passages. See **state of sea.** (2) A large body of salt water, second in rank to an ocean, more or less landlocked and generally part of, or connected with, an ocean or a larger sea. (3) Waves caused by wind at the place and time of observation. (4) State of the ocean or lake surface, in regard to waves. See **ocean.**

sea, state of See **state of sea.**

sea arch Roof of a cave cut by wave erosion if open at both ends. A rocky headland pierced by a sea cave.

seaboard Rather extensive coastal region bordering the sea.

sea breeze Wind blowing landward as a result of landward pressure gradient, usually best developed during afternoons. Commonly alternates daily with land breeze of early mornings.

sea cave   Cleft or cut of appreciable depth originating as a result of wave processes acting on a cliff or steep slope. In some cases open to the sea at both ends, producing one type of arch or natural bridge; in some cases connected by openings to a somewhat higher surface where spouting horns occur, or where there is detectable inhalation and expulsion of air associated with entering wave surges.

sea cliff   (1) Steep land surface facing a waterbody, ordinarily caused by undercutting of its base by processes associated with wave action. If inactive, called dead or false sea cliff. (2) A cliff situated at the seaward edge of the coast.

seacoast   The coast adjacent to the sea or ocean.

seafloor spreading   Addition of new crustal material at a midocean ridge accompanied by lateral movement of adjacent crustal plates.

sea island   A name applied in Georgia to a series of barrier islands of short length but considerable breadth.

sea level   The height of the water of the sea; but ordinarily the reference is to mean sea level, established as a result of measurements on tide gages for 19-year periods of observation. The elevation of sea level varies considerably along coasts, being higher if mountains are nearby (gravitational attraction) and depending on constancy of wind direction and other factors. Sea level changes according to the volume of water incorporated in masses of ice present on land (mainly Antarctic), displacement in areas of ocean floor, and many other factors. See **mean sea level.**

seas   Waves caused by wind at the place and time of observation.

seashore   (1) (Law) All the ground between the ordinary high-water and low-water mark. (2) The shore of the sea or ocean.

sea stack   Tall, isolated column of rock resulting from processes associated with wave action that have detached it from continuation into rock of the nearby sea cliff.

sea valley   A submarine depression of broad valley form without the steep side slopes that characterize a canyon.

seawall   Structure built with intent of halting the inland movement of the shore during times of particularly severe wave action or high water level, as behind a beach or in front of a highway, building, etc. It retains earth against its shoreward face. See also **bulkhead.**

seaweed   (1) Visible marine algae, plantlike in habit, ordinarily distinguished from microscopic forms, such as are abundant in plankton. By some, any plant growing in the sea. (2) A characteristic plant growth in sea water. Usually indicates the presence of rocks. See also **kelp** and **rockweed.**

seiche   (pronounced "sash") (1) A standing wave oscillation of an enclosed water body that continues, pendulum fashion, after the cessation of the originating force, that may have been either seismic or atmospheric. (2) An oscillation of a fluid body in response to a disturbing force having the same frequency as the natural frequency of the fluid system. Tides are now considered to be seiches induced primarily by the periodic forces caused by the sun and moon. (3) In the Great Lakes area, any sudden rise in the water of a harbor or a lake whether or not it is oscillatory. Although inaccurate in a strict sense, this usage is well-established in the Great Lakes area. (4) A stationary wave oscillation, found both in enclosed bodies of water and superimposed upon the tide waves of the ocean with a period varying from a few minutes to an hour or more but somewhat less than the tidal periods.

seif   Seif dune, characterized by linearity along the wind direction. Although modified when wind direction changes somewhat, so that one side becomes stoss and the other lee, with accompanying contrasts in packing or looseness of surface sand, the general position remains about constant, guides and landmarks for persons crossing a desert where such dunes are present.

seismic   Pertaining to, characteristic of, or produced by vibrations, ordinarily associated with shearing of rocks (along faults), earthquakes, explosions, or other impacts. Seismology is the science concerned with vibrations experienced and transmitted by the earth's crust. A seismograph records vibrations. Microseisms have extremely small amplitudes; a sharp increase in their number commonly precedes a larger earthquake, but others result from artificial disturbances, such as the shaking caused by a moving train or truck.

seismic sea wave (tsunami)   A long-period wave caused by an underwater seismic disturbance or volcanic eruption. Commonly misnamed tidal wave.

semidiurnal   (1) Having a period or cycle of approximately one-half of a tidal day. The predominating type of tide throughout the world is semidiurnal, with two high waters and two low waters each tidal day. The tidal current is said to be semidiurnal when there are two flood and two ebb periods each day. (2) Occurring twice a day; half of the length of a lunar day of 24.84 solar hours. Used specifically with reference to tides (land or sea) and other cyclic events.

semidiurnal tide   A tide with two high and two low waters in a tidal day with comparatively little diurnal inequality.

sheet piling   Interlocking member of wood, steel,

concrete, etc., subject to lateral pressure, driven individually to form an obstruction to percolation, to prevent movement of material, for cofferdams, sea walls, stabilization of foundations, etc.

shelf As used in describing continental margins, the continental shelf, a flat plain offshore, ordinarily sloping gently to the crest of the steeper continental slope toward the level of the sea floor. Various flats in other locations. Bench. freshwater ice extending into a lake or sea. Same as insular shelf.

shelf, continental See **continental shelf.**

shingle (1) Loosely and commonly, any beach material coarser than ordinary gravel, especially any having flat or flattish pebbles. (2) Strictly and accurately, beach material of smooth, well-rounded pebbles that are roughly the same size. The spaces between pebbles are not filled with finer materials. Shingle often gives out a musical sound when stepped on.

shoal (1) Any shallow area surrounded by deeper water, whether in a river or body of standing water (lake, sea), whatever the origin. Generally regarded as being within 10 fathoms of the water surface from the navigator's standpoint. (2) A detached area of any material except rock or coral. The depths over it are a danger to surface navigation. Similar continental or insular shelf features of greater depths are usually termed banks. (3) (Verb). To become shallow gradually. (4) To cause to become shallow. (5) To proceed from a greater to a lesser depth of water.

shore (1) Land close to a body of water, especially a sea or a lake. As a term in popular use, it has other, but similar, meanings; for example, shore dinner (featuring sea foods). Generally the extent is more restricted than that implied by coast. (2) That strip of ground bordering any body of water that is alternately exposed, or covered by tides and/or waves. A shore of unconsolidated material is usually called a beach.

shoreface The narrow zone seaward from the low tide shoreline permanently covered by water over which the beach sands and gravels actively oscillate with changing wave conditions.

shoreline (1) The intersection of a specified plane of water with the shore or beach; for example, the highwater shoreline would be the intersection of the plane of mean high water with the shore or beach. The line delineating the shoreline on U.S. Coast and Geodetic Survey nautical charts and surveys approximates the mean high water line. (2) Boundary between land and water surface of a lake, sea, etc., commonly regarded as at the time of high tide or high stage.

shore profile Intersection of the surface of land and nearby bottom with a vertical plane. Commonly extends inland to the top of the sea cliff or sand dune and seaward to some place on the lower (submerged)

beach, but may be extended any distance across the continental shelf.

shore terrace A terrace made along a coast by the action of waves and shore currents; it may become land by the uplifting of the shore or the lowering of the water.

sill Barrier to flow, as between deeper water in a fiord and the open sea, present as a result of irregular erosion of solid rock; also, rock locally obstructing the flow of ground water; as a geologic term, a tabular mass of intrusive rock more or less horizontal in attitude, in contrast to a dike, a tabular mass of rock with vertical or steeply inclined attitude.

sinkhole A hole due to the collapse of the roof above. A solution cavity in limestone, gypsum, salt, or dolomite. Surface streams are often carried underground along sinkholes. An area with sinkholes has karst topography.

slip A space between two piers, wharfs, etc., for berthing a vessel. A dock.

slip face The lee or downcurrent surface of a dune or similar feature, commonly composed of sand, shore accumulation occurs of materials that have crossed the crest from the upcurrent (stoss) face. The slope of the surface is approximately the angle of repose and is not increased by new accumulation because any added weight causes slippage. This slope is ordinarily close to 35° from the horizontal in dry sand, but steeper if the sand is moist.

slope The degree of inclination to the horizontal. Usually expressed as a ratio, such as 1:25, indicating one unit rise in 25 units of horizontal distance; or in a decimal fraction (0.04); degrees (2°18′); or percent (4%). It is sometimes expressed by such adjectives as steep, moderate, gentle, mild, flat. Also called gradient.

slope of foreshore (1) The Beach Erosion Board uses the following definition: The angle between the tangent to the beach at the high water line and the horizontal. (2) The angle between the tangent to the beach at the reference point and the horizontal.

slope wash Soil or rock materials in progress of moving downslope; the processes involved in the movement, mainly gravity and action of currents (chiefly water). The areas involved are broad in comparison with those of intervening definite channels or restricted ravines, etc. As a general rule the movement is slow.

slump Lowering of blocks of land or rock, chiefly as a result of gravitational stress producing shear, that leads to the sliding of an upper (slump) block across rock below down an inclined plain (sole), which commonly dips at some angle between 40 and 80°. As a verb, the process; as a noun, the displaced block. A type of caving along stream banks associated with flooding as a rule, called subsidence by engineers. On a large scale may affect considerable areas of mountain fronts.

soil (1) Earth material covering the surface of most land, more or less derived from parent (locally present) rock and modified by climatic and organic processes in the direction of differentiation into distinct layers that are parts of a soil profile. There is debate as to the best definition: agriculturists regard ability to grow plants as essential; in a strict sense, newly formed detritus and fresh alluvium are not soil, but become soil to the degree that they begin to form a profile (plants may grow luxuriantly in such materials, and they decrease the time required for profile characteristics to appear). From the standpoint of the pedologist, engineers misuse the term completely in regarding as soil any unconsolidated material in the vicinity of the surface (such as alluvium or accumulations of detrital fragments), but the usage is well established. Various systems of soil classification exist, the most comprehensive dividing into great groups that more or less coincide with climate distribution but that are more closely tied to vegetation. Microbiologic activities are of extreme importance in soil differentiation. (2) (Engineering). A natural aggregate of mineral grains that can be separated by such gentle mechanical means as agitation in water. The boundary between soil and rock is necessarily an arbitrary one; there are many natural aggregates of mineral particles that are difficult to classify either as soil or as rock. (3) (Geological). The top layer of the surface of the earth, composed of the finely divided disintegrated rock that is penetrated by the roots of plants. It includes the soil at the surface (Horizon A) in which life is most active and abundant and commonly includes the plowed layers; a denser and darker layer (Horizon B); and the upper portion of the substratum in either the weathered or unweathered state (Horizon C).

solifluction (solifluxion) Slow movement of soil or other surface cover from higher to lower ground associated with the presence of water—most rapid if saturated. Commonly misused as limited to the result of thrust and heave associated with freezing and hence an arctic phenomenon. Anderson, who coined the term, doubted whether there could be general peneplanation (conspicuous topographic flattening) in tropical regions were it not for widespread solifluction.

solitary wave A wave consisting of a single elevation (above the original water surface), its height not necessarily small compared to the depth, and neither followed nor preceded by another elevation or depression of the water surfaces.

sound (1) (Noun) A wide waterway between the mainland and an island, or a wide waterway connect-

ing two sea areas. (2) A relatively long arm of the sea or ocean forming a channel between an island and a mainland or connecting two larger bodies, as a sea and the ocean, or two parts of the same body; usually wider and more extensive than a strait. (3) (Verb). To measure the depth of the water.

sounding A measured depth of water. On hydrographic charts the soundings are adjusted to a specific plan of reference (sounding datum).

spilling breaker (1) Breaker characterized by more or less orderly appearance for a considerable distance along its crest and much less water disturbance than occurs in a plunging breaker. See **breaker.** (2) Waves near shore that break gradually over quite a distance.

spit A small point composed of sand or gravel projecting from the shore into a body of water, whether exposed above water level or in part submerged; an incomplete bar. Spits form for various reasons but most commonly as a result of diminishing transport capability of currents; for example, where a current diverges from the shore. Elongate sand deposit extending down-current from a headland; a hook is a curved spit.

spit, barrier See **barrier spit.**

spit, sand See **sand spit.**

spouting horn Orifice of a marine cave opening upward to the air through which water issues or sprays when larger waves surge into the submerged part of the cave.

spray Water (or other liquid) moving as small drops, commonly as a result of wind blowing across the surface of the sea or lake. Sea spray carries a considerable amount of salt and other contaminants. Spray is generated at waterfalls, spouting horns, etc., by impact of waves against solid surfaces, on emergence from nozzles, etc.

spray zone Area subject to precipitation of sea spray.

spring range The average semidiurnal range occurring at the time of spring tides and most conveniently computed from the harmonic constants. It is larger than the mean range where the type of tide is either semidiurnal or mixed, and is of no practical significance where the type of tide is diurnal.

spring tide (1) A tide that occurs at or near the time of new or full moon (syzygy), and which rises highest and falls lowest from the mean sea level. (2) Tides of increased range occurring semimonthly as the result of the moon being new or full.

squall Wind of considerable intensity caused by local atmospheric instability, ordinarily appearing suddenly and quickly dying out.

stabilized dune A dune protected from modification by wind because of vegetational cover, cementation, etc.; also called a fixed dune.

stack   An isolated rock rising from the shallow sea floor near shore, detached from shore cliffs by erosion. See **sea stack**.

star (oghurd) dune   Ovate dune with many radiating ridges.

state of sea   (1) Description of the state of the sea surface, in regard to wave action; surface roughness; the wave structure on the ocean surface. (2) Commonly regarded in terms of the heights of the highest one-third of waves present; expressed in a code (Douglas scale) ranging from 0 to 9, covering heights ranging from 0 to over 45 feet (9).

stationary wave   A wave of essentially stable form that does not move with respect to a selected reference point; a fixed swelling. Sometimes called standing wave.

step   (1) The nearly horizontal section that more or less divides the beach from the shoreface. (2) A localized steepening, not necessarily permanent, close to low-tide level separating upper from lower beach. In many cases the step is marked by the presence of coarser sediment—gravel on a sand beach, etc. It occurs shoreward from the surf zone. An abrupt rise of land surfaces, and many other usages.

step zone   A band along a shoreline located slightly below mean sea level and characterized by sediments coarser than those above, on the upper beach, or below, on the lower (submerged) beach.

stillstand   Stationary position, or nearly so. Applied to sea level, particularly over long intervals of time; for example, 2,000 years or more, and specifically to the relatively high sea level at the present time. It is commonly recognized that the recent stillstand refers to slowly rising level, at a rate contrasting with the more rapid general rise preceding it, when the volumes of continental ice diminished more rapidly.

still-water level   (1) The level water would have in the absence of waves or other surface irregularities, commonly measured in gages that are tubes open at depth and in which some buoyant object floats. The dampening of waves, etc., is regulated by the size of the intake openings in the tubes. Still-water level may also be calculated by examination of recorded changes in pressure as indicated by a pressure cell or other submerged instrument. (2) The surface of the water if all wave and wind action were to cease. In deep water this level approximates the midpoint of the wave height. In shallow water it is nearer to the trough than the crest. Also called undisturbed water level. (3) The elevation that the surface of the water would assume if all wave action were absent.

stockpile   Sand piled on a beach foreshore to nourish downdrift beaches by natural littoral currents or forces. See **feeder beach**.

storm beach   High level on the upper beach deposited during storms, or at least when local sea level or wave energy was high. These highest berms may persist for several years or even decades, whereas lower berms are ephemeral. In the Seychelles they are called plateaus.

storm surge   A rise above normal water level on the open coast due to the action of wind stress on the water surface. Storm surge resulting from a hurricane also includes that rise in level due to atmospheric pressure reduction as well as that due to wind stress.

storm tide   See **storm surge**.

stoss   Descriptive of side facing the current direction; in distinction to lee.

strait   A relatively narrow waterway between two larger bodies of water.

strand   (1) The shore or beach of the ocean or a large lake. The land bordering any large body of water, especially a sea or an arm of the ocean. (2) (Verb). Same as beach. (3) Specifically, the part of the seashore between high and low waterlines, but popularly and by extension a seashore generally, particularly along a sandy beach.

strandflat   A wide bedrock platform along the fiorded coast of Norway at the base of steep slopes, and in some places submerged.

subaqueous   Under the surface of water; submarine.

subdelta   A portion of a large compound delta, like that of the Mississippi River where breaches in the natural levees of old channels have provided shorter routes to the sea for new channels with the development of new deltaic lobes.

submarine bank   An elevation or ridge in bed of lake or ocean of appreciable magnitude in relation to the surrounding depths.

submarine canyon   (1) A V-shaped submarine depression of valley form with relatively steep slope and progressive deepening in a direction away from shore. (2) A deep, narrow, steep-sided valley entirely below sea level, but commonly located seaward of a stream valley on land. (3) Valleylike, typically rather linear, steep-sided cut running down the continental slope and in some cases extending back various distances into the continental shelf. In most cases they are located out from the mouths of rivers or valleys on the land. Some are over a kilometer deep; some, several kilometers in width.

submarine natural levees   Deposits formed under water along sides of channels in areas where turbulence, and ordinarily the velocity of a current, diminishes in intensity, whether ahead of distributaries in a delta or elsewhere. Ordinarily these occur as ridges, shoal at first but increasing in size in many cases becoming normal natural levees after their crests rise above water level. The patterns in which submarine ridges form commonly determine those of natural levees and stream courses between them in a delta or fill in an estuary.

submarine valley   A prolongation of a land valley into or across a continental or insular shelf, which generally gives evidence of having been formed by stream erosion.

submerged coast   A coastal area that recently subsided due to land movement, like parts of the Mississippi Delta. Many coasts that appear submerged have been affected only by postglacial rise in sea level, inundating stream valleys. Such coasts are not truly submerged.

subsidence   Lowering of level affecting land or rock areas, a process that may have various causes; for example, convection current or other process within the earth's crust, overloading (by sediment, ice, water, highway fill, dams, etc.). Sinking or collapse of caverns below the surface (including those made artificially; for example, mines); lowering of banks along channels, mainly as a result of slumping or bank caving, etc. Both local and regional expressions occur.

summer beach   Upper beach of maximum volume and steep front accumulated during summers in regions where lowest wave energies characterize that season, but the accumulation may occur at other seasons as well, and tendencies to develop summer beach characteristics occur during brief intervals whenever sea state is low and to a small degree with falling tide.

superficial deposits   Accumulations of unconsolidated sediments above bedrock; for example, alluvium, glacial moraines, dunes.

surf   (1) Breakers; wave activity concentrated close to the shoreline; swell of the sea that breaks along the shore, as on a sloping beach. Popularly extended to various meanings: state of the sea, broad areas of waves close to a coast, etc. (2) Collective term for breakers. (3) The wave activity in the area between the shoreline and the outermost limit of breaking. (4) The term surf in literature usually refers to the breaking of waves on shore and on reefs when accompanied by a roaring noise caused by the larger waves breaking.

swale   (1) The depression between two beach ridges. (2) See **ridge and swale topography.** A linear depression between somewhat higher surfaces.

swamp   (1) Low, wet area covered by trees or high bushes, as distinguished from marsh (reed-, sedge-, or grass-covered). Mangrove swamps occur widely in tropical climates. Swamp is used less scientifically to include marshes, bogs, and other wet areas regardless of vegetational cover, but not to include areas that are

water-covered. (2) (Noun). A tract of wet spongy land, frequently inundated by fresh or salt water, and characteristically dominated by trees and shrubs. (3) (Verb). To sink or fill up a craft with water.

swash   (1) Uprush, run-up, etc., of water brought by waves to an inclined surface, ordinarily a beach. The swash or swash zone is the area covered by the uprush. Commonly the limit of the swash is indicated by irregular lines of foam and fine debris (swash marks) that may be erased by any higher uprush; in these swash lines there may be accumulations worth collecting of microorganisms, small shells, etc. (2) The rush of water up onto the beach face following the breaking of a wave. (3) Same as uprush, runup. (4) A body of dashing, splashing water. (5) A bar over which the sea washes.

swash bar   Bar resulting from uprush and backwash of waves shoreward from the surf-zone breakpoint. Regarded as typical of the summer beach.

swash channel   (1) On the open shore, a channel cut by flowing water in its return to the parent body (for example, a rip channel). (2) A secondary channel passing through or shoreward of an inlet or river bar. (3) A narrow sound or channel of water lying within a sand bank, or between a sand bank and a shore.

swash mark   (1) The thin wavy line of fine sand, mica scales, bits of seaweed, etc., left by the swash when it recedes from its upward limit of movement over the beach face. (2) Lines left at upper limits of uprush on a beach, consisting commonly of fine debris, concentrations of mica or other minerals, and in recent years of foam derived from detergents. Microorganisms may be concentrated sufficiently to justify collection of these deposits for various biological reasons.

sweep zone   The part of a beach subject to movement of beach material imparting morphologic changes on either short- or long-term bases, marine processes being the agents involved. The lower limit is that of entrainment of bottom sediment on the lower beach.

swell   (1) Ocean waves advancing beyond the area in which they were generated, as by local high winds. Swell is ordinarily characterized by long periods, flat crests, and regularity in approach. Swell is particularly high on the southernmost continents surrounding the Southern (Antarctic, South Pacific, etc.) Ocean, and commonly is higher around Pacific than around Atlantic shores. The distance traveled may be several thousand miles, greater fetch ordinarily being associated with more intense swell. (2) Wind-generated calm. (3) Wind-generated waves that have traveled out of their generating area. Swell characteristically exhibits a more regular and longer period, and has flatter crests than waves within their fetch (seas).

syncline   Elongate geologic structure more or less

trough-shaped, with limbs dipping toward an axis and youngest rocks located centrally on the surface.

synclinorum   As defined originally (using *synclinorium*) by Dana, a mountain range formed out of sedimentary rocks that accumulated in a geosyncline (syncline + oros, the Greek word for mountain). Without stated reason, the term later came to mean a synclinal fold complicated by the presence of minor folds, a common usage today among U.S. geologists.

tectonic   Pertaining to the geological structural features of the earth's crust—their origin, etc.—ordinarily in a specific sense implying diastrophic changes associated with orogeny occurring at some definite time. The word is derived from the Greek for architect, hence the original meaning is earth architecture, the ruins of which are observable in the crust.

tephra   Clastic volcanic material ejected into the air when erupted and settling to the earth as rock; includes volcanic dust, tuff, cinders, etc.

terminal (end) moraine   Ridge of debris deposited at the line of the farthest glacier advance.

terrace   Relatively flat surface at some elevation above another surface. Alluvial terrace, an abandoned flood plain no longer subject to flooding because it stands higher than areas submerged at times of band overtopping. Also, flats of erosional origin. Marine terrace, bench more or less horizontal and parallel to the shore related to a higher-than-present stand of sea level, whether alluvial or erosional in origin (smaller ones are called benches and larger are plateaus). Flat formed by deposits of mineral springs, organisms, etc. Submarine terraces are located below sea level.

terrigenous coast (disequilibrium type)   A coast mainly composed of inorganic materials, for the most part, which is also highly irregular in shape.

terrigenous coast (equilibrium type)   A coast mainly composed of inorganic materials, straight to curvilinear.

thaw lake   In arctic areas underlain by permafrost, the summer sun thaws the ground ice unevenly and areas of local thaw become small ponds.

tidal bore   Bore, q.v., associated with rising tide.

tidal current   The alternating horizontal movement of water associated with the rise and fall of the tide. In open seas the direction rotates continuously through 360° with each tide. In locations near the shore the directions and velocities are influenced by local topography (including submarine).

tidal delta   When flood tides enter a tidal inlet across a barrier, they deposit part of their load in the lagoon just inside the inlet, forming a delta supplied with sediment from the ocean rather than from a river. See **delta.**

tidal flat   A marshy or muddy land covered and uncovered by rise and fall of the tides. Tidal flats are largest where land slopes are low and tidal range is high, as in northern Maine. If muddy, slikke. A tidal marsh.

tidal inlet   (1) A natural inlet maintained by tidal flow. (2) Loosely, any inlet in which the tide ebbs and flows. Also tidal outlet. (3) Waterway admitting ocean water into a lagoon or similar waterbody on a coast. (4) A breach in a coastal barrier generally opened by a major storm and maintained by tidal flow.

tidal marsh   Marshy tidal flat. Marsh may eventually occupy most of a lagoon that has been filled by tidal delta sediments. Same as tidal flats.

tidal period   The interval of time between two consecutive like phases of the tide or tidal current.

tidal pool   A pool of water remaining on a beach or reef after recession of the tide.

tidal range   The difference in elevation of coastal waters at high and low tides. A maximum in North America is about 18 meters (60 feet) near the head of the Bay of Fundy in New Brunswick. See **range of tide.**

tidal scour   Erosion by tidal currents may form deep channels in bay entrances or in shallow marshy lagoons, as in the channels.

tidal stand   An interval at high or low water when there is no appreciable change in the height of the tide. The water level is stationary at high and low water for only an instant, but the change in level near these times is so slow that it is not usually perceptible.

tidal stream   (1) A flow of water through a channel in a marsh where the current is due to the rising or falling tide. (2) In British usage, the expression is applied to a tidal current, their use of the word "current" being confined exclusively to the nontidal horizontal flow of water.

tide   (1) The periodic rising and falling of the water that results from gravitational attraction of the moon and sun and other astronomical bodies acting upon the rotating earth. Although the accompanying horizontal movement of the water resulting from the same cause is also sometimes called the tide, it is preferable to designate the latter as "tidal current," reserving the name "tide" for the vertical movement. (2) In popular usage, any unusually high and destructive water level along a shore. It usually refers to storm surge or tsunami. See **tsunami** and **long wave.**

tide amplitude   The semirange of a constituent tide. By analogy, it may be applied also to the maximum velocity of constituent current.

tide, daily retardation of   The amount of time by which corresponding tides grow later day by day (about 50 minutes).

tide, diurnal   See **diurnal tide.**

tide, ebb   See **ebb tide.**

tide, mixed   See **mixed tides.**

tide, neap   See **neap tide.**

tide, rip   See **rip tide.**

tide, semidiurnal   See **semidiurnal tide.**

tide, spring   See **spring tide.**

tide, type of   The characteristic form of the tide with special reference to the relation of the diurnal and semidiurnal waves. Tides are sometimes classified as diurnal, semidiurnal and mixed, but there are no sharply defined limits separating the groups. The tide is said to be diurnal when the diurnal wave predominates and only a single high and single low water occur each day during the greater part of the month. The tide is semidiurnal when the semidiurnal wave predominates and two high and two low waters occur each tidal day with a relatively small inequality in the high and low water heights. In the mixed type of tide the diurnal and semidiurnal waves are both important factors and the tide is characterized by a large inequality in the high or low water heights or in both. There will usually be two high and two low waters each day, but occasionally the tide will become diurnal. Also applicable to tidal currents.

tide wave   A long-period gravity wave that has its origin in the tide-producing force and that manifests itself in the rising and falling of the tide. A long wave.

till   Glacially deposited rock debris.

tombolo   (1) A barrier that ties an island to the mainland, such as Marblehead Neck, Massachusetts. Some islands are attached to the mainland by two barriers (double tombolo). (2) A spit, bar, or beach that extends from the mainland or an island to another island that thereby becomes tied to the shore (not the island itself). (3) An area of unconsolidated material, deposited by wave or current action, that connects a rock, island, etc., to the main shore, or other body of land.

tongue   A long, narrow strip of land, projecting into a body of water.

trade wind   Type of wind characteristic of tropical oceans and adjacent lands in which air moves from subtropical high-pressure areas (horse latitudes) toward equatorial low-pressure areas (doldrums), with a strong easterly component (from the northeast in the northern hemisphere; southeast in the southern) and comparative steadiness. Used to designate climates or meteorological characteristics within trade wind belts. Effects die out poleward from about 30° latitude.

training wall   A wall or jetty to direct current flow.

transgression   Invasion of or advance toward something, as a coast, sediments being superimposed over others with such advance. There have been notable transgressions of the sea over continents during earth history.

transitional water   In regard to progressive gravity waves, water whose depth is less than 1/2 but more than 1/25 the wave length. Often called a shallow water wave, deepwater wave, gravity wave.

transitional zone (transitional water)   In regard to progressive gravity waves, water whose depth is less than 1/2 but more than 1/25 the wave length. Often called shallow water.

translatory wave   See **wave of translation.**

transport   Movement of material, as sediment, individual particles, dissolved substances, etc., by a current (in air, ice, or deposition, and may be considered to take place over any distance between points of temporary or permanent rest). In streams, any load whatever, and however brought up into a current (including microturbulent), and by whatever means remaining in a current, is transported, not necessarily in the direction of flow. Material on beds of other bodies of water is also transported when moved.

transverse bar   (1) A bar that extends at approximately right angles to shorelines. (2) Slightly submerged sand ridges extending at comparatively high angles from the shore. When several are present the local topography is regarded as rhythmic.

transverse dune   Asymmetrical sand dune trending at about right angles to predominant wind direction, ordinarily with slope and other contrasts between stoss and lee sides. The windward side of the ridge is less steep than the leeward.

trench   Linear, narrow, and deep depression below the level of the seafloor, with relatively steep sides, and commonly located near coasts of continents or island arcs; also called trough or deeps; many other usages, for example, an elongate, relatively low area on land.

tributary   Branch or smaller stream that flows into a larger one or into a lake or other waterbody. Also applied to glaciers, parts of watersheds, etc.

trochoidal wave   A theoretical, progressive oscillatory wave first proposed by F. J. Gerstner in 1802 to describe the surface profile and particle orbits of finite amplitude, nonsinusoidal waves. The wave form is that of a prolate cycloid or trochoid, and the fluid particle motion is rotational as opposed to the usual irrotational particle motion for waves generated by normal forces.

tropic currents   Tidal currents occurring semimonthly when the effect of the moon's maximum declination is greatest. At these times the tendency of the moon to produce a diurnal inequality in the current is at a maximum.

trough   (1) A long and broad submarine depression with gently sloping sides. (2) Elongate depression on land, sea floor, between wave crests, etc.; trench, q.v.

trough of wave   The lowest part of a wave form between successive crests. Also that part of a wave below stillwater level. See **wave trough.**

true oceanic islands Islands either composed of basalt or of biogenic origin (coral reef, etc.), as distinguished from islands having rocks characteristic of continents. The Hawaiian and most islands in the Pacific Ocean are oceanic, whereas Japan, the Philippines, New Zealand, and most of the larger islands toward the western side of the basin are continental. Beaches of true oceanic islands consist of rock fragments or of coral and shell debris, and have a dark, white, or reddish appearance. They lack white quartz sand, the most characteristic component of continental beaches.

truncate To cut off the top or end; to level off; to change an outline, etc., abruptly. Thus ridges are truncated by the sea, rocks are truncated by wear, ends of spired shells may be truncated by being broken off or may grow naturally into a similar form. To remove upper parts of a soil profile.

tsunami (1) Seismic sea wave with long period generated by submarine earth displacements or volcanic explosions. Tsunami travel at terrific velocity across oceans with small amplitude in deep water, but grow higher as the disturbance feels the bottom and may reach tremendous heights as they cross platforms of shoaling water, at times producing disasters along coasts. The word is of Japanese origin and hence includes both the singular and plural. Also called seismic sea wave. (2) A long-period wave caused by underwater disturbance such as a volcanic eruption or earthquake. Commonly miscalled "tidal wave."

tufa Chemical sedimentary rock, ordinarily composed of calcium carbonate or silica, precipitated from groundwater along seepages or distinct vents, as in the case of mineral springs.

tuff Tephra; finer materials of explosive volcanic origin, whether in process of accumulation or forming an indurated rock. Commonly only cinders or sand-sized particles of rock, but some tuff contains crystals of considerable size. When huge quantities of gas are vented, rock material of all sizes, even some large blocks, are transported downslope at terrific speed (as glowing avalanches; nuèes ardentes) and have caused many disasters such as wiping out the population of St. Pierre, Martinique. Deposits resulting from these glowing avalanches are called welded tuff.

tundra Ordinarily treeless plain characteristic of arctic regions; the vegetation, commonly consisting of annuals, mosses, etc., found in such regions; the climate responsible, commonly defined as having a mean warmest month temperature between 0 and 10°C (32 and 50°F). Permafrost develops under many tundra regions, preventing water seepage and causing soil

saturation, etc. Also alpine varieties, where great elevation, rather than high latitude, is responsible.

turbidity current A density current caused by the weight of sand, silt, or clay it contains. Examples occur in lakes, reservoirs, and down continental slopes, where the rock resulting from deposition is known as turbidite. The force of flow may be sufficient to break submarine cables. Entrainment of sediment from a bottom crossed by a density current may leave furrows downslope, a common type of bottom in the vicinity of deltas. A gravity current or suspension current.

turtle grass A widely dispersed plant of the genus *Thallasia* that commonly forms the dominant growth over sandy, calcareous bottoms down to depths of 3 meters (10 feet) or so in lagoons, pools, or moats associated with coral reefs, etc. Individual plants seldom grow to more than half a meter high but commonly form dense, interwoven mats. The name popularly is also applied to eelgrass, which actually is a very different plant.

tussock A dense tuft of grass or sedge standing somewhat above its surroundings. Typical of muskeg, bog, or marsh.

undercutting Removing material at the base of a cliff or steep slope, as in the case of effects of wave action on a sea cliff or concentrated abrasion or turbulence on the wall of a channel.

undertow (1) A seaward current near the bottom on a sloping inshore zone. It is caused by the return, under the action of gravity, of the water carried up on the shore by waves. Often a misnomer for rip current. (2) The misconception that the backwash from a wave forms a powerful seaward current beneath the next advancing wave. Such currents are largely fictitious and based on a misinterpretation of rip currents, which move seaward mostly near the surface. (3) A current below water surface flowing seaward; the receding water below the surface from waves breaking on a shelving beach. (4) Actually "undertow" is largely mythical. As the backwash of each wave flows down the beach, a current is formed that flows seaward. However, it is a periodic phenomenon. The most common phenomena expressed as "undertow" are actually the rip currents in the surf.

underwater gradient The slope of the sea bottom. See also **slope.**

undulation (1) A continuously propagated motion to and fro, in any fluid or elastic medium, with no permanent translation of the particles themselves. (2) Wavy appearance of a surface (of water, sand, etc.). In physics, a motion to and fro, up and down, or from side to side in a fluid or elastic medium, in which the force of propagation results in little or no translation of particles; a wave; a vibration.

upcoast   In U.S. usage, the coastal direction generally trending toward the north.

updrift   The direction opposite that of the predominant movement of littoral materials.

uprush   The rush of water up onto the beach or foreshore following the breaking of a wave. Also swash, runup.

upwelling   (1) Rising of water toward the surface, ordinarily as a result of more rapid surface flow that removes upper layers, requiring replenishment from below to retain surface equilibrium. A common cause is increased wind velocity that drags water along with accelerating velocities. The rising water is ordinarily cooler, producing important effects climatically, contains more food and nutrients, hence attracts animal populations and provides favorable environments for increase in numbers of individuals. Many parts of oceans are subject to more or less persistent upwelling. On a small scale upwelling is an expression of macroturbulence in stream channels or occurs locally and temporarily in surf zones. (2) An upward flow of water from a subsurface current.

upwind   In the direction from which the wind blows.

U-shaped valley   A valley with steep walls and rounded floor curved by a former valley glacier.

valley   An elongated depression, usually with an outlet, between bluffs or between ranges of hills or mountains.

valley, sea   See **sea valley.**

valley, submarine   See **submarine valley.**

valley train   Outwash of a melting glacier carried downstream along a valley below the glacial front. For example, the valley train on which Valdez, Alaska, was located.

variability of waves   See **wave variability.**

velocity of waves   See **wave velocity.**

volcanic ash   The finely divided, fragmental rock material violently blown from volcanoes during explosive eruptions. Coarse ash is from 4 to 1/4 millimeters (-2 phi to 2 phi) in grain size; fine ash is under 1/4 millimeters.

volcanic caldera   A large, circular depression in the center of a large volcanic cone generally formed by collapse of the top of a mountain but occasionally by removal of the mountain by explosive eruption. For example, Aleutian Islands, Alaska.

volcanic sand   Fine detritus erupted during volcanic explosions, with fragments the size of a pea or smaller. The particles are also called lapilli.

volcanic tuff   The particles smaller than sand size resulting from volcanic explosions, also called volcanic ash. A volume of tuff equal to 11.3 cubic kilometers (7

cubic miles) was produced by the Mt. Katmai eruption of 1912.

volcano   Vent in the earth's crust through which magma, lava, fragmental materials gas, water, and various solutions, etc., are ejected. A mountain resulting from local accumulation of such material. Used also for mounds, etc., resulting from other than igneous activity, for example, mud volcano.

wadi, wady, waddy   (from oued). Arid-climate (typically desert) stream channel, ordinarily dry but capable of flowing, at times with considerable velocity, when concentrating local runoff. The term originated in Mediterranean Africa but has come into general use. Also, arroyo, wash, barranca, etc.

wash   Wadi, q.v.; to cover by a fluid, ordinarily water; to waste or abrade by flowing water; to remove by water; backward current or disturbed water, as by movement of oars or rotation of a ship's screw; gravel or rock debris transported by water and deposited. Many other usages.

wash, wave   See **wave wash.**

washover (overwash)   (1) Advance of water beyond normal limits, specifically across a beach or belt of low dunes, forming washover deltas or other deposits as a result of deposition or sediment carried along with the flow of water or wind. An area where temporary submergence has occurred. (2) The transfer of beach sand across to the lagoon side of the barrier through sluiceways during a hurricane.

washover delta (fan)   A triangular deposit on the lagoon side of a barrier transported from the beach through a gap in a barrier during a hurricane or other violent storm.

watercourse   Stream of surface water, whether natural or artificial, ordinarily having a definite channel and active, in at least some years. Runoff channel.

waterline   (1) A juncture of land and sea. This line migrates, changing with the tide or other fluctuation in the water level. Where waves are present on the beach, this line is also known as the limit of backrush. (Approximately the intersection of the land with the stillwater level.) (2) The common boundary between the water surface and any immersed structure.

water-table rock   Rock cemented along or close to the level of the water table. Common varieties are beach rock exposed as a result of retreat of the shore, stream rock cropping out along eroding banks of streams, and hardpans encountered at water-table level over extensive inland areas where rocks are unconsolidated, especially if the cement is calcium carbonate. A specific type of hardpan.

wave   (1) A ridge deforming the upper surface of water, whether fixed in position or changing position, as illustrated by lake or sea waves created and moved forward by shear caused by wind or reflected back from barriers (such as vertical sea walls); deformation resembling waves, as produced by tidal forces, explosions, sudden changes in bottom configuration, as tsunami. Waves alternate with troughs. Also many other usages; for example, complete cyclic changes in amplitude. See **sand wave**. (2) An oscillatory movement in a body of water manifested by an alternate rise and fall of the surface. (3) A disturbance of the surface of a liquid body, as the sea or a lake, in the form of a ridge, swell or hum. (4) the term "wave" by itself usually refers to the term "surface gravity wave," "progressive wave," "standing wave," "tide wave," "tsunami." (5) A ridge, deformation, or undulation of the surface of a liquid.

wave, oscillatory   See **oscillatory wave**.

wave, reflected   See **reflected wave**.

wave, trochoidal   See **trochoidal wave**.

wave amplitude   (1) The magnitude of the displacement of a wave from a mean value. An ocean wave has an amplitude equal to the vertical distance from still-water level to wave crest. For a sinusoidal wave, amplitude is one-half the wave height. (2) The semirange of a constituent tide. Half the wave height.

wave amplitude (height)   Vertical distance between crest and adjacent trough.

wave base   Lower limit of wave action, especially in ability to entrain sediment or erode rock. For many years it was presumed that continental shelves were eroded to a wave base of about 182 meters (600 feet), but this concept has been discarded by almost everyone, some favoring the datum of surf base, and others, somewhat deeper water. The significance of these terms is reduced by greater appreciation of depositional origin of numerous submarine flats.

wave celerity   Wave speed.

wave convergence   Where the crest of a wave is bent so that the two arms converge on a point, which produces high waves at the point.

wave crest   (1) The highest part of a wave. (2) That part of the wave above still water level.

wave-cut platform   A relatively smooth surface just below low tide extending seaward from the shore, resulting from wave erosion.

wave direction   See **direction of waves**.

wave height   The vertical difference between the wave crest and trough, the equivalent to the wave amplitude.

wave hollow   See **wave trough**.

wave length (wavelength)   The horizontal distance between similar points on two successive waves measured perpendicular to the crest.

wave of translation   Wave characterized by movement of water particles in its direction of advance, in contrast with wave of oscillation in which water particles travel in more or less circular orbits. In some cases a bore is associated with tidal rise, but commonly it is the result of waves feeling the bottom and slowing down at depth, whereas toward the surface the flow is not retarded as much by friction, so moves ahead more rapidly, commonly overturning to form breakers. Translatory movement is characteristic of shoaling bottoms, approach to beaches, in swash, etc. Distinguished from an oscillatory wave.

wave period   (1) The time for a wave crest to traverse a distance equal to one wave length. The time for two successive wave crests to pass a fixed point such as a rock or an anchored buoy. (2) Time required for two adjacent wave crests to pass a point, commonly less than 15 seconds in the case of sea waves, shorter periods occurring in shoal water.

wave propagation   The transmission of waves through water.

wave refraction   A bending of wave trains where their orbiting water particles encounter bottom. See **refraction of water waves**.

wave steepness   The ratio of the wave's height to its length.

wave train   A series of waves from the same direction.

wave trough   The lowest part of the wave form between crests. Also that part of a wave below still water level. Sometimes called wave hollow. More or less linear depression between adjacent wave crests.

wave variability   (1) The variation of heights and periods between individual waves within a wave train. Wave trains are not composed of waves of equal height and periods, but rather of heights and periods that vary in a statistical manner (2) The variability in direction of wave travel when leaving the generation area. (3) The variation in height along the crest.

wave velocity   The speed with which an individual wave advances.

wave wash   The erosive action on shores or embankments caused by the lapping or breaking of waves.

wave of oscillation   See **oscillatory wave**.

wave of translation   Waves of oscillation that acquire lateral motion through water-particle contact with the bottom.

weathering   Changes, especially in rock, associated with differences in temperature, freezing of water, exposure to atmospheric gases, solution, etc., that result from processes along the interface between the atmosphere and solid earth. Both disintegration (mechanical fragmentation) and decomposition (chemical change) are included.

weir   Submerged barrier to flow, typically of artificial origin; for example, for the purpose of deflecting flow direction into the head of a canal, etc., or to direct the movements of fish heading upstream.

weir jetty   An updrift jetty with a low section or weir over which littoral drift moves into a predredged deposition basin which is dredged periodically.

welded tuff   Rock resulting from consolidation of materials transported by a glowing avalanche associated with expulsion of heavy gases, water, etc., from volcanoes.

whaleback dune   Sand dune with rounded crest. Whaleback dunes are commonly elongate in the direction of prevailing wind off the horns of barchan dunes.

wharf   A structure built on the shore of a harbor, river, or canal, so that vessels may lie alongside to receive and discharge cargo and passengers. Any structure such as a pier, dock or quay, alongside which a vessel may lie.

whirlpool   (1) A conspicuous vortex, typically fixed in position and associated with current movement along a channel. The water in the central part of the structure moves downward; in extreme cases a whirling depression is present at the core. (2) An eddy or vortex of water. Water moving rapidly in a circle.

whitecap   White froth resulting from wind shear at the crest of a wave. Scattered whitecaps appear with wind of Beaufort scale 3, 12.8 to 19.3 kilometers (8 to 12 miles) per hour; they become general at force 6, 40.2 to 49.8 kilometers (25 to 31 miles) per hour. With gales the white foam is blown into streaks.

wind, offshore   See **offshore wind.**

wind, onshore   See **onshore wind.**

wind current (wind-driven current)   (1) A current created by the action of the wind. From theoretical considerations, currents produced by winds in the open sea will set to the right of the direction toward which the wind is blowing if in the Northern Hemisphere and to the left of this direction if in the Southern Hemisphere. (2) A current formed by shear caused by the force of the wind against a water surface, in streams, lagoons, open seas, etc.

windward   (1) Term to designate the side of a ship, island, or other object against which the wind blows, in distinction to lee. (2) The direction from which the wind is blowing. The weather side.

wind waves   (1) Waves formed and growing in height under the influence of wind. (2) Loosely, any wave generated by wind.

winter beach   Depleted upper beach resulting from erosion associated with high wave energy. Storms are particularly effective in removing the upper beach, lowering its level and flattening its profile. Storms may occur at any season, as may other periods of high sea state, but in many regions are most characteristic of winters. Tendencies toward winter beach development occur during short periods of high wave energy and also during rising tides.

worm rock   Hardened deposits of tubular structures originating at about sea level as a result of activities of various segmented worms. Typically calcareous secretions form or bind together the tubes by cementation of inorganic materials, such as coarse silt or fine sand. Most worm rock is gray, but in some cases amber or other colors. When first formed the masses may be crushed when stepped upon, but later acquire greater bearing strength, and in some cases become hard and durable.

xerophyte   Plant that lives in an arid environment. A plant structurally adapted for life and growth with a limited water supply.

yardang   Grooves and intervening pinnacles eroded in deserts by the wind.

zone of aeration   Space above the water table where voids in soil or rock are not filled with water except for brief intervals.

zone of saturation (cementation)   Space below the water table where voids are normally filled with water having a pressure in excess of one atmosphere. The zone of groundwater, characterized by tendencies toward cementation, ordinarily by carbonates, silica, iron compounds, etc., that indurate rock.

REFERENCES

American Geological Institute, 1962, *Dictionary of Geological Terms*, Dolphin Books, Doubleday, Garden City, N.Y., 545 p.

Allen, Richard H., 1972, A Glossary of Coastal Engineering Terms, *Miscellaneous Paper 2-72*, U.S. Army, Corps of Engineers, Coastal Engineering Research Center, Washington, D.C., 55 p.

Garner, H. F., 1974, *The Origin of Landscapes: A Synthesis of Geomorphology*, Oxford University Press, New York, pp. 695-709.

Russell, Richard J., 1968, Glossary of Terms Used in Fluvial, Deltaic, and Coastal Morphology and Processes, *Coastal Studies Institute Technical Report No. 63*, Louisiana State University, Baton Rouge, 97 p.

Shepart, Francis P., and Harold R. Wanless, 1971, *Our Changing Coastlines*, McGraw-Hill, New York, pp. 551-579.

Wiegel, Robert L., 1953, *Waves, Tides, Currents and Beaches: Glossary of Terms and List of Standard Symbols*, Council on Wave Research, The Engineering Foundation, 113 p.

Bibliography

Abbe, C. J., 1895, Remarks on the Cuspate Capes of the Carolina Coast, *Boston Soc. Nat. Hist. Proc.* **26:**489-497.

Agassiz, A., 1893, A Visit to the Great Barrier Reef of Australia in the Steamer *Croydon, Mus. Comp. Zool. Bull.* (Harvard College, Cambridge) **28:**95-148.

Agassiz, A., 1903, On the Formation of Barrier Reefs and of the Different Types of Atolls, *Royal Soc. London Proc.* **71:**412-414.

Allen, R. H., 1972, A Glossary of Coastal Engineering Terms, *U.S. Army Coastal Engineering Research Center Misc. Paper 2-72,* U.S. Army Corps of Engineers, Coastal Engineering Research Center, Washington, D.C., 55 p.

Athearn, W. D., and F. C. Ronne, 1963, Shoreline Changes at Cape Hatteras: An Aerial Photographic Study of a 17-Year Period, *Office of Naval Res. Rev.* **6:**17-24.

Axelrod, D. I., 1958, Map of Coastal Vegetation of the World, Scale 1:50,000,000, American Geographical Society, New York.

Bagnold, R. A., 1941, *Physics of Blown Sand and Desert Dunes,* William Morrow & Co., New York, 265 p.

Bailey, H. P., 1958, Map of Coastal Climates of the World, Scale 1:50,000,000, American Geographical Society, New York.

Ball, M. M., and A. C. Neuman, 1968, Crescentic Landforms Along the Atlantic Coast of the United States, *Science* **161:**710.

Bascom, W. H., 1951, The Relationship Between Sand Size and Beach Face Slope, *Am. Geophys. Union Trans.* **32:**866-874.

Bascom, W. H., 1951, *Investigation of Coastal Sand Movements Near Santa Barbara, California, Part I,* Council on Wave Research, Engineering Foundation, University of California, Berkeley, 38 p.

Bascom, W. H., 1951, *Investigation of Coastal Sand Movements Near Santa Barbara, California, Part II,* Council on Wave Research, Engineering Foundation, University of California, Berkeley, 78 p.

Bird, E. C. F., 1967, Depositional Features in Estuaries and Lagoons on the South Coast of New South Wales, *Australia Geog. Studies* **5:**113-124.

Bloom, A. L., 1963, Late-Pleistocene Fluctuations of Sea Level and Post-glacial Crustal Rebound in Coastal Maine, *Am. Jour. Sci.* **261:**862-879.

Bloom, A. L., 1965, The Explanatory Description of Coasts, *Zeitschr. Geomorphologie* **9:**422-436.

Bloom, A. L., 1971, Glacial-Eustatic and Isostatic Controls of Sea Level, in *Late Cenozoic Glacial Ages,* K. K. Turekian, ed., Yale University Press, New Haven, pp. 355-378.

Bradley, W., 1958, Submarine Abrasion and Wave-Cut Platforms, *Geol. Soc. America Bull.* **69:**967-974.

Brown, C. W., 1939, Hurricanes and Shoreline Changes in Rhode Island, *Geog. Rev.* **29:**416-420.

Brown, E. I., 1928, Inlets on Sandy Coasts, *Am. Soc. Civil Engineers Proc.* **54(2):**505-553.

Brown, R. C., 1953, Birth of an Inlet—Carolina Beach Inlet, N. Carolina, *Shore and Beach* **21:**20-21.

Burton, I., and R. W. Kates, 1964, The Flood Plain and the Sea-Shore: A Comparative Study of Hazard Zone Occupance, *Geog. Rev.* **54(3):**366-385.

Burton, I., R. W. Kates, and R. E. Snead, 1969, The Human Ecology of Coastal Flood Hazard in Megalopolis, *Department of Geography Research Paper No. 115,* University of Chicago, Chicago, 196 p.

Caldwell, J. M., 1949, Beach Erosion, *Scientific Monthly* **69:**229-235.

Caldwell, J. M., 1959, Shore Erosion by Storm Waves, *U.S. Army Corps of Engineers, Beach Erosion Board Misc. Paper 1,* p. 59.

Carson, R., 1955, *The Edge of the Sea,* New American Library, New York, 238 p.

Carson, R., 1961, *The Sea Around Us,* New American Library, New York, 221 p.

Coates, D. R., ed., 1973, *Coastal Geomorphology,* Publication in Geomorphology, State University of New York, Binghamton, 403 p.

Coleman, J. M., and W. G. Smith, 1964, Late Recent Rise of Sea Level, *Geol. Soc. American Bull.* **75:**833-840.

Cotton, C. A., 1918, The Outline of New Zealand, *Geog. Rev.* **6:**320-340.

Cotton, C. A., 1922, Geomorphology of New Zealand, Part I:

Systematic, *New Zealand Board Sci. and Art* **3**:442.

Cotton, C. A., 1942, Shorelines of Transverse Deformation, *Jour. Geomorphology* **5**:45-58.

Cotton, C. A., 1945, *Geomorphology*, John Wiley and Sons, New York, 505 p.

Cotton, C. A., 1951a, Atlantic Gulfs, Estuaries, and Cliffs, *Geol. Mag.* **88**:113-128.

Cotton, C. A., 1951b, Accidents and Interruptions in the Cycle of Marine Erosion, *Geog. Jour.* **117**:343-349.

Cotton, C. A., 1951c, Une Cole de'Deformation Transverse a Wellington (N.Z.), *Rev. Géomorphologie Dynam.* **2**:97-109.

Cotton, C. A., 1951d, Sea Cliffs of Banks Peninsula and Wellington: Some Criteria for Coastal Classification, *New Zealand Geogr.* **7**:103-120.

Cotton, C. A., 1952a, Cyclic Resection of Headlands by Marine Erosion, *Geol. Mag.* **89**:221-225.

Cotton, C. A., 1954, Deductive Morphology and the Genetic Classification of Coasts, *Scientific Monthly* **78**(3):163-181.

Crandell, D. R., 1965, The Glacial History of Western Washington and Oregon, in *The Quaternary of the United States*, H. W. Wright, Jr. and D. G. Frey, eds., Princeton University Press, Princeton, pp. 341-353.

Daly, R. A., 1910, Pleistocene Glaciation and the Coral Reef Problem, *Am. Jour. Sci.* **30**:297-308.

Davies, J. L., 1964, A Morphogenic Approach to World Shorelines, *Zeitschr. Geomorphologie* **8**:127-142.

Davis, J. H., 1938, Mangroves, Makers of Lands, *Nature* **31**:551-553.

Davis, J. H., 1940, The Ecology and Geologic Role of Mangroves in Florida, *Carnegie Inst. Washington Pub.* **517**:303-412.

Davis, R. A., and W. T. Fox, 1972, Coastal Processes and Nearshore Sand Bars, *Journ. Sed. Petrology* **42**:401-412.

Davis, W. M., 1898, *Physical Geography*, Ginn and Company, Boston, 428 p.

Davis, W. M., 1928, The Coral Reef Problem, *Am. Geog. Soc. Spec. Pub. 9*, 596 p.

Dolan, R., 1965, Relationships Between Nearshore Processes and Beach Changes Along the Outer Banks of North Carolina, Ph.D. dissertation, Louisiana State University, Baton Rouge, 51 p.

Dolan, R., 1973, Barrier Islands: Natural and Controlled, in *Coastal Geomorphology*, D. R. Coates, ed., Publication in Geomorphology, State University of New York, Binghamton, pp. 263-278.

Dolan, R., and J. C. Ferm, 1968, Concentric Landforms Along the Atlantic Coast of the United States, *Science* **159**:627-629.

Dolan, R., and J. McCloy, 1964, *Selected Bibliography on Beach Features and Related Nearshore Processes*, Louisiana State University Press, Baton Rouge, 59 p.

Dolan, R., B. Hayden, G. Hornberger, J. Zieman, and M. Vincent, 1972, Classification of the Coastal Environments of the World, Part I: The Americas, *Office of Naval Research Technical Report No. 1*, Department of Environmental Sciences, University of Virginia, Charlottesville, 163 p.

Dolan, R., P. J. Godfrey, and W. E. Odum, 1973, Man's Impact on the Barrier Islands of North Carolina, *Am. Scientist* **61**:152-162.

Dolan, R., L. Vincent, and B. Hayden, 1974, Crescentic Coastal Landforms, *Zeitschr. Geomorphologie* **18**:1-2.

Easterbrook, D. J., 1963, Late Pleistocene Glacial Events and Relative Sea Level Changes in the Northern Puget Sound Lowland, Washington, *Geol. Soc. America Bull.* **74**:1465-1483.

El-Ashry, M. T., 1968, Photo Interpretation of Shoreline Changes Between Capes Hatteras and Fear (North Carolina), *Marine Geology* **6**(5):347-379.

Emery, K. O., 1960, *The Sea Off Southern California*, John Wiley and Sons, New York, 366 p.

Emery, K. O., 1961, Submerged Marine Terraces and Their Sediments, *Zeitschr. Geomorphologie Supp.*, **3**:17-29.

Evans, O. F., 1938, Classification and Origin of Beach Cusps, *Jour. Geology* **47**:324-334.

Fairbridge, R. W., 1947, A Contemporary Eustatic Rise in Sea Level, *Geog. Jour.* **109**:157.

Fairbridge, R. W., 1950a, Recent and Pleistocene Coral Reefs in Australia, *Jour. Geology* **58**:330-401.

Fairbridge, R. W., 1950b, The Geology and Geomorphology of Point Peron, Western Australia, *Royal Soc. Western Australia Jour.* **34**(3):35-72.

Fairbridge, R. W., 1961. Eustatic Changes in Sea Level, in *Physics and Chemistry of the Earth*, vol. 4, L. H. Ahrens et al., eds., Pergamon Press, London, pp. 99-185.

Fairbridge, R. W., ed., 1968, *The Encyclopedia of Geomorphology*, Reinhold Book Corporation, New York, 1295 p.

Fairbridge, R. W., 1980, The Estuary: Its Definition and Geodynamic Cycle, in *Chemistry and Biogeochemistry of Estuaries*, E. Olavsson and I. Cato, eds., John Wiley and Sons, New York, pp. 1-35.

Freeman, O. W., and J. W. Morris, 1958, *World Geography*, McGraw-Hill Book Co., New York, 623 p.

Garner, H. F., 1974, *The Origin of Landscapes: A Synthesis of Geomorphology*, Oxford University Press, New York, 734 p.

Ginsberg, R. N., 1953, Beachrock in South Florida, *Jour. Sed. Petrology* **23**:85-92.

Godfrey, P. J., and M. M. Godfrey, 1973, Comparison of Ecological and Geomorphic Interactions Between Altered and Unaltered Barrier Island Systems in North Carolina, in *Coastal Geomorphology*, D. R. Coates, ed., Publication in Geomorphology, State University of New York, Binghamton, pp. 239-258.

Green, J., and N. M. Short, 1971, *Volcanic Landforms and Surface Features: A Photographic Atlas and Glossary*, Springer-Verlag, New York, 519 p.

Guilcher, A., 1958, Coastal Corrosion Forms in Limestone Around the Bay of Biscay, *Scottish Geog. Mag.* **74**:137-149.

Gulliver, F. P., 1896, Cuspate Forelands, *Geog. Soc. American Bull.* **7**:399-422.

Haferkorn, H. E., 1929, *Sand Movement and Beaches*, a Bibliography prepared under the Chief of Engineers, U.S. Army, U.S. Army Engineering School, Fort Humphreys, Virginia, 114 p.

Hails, J. R., 1967, Significance of Statistical Parameters for Distinguishing Sedimentary Environments in New South Wales, Australia, *Jour. Sed. Petrology* **37**:1059-1069.

Hansen, W. R., 1965, Effects of the Earthquake of March 27,

1964 at Anchorage, Alaska, *U.S. Geol. Survey Prof. Paper 542-A*, pp. A1-A68.

Hansen, W. R., E. B. Eckel, W. E. Schaem, R. E. Lyle, W. George, and G. Chance, 1966, The Alaska Earthquake, March 27, 1964: Field Investigations and Reconstruction Effort, *U.S. Geol. Survey Prof. Paper 541*, 111 p.

Harrison, W., and K. A. Wagner, 1964, Beach Changes at Virginia Beach, *U.S. Army Coastal Engineering Research Center Misc. Paper 6-64*, U.S. Army Corps of Engineers, Coastal Engineering Research Center, Washington, D.C., 25 p.

Hayden, B., M. Vincent, D. Resio, C. Biscoe, Jr., and R. Dolan, 1973, Classification of the Coastal Environments of the World, Part II: Africa, *Office of Naval Research Technical Report No. 3*, Department of Environmental Sciences, University of Virginia, Charlottesville, 46 p.

Hayes, M. O., 1967, Hurricanes as Geological Agents, in *Case Studies of Hurricanes Carla, 1961, and Cindy, 1963*, Bureau of Economic Geology, Report of Investigations No. 61, University of Texas, Austin, 54 p.

Hayes, M. O., 1972, Forms of Sediment Accumulation in the Beach Zone, in *Waves on Beaches*, R. E. Meyer, ed., Academic Press, New York, pp. 297-356.

Heezen, B. C., and M. Ewing, 1952, Turbidity Currents and Submarine Slumps, and the 1929 Grand Banks Earthquake, *Am. Jour. Sci.* **250**:849-873.

Hills, E. S., 1949, Shore Platforms, *Geol. Mag.* **86**:137-152.

Hoffmeister, J. E., and H. G. Multer, 1965, Fossil Mangrove Reef of Key Biscayne, Florida, *Geol. Soc. America Bull.* **76**(8):845-852.

Hoffmeister, J. E., and K. W. Stockman, 1967, Miami Limestone of Florida and Its Recent Bahamian Counterpart, *Geol. Soc. America Bull.* **78**:175-190.

Hollister, C. D., 1973, Atlantic Continental Shelf and Slope of the United States—Texture of Surface Sediments from New Jersey to Southern Florida, *U.S. Geol. Survey Prof. Paper 529-M*, 23 p.

Hopley, D., and P. Isdale, 1977, Coral Microatolls, Tropical Cyclones and Reef Flat Morphology: A North Queensland Example, *Search* **8**(3):79-81.

Howard, A. D., 1939, Hurricane Modification of the Offshore Bar of Long Island, New York, *Geog. Rev.* **29**(3):400-415.

Hoyt, J. H., 1967, Barrier Island Formation, *Geol. Soc. America Bull.* **78**:1125-1136.

Hoyt, J. H., 1970, Development and Migration of Barrier Islands, Northern Gulf of Mexico: Discussion, *Geol. Soc. America Bull.* **81**:3779-3782.

Hunt, A. R., 1884, Description of Oscillation Ripple Marks, *Royal Soc. Dublin Proc.* **4**:261-262.

Inman, D. L., C. E. Nordstrom, and R. E. Flick, 1976, Currents in Submarine Canyons: An Air-Sea Interaction, in *Ann. Rev. Fluid Mechanics* **8**:205-310.

Kates, R. W., 1962, Hazard and Choice Perception of Flood Plain Management, *Department of Geography Research Paper No. 78*, University of Chicago, Chicago, 157 p.

King, C. A. M., and W. W. Williams, 1949, The Formation and Movement of Sand Bars by Wave Action, *Geog. Jour.* **107**:70-84.

King, P. B., 1969, Tectonics of North America: A Discussion to Accompany the Tectonic Map of North America, scale 1:5,000,000, *U.S. Geol. Survey Prof. Paper 628*, 95 p.

Komar, P. D., 1975, On the Comparison Between the Threshold of Sediment Motion Under Waves and Unidirectional Currents with a Discussion of the Practical Evaluation of the Threshold, *Jour. Sed. Petrology* **45**:362-367.

Komar, P. D., and M. C. Miller, 1973, The Threshold of Sediment Movement Under Oscillatory Water Waves, *Jour. Sed. Petrology* **43**:1101-1110.

Lizarraga-Arciniega, J. R., and P. D. Komar, 1975, Shoreline Changes Due to Jetty Construction on the Oregon Coast, *Sea Grant Program Pub. ORESU-T-75-004*, Oregon State University, 85 p.

Loebeck, A. K., 1939, *Geomorphology: An Introduction to the Study of Landscapes*, McGraw-Hill Book Co., New York, 731 p.

Lugo, A. E., and S. C. Snedaker, 1974, Ecology of Mangroves, *Ann. Rev. Ecology and Systematics* **5**:39-64.

McGill, J. T., 1958, Map of Coastal Landforms of the World, *Geog. Rev.* **48**:402-405.

McGill, J. T., 1960, *Selected Bibliography of Coastal Geomorphology of the World*, University of California, Los Angeles, 50 p.

McKenzie, R., 1958, Rip Current Systems, *Jour. Geology* **66**(2):103-113.

Merriam, R., 1960, Portuguese Bend Landslide, Palos Verdes Hills, California, *Jour. Geology* **68**:140-153.

Moore, J. G., R. L. Phillips, R. W. Grigg, D. W. Peterson, and D. A. Swanson, 1973, Flow of Lava into the Sea, 1969-1971, Kilauea Volcano, Hawaii, *Geol. Soc. America Bull.* **84**:537-546.

Morton, R. A., 1976, Effects of Hurricane Eloise on Beach and Coastal Structures, Florida Panhandle, *Geology* **4**(5):277-280.

Neumann, G., 1966, *Principles of Physical Oceanography*, Prentice-Hall, Englewood Cliffs, N.J., 545 p.

Niering, W. A., 1970, The Dilemma of the Coastal Wetlands: Conflict of Local, National, and World Priorities, in *The Environmental Crises*, H. W. Helfrich, ed., Yale University Press, New Haven, pp. 142-156.

Otvos, E. G., 1970, Development and Migration of Barrier Island, Northern Gulf of Mexico, *Geol. Soc. America Bull.* **81**:241-246.

Psuty, N. P., 1965, Beach-Ridge Development in Tabasco, Mexico, *Assoc. Am. Geographers Annals* **55**:112-124.

Putnam, W. C., D. I. Axelrod, H. P. Bailey, and J. T. McGill, 1960, *Natural Coastal Environments of the World*, University of California, Los Angeles, 140 p.

Quinn, A. D. C., 1972, *Design and Construction of Ports and Marine Structures*, McGraw Hill Book Co., New York, 611 p.

Russell, R. J., 1953, Coastal Advance and Retreat in Louisiana, Internat. Geol. Congress, 19th Sess., *Comptes Rendus* **4**:108-118.

Russell, R. J., 1958, Long Straight Beaches, *Eclog. Geol. Helv.* **51**:591-598.

Russell, R. J., 1962, Origin of Beach Rock, *Zeitschr. Geomorphologie* **6**:1-6.

Russell, R. J., 1963, Recent Recession of Tropical Cliffy Coasts, *Science* **139**:9-15.

Russell, R. J., 1964, Duration of the Quaternary and Its Subdivisions, *Natl. Acad. Sci. Proc.* **52**:790-796.

Russell, R. J., 1965b, Southern Hemisphere Beach Rock, *Geog. Rev.* **55**:17-45.

Russell, R. J., 1965c, Beach Cusps, *Geol. Soc. America Bull.* **76**:307-350.

Russell, R. J., 1968, Glossary of Terms Used in Fluvial, Deltaic, and Coastal Morphology and Processes, *Coastal Studies Institute Technical Report 63,* Louisiana State University, Baton Rouge, 97 p.

Russell, R. J., and H. V. Howe, 1935, Cheniers of Southwestern Louisiana, *Geog. Rev.* **25**:449-461.

Russell, R. J., and W. G. McIntire, 1965, Beach Cusps, *Geol. Soc. America Bull.* **76**:307-320.

Savage, R. P., 1959, Laboratory Study of the Effect of Groins in the Rate of Littoral Transport, *U.S. Army Corps Engineers Beach Erosion Board Tech. Memo. 114,* 55 p.

Schureman, P., 1941, Tide and Current Glossary, *U.S. Coast and Geod. Survey Spec. Pub. 228,* 40 p.

Schwartz, M. L., 1972, *Spits and Bars,* Dowden, Hutchinson & Ross, Stroudsburg, Penna., 452 p.

Shepard, F. P., 1951a, Transportation of Sand into Deep Water, *Soc. Econ. Paleontologists and Mineralogists Spec. Pub. 3,* pp. 53-65.

Shepard, F. P., 1951b, Mass Movements in Submarine Canyon Heads, *Am. Geophys. Union Trans.* **32**:405-418.

Shepard, F. P., 1973, *Submarine Geology,* 3rd ed., Harper and Row, New York, 557 p.

Sonu, C. J., J. M. McCloy, and D. S. McArthur, 1967, Longshore Currents and Nearshore Topographies, *10th Conf. on Coastal Engineering Proc.,* pp. 525-549.

Steers, J. A., 1962, *The Sea Coast,* 2nd ed., Collins, London, 292 p.

Sverdrup, H. U., R. Fleming, and M. W. Johnson, 1942, *The Oceans,* Prentice-Hall, Englewood Cliffs, N.J., 1987 p.

Tanner, W. F., 1958, The Equilibrium Beach, *Am. Geophys. Union Trans.* **39**:889.

Tanner, W. F., 1963, Origin and Maintenance of Ripple Marks, *Sedimentology* **2**:307-311.

Thom, B. G., 1964, Origin of Sand Beach Ridges, *Australian Journ. Sci.* **26**:351-352.

U.S. Geological Survey, 1970, *Natural Atlas of the United States of America,* U.S. Government Printing Office, Washington, D.C., 417 p.

Veen, J. V., 1962, *Dredge Drain Reclaim, the Art of a Nation,* 5th ed. Martinius Nijhoff, The Hague, 200 p.

Vesper, W. H., 1967, Behavior of Beach Fill and Borrow Area at Sherwood Island State Park, Westport, Connecticut, *U.S. Army Corps Engineers Coastal Eng. Research Center Tech. Mem. 20,* U.S. Army Corps of Engineers, Coastal Engineering Research Center, Washington, D.C., 25 p.

Walker, H. J., 1962, The Colville River Delta, *1st Natl. Coast and Shallow Water Conf. Proc.,* pp. 472-474.

West, R. C., 1957, *The Pacific Lowlands of Colombia,* Louisiana State University Press, Baton Rouge, 278 p.

West, R. C., N. P. Psuty, and B. C. Thom, 1969, The Tabasco Lowlands of Southeastern Mexico, *Coastal Studies Institute Technical Report 70,* Louisiana State University, Baton Rouge, 193 p.

Woodhouse, W. W., Jr., 1978, Dune Building and Stabilization with Vegetation, *U.S. Army Coastal Engineering Research Center Special Report SR-3,* U.S. Army Corps of Engineers, Coastal Engineering Research Center, Washington, D.C., 99 p.

Woodhouse, W. W., Jr., and R. E. Hanes, 1967, Dune Stabilization with Vegetation on the Outer Banks of North Carolina, *U.S. Army Coastal Engineering Research Center Tech. Mem. 22,* U.S. Army Corps of Engineers, Coastal Engineering Research Center, Washington, D.C., 45 p.

Ziegler, J. M., 1959, Origin of the Sea Islands of the Southeastern United States, *Geog. Rev.* **49**(2):222-237.

Ziegler, J. M., R. H. Hayes, and S. D. Tuttle, 1959, Beach Changes During Storms on Outer Cape Cod, Massachusetts, *Jour. Geology* **67**:318-336.

Index

About the Author

Rodman E. Snead is Professor of Geography at the University of New Mexico in Albuquerque. His major fields of research and teaching include arid coastal geomorphology, physical geography, climatology, aerial photographic interpretation, remote sensing techniques, and the geographic regions of South Asia and the Middle East. Dr. Snead spent his early years near the coast of southern New Jersey, which led to his early interest in the problems of coastal erosion and human settlement in the coastal zone. His undergraduate degree in geography and geology is from the University of Virginia, and his Master's degree is in geography from Syracuse University. He received the Ph.D. in geography in 1963 from the coastal Studies Institute at Louisiana State University. From 1961 to 1969 he taught at the Graduate School of Geography, Clark University, Worcester, Massachusetts. In 1969 he joined the faculty of the University of New Mexico.

Professor Snead has travelled extensively, which has enabled him to observe and record a great diversity of coastal landform types around the world. From the fjord coast of Alaska to the desert coast of Australia and the tropical coasts of Jamica and Puerto Rico, this geographer/geomorphologist has observed and noted firsthand the many types of coastal features. The information collected through thirty years of travel in over ninty-four countries has enabled him to compile this coastal photographic atlas and compendium. Coastal regions on which Dr. Snead has done detailed studies include the mapping and interpretation of landforms along the coast of Pakistan and Iran, sections of coast around the Gulf of California, arcuate bays in western Jamaica and northern Puerto Rico, beach rock studies in the lower Caribbean islands, and storm damage from hurricanes and severe "northeasters" along the east coast of the United States and Mexico. In recent years Dr. Snead has been working with archaeologists in Afghanistan, Iran, and Pakistan. In 1975 he joined Professor George F. Dales, a Berkeley archaeologist, in the Las Bela region of Pakistan. Professor Snead helped to identify an inner 3000-year-old coastline near the Harappan site of Balakot. He is the author of *World Atlas of Geomorphic Features*.